BLOOM'S

HOW TO WRITE ABOUT

Jane Austen

CATHERINE J. KORDICH

BLOOM'S
LITERARY CRITICISM
An imprint of Infobase Publishing

Bloom's How to Write about Jane Austen

Bloom's Literary Criticism
An imprint of Infobase Publishing
132 West 31st Street
New York NY 10001

Library of Congress Cataloging-in-Publication Data
Kordich, Catherine J.
  Bloom's how to write about Jane Austen / Catherine J. Kordich; introduction by Harold Bloom.
    p. cm. — (Bloom's how to write about literature)
    Includes bibliographical references and index.
    ISBN 978-0-7910-9743-4
    1. Austen, Jane, 1775–1817—Criticism and interpretation. 2. Criticism—Authorship. 3. Report writing. I. Bloom, Harold. II. Title. III. Title: How to write about Jane Austen. IV. Series.
    PR4037.K67 2008
    823'.7—dc22   2008004865

Bloom's Literary Criticism books are available at special discounts when purchased in bulk quantities for businesses, associations, institutions, or sales promotions. Please call our Special Sales Department in New York at (212) 967-8800 or (800) 322-8755.

You can find Bloom's Literary Criticism on the World Wide Web
at http://www.chelseahouse.com

Text design by Annie O'Donnell
Cover design by Ben Peterson

Printed in the United States of America

Bang MSRF 10 9 8 7 6 5 4 3 2 1

This book is printed on acid-free paper.

CONTENTS

ACKNOWLEDGMENTS

I GRATEFULLY ACKNOWLEDGE the Fund for Teachers program, which profoundly enhanced my scholarship of Jane Austen by sending me on a literary pilgrimage to England. Thanks to my many outstanding teachers, students, and colleagues for their guidance, feedback, and shenanigans. Thanks to the libraries of the world, especially the Alameda Free Library and the Berkeley Public Library. I genuflect at the altar of Douglas Smith for his tireless editing and superb company. This book is dedicated to Judy and John Kordich, my rousing parents, for all they have done and for all they are.

SERIES
INTRODUCTION

BLOOM's How to Write about Literature series is designed to inspire students to write fine essays on great writers and their works. Each volume in the series begins with an introduction by Harold Bloom, meditating on the challenges and rewards of writing about the volume's subject author. The first chapter then provides detailed instructions on how to write a good essay, including how to find a thesis; how to develop an outline; how to write a good introduction, body text, and conclusions; how to cite sources; and more. The second chapter provides a brief overview of the issues involved in writing about the subject author and then a number of suggestions for paper topics, with accompanying strategies for addressing each topic. Succeeding chapters cover the author's major works.

The paper topics suggested within this book are open-ended, and the brief strategies provided are designed to give students a push forward on the writing process rather than a road map to success. The aim of the book is to pose questions, not answer them. Many different kinds of papers could result from each topic. As always, the success of each paper will depend completely on the writer's skill and imagination.

HOW TO WRITE ABOUT JANE AUSTEN: INTRODUCTION

A LIFELONG STUDENT of literary influence, in both my teaching and my writing, I urge readers to make themselves aware of the genealogy of major writers. I mean "genealogy" in the Nietzschean sense: Who are the cognitive and aesthetic parents of an individual creative imagination? Jane Austen is rightly regarded as an indispensable novelist, at least the peer of Charles Dickens, George Eliot, Nathaniel Hawthorne, and Henry James. With Shakespeare and Dickens, she survives triumphantly in our Age of the Screen—whether computer, television, or motion picture. The waning of the deep reader does not greatly affect Austen's reception, since, like Shakespeare and Dickens, she engages an audience at all levels of its response.

Austen's precursors, of whom she was always aware, were Shakespeare and two great authors of the English 18th century: the novelist Samuel Richardson and the critic Dr. Samuel Johnson. Unfortunately, the length and complexity of Richardson's magnificent novel *Clarissa* limits its current readership, but that indicts our increasing educational failure and not that of *Clarissa*, which I judge to be the best novel ever written. Only Marcel Proust's *In Search of Lost Time* rivals *Clarissa* as an aesthetic achievement in the realm of prose fiction. From Shakespeare's heroines and from Richardson's Clarissa Harlowe, Austen derived and transformed her own protagonists: Elizabeth Bennet, Emma Woodhouse, Fanny Price, and Anne Elliot. As Austen is a superbly ironic comic novelist, her heroines have a stronger apparent resemblance to Rosalind in *As You Like It* and Beatrice in *Much Ado About Nothing* than to the tragic Clarissa Harlowe, but they inherit from her what I have learned to call the tradition of the Protestant will, profoundly secularized in a great comic wit like Elizabeth Bennet's.

I suggest that to write well about Jane Austen you must brood on the Protestant will, the strongest element in the English Protestant sensibility. Austen's art is supremely deft in avoiding metaphysical or theological abstractions, and her famous irony has, in only one of its myriad functions, the task of defending her mind from its own fierce drive for order. I cite Samuel Johnson as one of Austen's three prime precursors, with Shakespeare and Samuel Richardson, because Johnson's deep trust in the common reader is shared by Austen. Her intricately balanced social dialectic makes irrelevant the recent critiques that indict her for not addressing the political and social injustices of her own era. Like Dr. Johnson, she knows implicitly that every society is founded on unfair exclusions, and she knows also that her vocation is to perfect her art. Her strongest belief, and here she joins Richardson and not Johnson, is that her heroines have the right of private judgment, particularly in the sphere of marital choice.

When we think of an English Protestant literary sensibility, the epic poet John Milton is likely to come first to mind. Milton finally became a sect of one, allied to but not affiliating with such Inner Light English persuasions as the 17th-century Quakers and Muggletonians (delightful name!). They, too, emphasized the principle that each Protestant was to read and interpret the Bible by his or her own Inner Light, "the Candle of the Lord." This freedom of spirit is secularized by Austen as the entitlement of the soul's self-esteem and its allied endowment of conferring esteem on others only by the operation of individual will. Love in Jane Austen's novels is the free exchange of mutual esteem between two legitimate prides in the integrity of their wills.

HOW TO WRITE
A GOOD ESSAY

ALTHOUGH THERE are many ways to write about literature, most assignments for high school and college English classes call for analytical papers. In these assignments, you are presenting your interpretation of a text to your reader. Your objective is to interpret the text's meaning in order to enhance your reader's understanding and enjoyment of the work. Without exception, strong papers about the meaning of a literary work are built upon a careful, close reading of the text or texts. Careful, analytical reading should always be the first step in your writing process. This volume provides models of such close, analytical reading, and these should help you develop your own skills as a reader and as a writer.

As the examples throughout this book demonstrate, attentive reading entails thinking about and evaluating the formal (textual) aspects of the author's works: theme, character, form, and language. In addition, when writing about a work, many readers choose to move beyond the text itself to consider the work's cultural context. In these instances, writers might explore the historical circumstances of the time period in which the work was written. Alternatively, they might examine the philosophies and ideas that a work addresses. Even in cases where writers explore a work's cultural context, though, papers must still address the more formal aspects of the work itself. A good interpretative essay that evaluates Charles Dickens's use of the philosophy of utilitarianism in his novel *Hard Times,* for example, cannot adequately address the author's treatment of the philosophy without firmly grounding this discussion in the book itself. In other words, any analytical paper about a text, even

1

one that seeks to evaluate the work's cultural context, must also have a solid understanding of the work's themes, characters, and language. You must look for and evaluate these aspects of a work, then, as you read a text and as you prepare to write about it.

WRITING ABOUT THEMES

Literary themes are more than just topics or subjects treated in a work; they are attitudes or points about these topics that often structure other elements in that work. To write about theme therefore you must not just identify a topic that a literary work addresses but also discuss what that work says about that topic. For example, if you were writing about the culture of the American South in William Faulkner's story "A Rose for Emily," you would need to discuss what Faulkner says, argues, or implies about that culture and its passing.

When you prepare to write about thematic concerns in a work of literature, you will probably discover that, like most works of literature, your text touches upon other themes in addition to its central theme. These secondary themes also provide rich ground for paper topics. A thematic paper on "A Rose for Emily" might consider gender or race in the story. While neither of these could be said to be the central theme of the story, each is clearly related to the passing of the "old South" and could provide plenty of good material for papers.

As you prepare to write about themes in literature, you might find a number of strategies helpful. After you identify a theme or themes in the story, you should begin by evaluating how other elements of the story—such as character, point of view, imagery, and symbolism—help develop the theme. You might ask yourself what your own responses are to the author's treatment of the subject matter. Do not neglect the obvious: What expectations does the title set up? How does the title help develop thematic concerns? Clearly, the title "A Rose for Emily" says something about the narrator's attitude toward the title character, Emily Grierson, and all she represents.

WRITING ABOUT CHARACTER

Generally, characters are essential components of fiction and drama. (This is not always the case, though; Ray Bradbury's "August 2026: There

Will Come Soft Rains" is technically a story without characters, at least any human characters.) Often, you can discuss character in poetry, as in T. S. Eliot's "The Love Song of J. Alfred Prufrock" or Robert Browning's "My Last Duchess." Many writers find that analyzing character is one of the most interesting and engaging ways to work with a piece of literature and to shape a paper. After all, characters generally are human, and we all know something about being human and living in the world. Although it is always important to remember that these figures are not real people but creations of the writer's imagination, it can be fruitful to begin evaluating them as you might evaluate a real person. Often, you can start with your own response to a character. Did you like or dislike the character? Did you sympathize with the character? Why or why not?

Keep in mind, though, that emotional responses like these are just starting places. To explore and evaluate literary characters truly, you need to return to the formal aspects of the text and evaluate how the author has drawn these characters. The 20th-century writer E. M. Forster coined the terms *flat characters* and *round characters.* Flat characters are fixed and unchanging; they frequently represent a particular concept or idea. In contrast, round characters are fully drawn and much more realistic characters who develop over the course of a work. Are the characters you are studying flat or round? What elements of the characters lead you to this conclusion? Why might the author have drawn such characters? How does their development affect the meaning of the work? Similarly, you should explore the author's techniques to develop characters. Do you hear a character's own words, or do you hear only other characters' assessments of him or her? Or does the author use an omniscient or limited omniscient narrator to allow you access to the workings of the characters' minds? If so, how does that help develop the characterization? Often you can even evaluate the narrator as a character. How trustworthy are the opinions and assessments of the narrator? You should also think about characters' names. Do they mean anything? If you encounter a hero named Sophia or Sophie, you should probably think about her wisdom (or lack thereof), since *sophia* means "wisdom" in Greek. Similarly, since the name *Sylvia* is derived from the word *sylvan,* meaning "of the wood," you might want to evaluate that character's relationship with nature. Once again, you might look to the title of the work. Does Herman Melville's "Bartleby, the Scrivener" signal anything about Bartleby himself? Is Bartleby adequately defined by his job as scrivener? Is this part of Melville's point? Pursuing questions like these can help you develop thorough papers about characters from psychological, sociological, or more formalistic perspectives.

WRITING ABOUT FORM AND GENRE

Genre, a word derived from French, means "type" or "class." Literary genres are distinctive classes or categories of literary composition. On the most general level, literary works can be divided into the genres of drama, poetry, fiction, and essays, yet within those genres there are classifications that are also referred to as genres. Tragedy and comedy, for example, are genres of drama. Epic, lyric, and pastoral are genres of poetry. *Form,* on the other hand, generally refers to the shape or structure of a work. There are many clearly defined forms of poetry that follow specific patterns of meter, rhyme, and stanza. Sonnets, for example, are poems that follow a fixed form of 14 lines. Sonnets generally follow one of two sonnet forms, each with its own distinct rhyme scheme. Haiku is another example of a poetic form, traditionally consisting of three unrhymed lines of five, seven, and five syllables.

You might think that writing about form or genre might leave little room for argument, but many of these forms and genres are very fluid. Remember that literature is evolving and ever changing, and so are its forms. As you study poetry, you may find that poets, especially more modern poets, play with traditional poetic forms, bringing about new effects. Similarly, dramatic tragedy was once quite narrowly defined, but over the centuries playwrights have broadened and challenged traditional definitions, changing the shape of tragedy. When Arthur Miller wrote *Death of a Salesman,* many critics challenged the idea that tragic drama could encompass a common man like Willy Loman.

Evaluating how a work of literature fits into or challenges the boundaries of its form or genre can provide you with fruitful avenues of investigation. You might find it helpful to ask whether or not the work fits into traditional categories. Why might Miller have thought it appropriate to write a tragedy of the common man? Similarly, you might compare the content or theme of a work with its form. How well do they go together?

Many of Emily Dickinson's poems, for instance, follow the meter of traditional hymns. While some of her poems seem to express traditional religious doctrines, many seem to challenge or strain against traditional conceptions of God and theology. What is the effect, then, of her use of traditional hymn meter?

WRITING ABOUT LANGUAGE, SYMBOLS, AND IMAGERY

No matter what the genre, writers use words as their most basic tool. Language is the most fundamental building block of literature. It is essential that you pay careful attention to the author's language and word choice as you read, reread, and analyze a text. Imagery is language that appeals to the senses. Most commonly, imagery appeals to our sense of vision, creating a mental picture, but authors also use language that appeals to our other senses. Images can be literal or figurative. Literal images use sensory language to describe an actual thing. In the broadest terms, figurative language uses one thing to speak about something else. For example, if I call my boss a snake, I am not saying that he is literally a reptile. Instead, I am using figurative language to communicate my opinions about him. Since we think of snakes as sneaky, slimy, and sinister, I am using the concrete image of a snake to communicate these abstract opinions and impressions.

The two most common figures of speech are similes and metaphors. Both are comparisons between two apparently dissimilar things. Similes are explicit comparisons using the words *like* or *as*; metaphors are implicit comparisons. To return to the previous example, if I say, "My boss, Bob, was waiting for me when I showed up to work five minutes late today—the snake!" I have constructed a metaphor. Writing about his experiences fighting in World War I, Wilfred Owen begins his poem "Dulce et decorum est" with a string of similes: "Bent double, like old beggars under sacks, / Knock-kneed, coughing like hags, we cursed through sludge." Owen's goal was to undercut clichéd notions that war and dying in battle were glorious. Certainly, comparing soldiers to coughing hags and to beggars underscores his point.

"Fog," a short poem by Carl Sandburg, provides a clear example of a metaphor. Sandburg's poem reads:

The fog comes
on little cat feet.

It sits looking
over harbor and city
on silent haunches
and then moves on.

Notice how effectively Sandburg conveys surprising impressions of the fog by comparing two seemingly disparate things—the fog and a cat.

Symbols, by contrast, are things that stand for, or represent, other things. Often they represent something intangible, such as concepts or ideas. In everyday life, we use and understand symbols easily. Babies at christenings and brides at weddings wear white to represent purity. Think, too, of a dollar bill. The paper itself has no value in and of itself. Instead, that paper bill is a symbol of something else, the precious metal in a nation's treasury. Symbols in literature work similarly. Authors use symbols to evoke more than a simple, straightforward, literal meaning. Characters, objects, and places can all function as symbols. Famous literary examples of symbols include Moby Dick, the white whale of Herman Melville's novel, and the scarlet *A* of Nathaniel Hawthorne's *The Scarlet Letter.* As both of these symbols suggest, a literary symbol cannot be adequately defined or explained by any one meaning. Hester Prynne's Puritan community clearly intends her scarlet *A* as a symbol of her adultery, but as the novel progresses, even her own community reads the letter as representing not just *adultery*, but *able*, *angel*, and a host of other meanings.

Writing about imagery and symbols requires close attention to the author's language. To prepare a paper on symbolism or imagery in a work, identify and trace the images and symbols and then try to draw some conclusions about how they function. Ask yourself how any symbols or images help contribute to the themes or meanings of the work. What connotations do they carry? How do they affect your reception of the work? Do they shed light on characters or settings? A strong paper on imagery or symbolism will thoroughly consider the use of figures in the text and will try to reach some conclusions about how or why the author uses them.

WRITING ABOUT HISTORY AND CONTEXT

As noted above, it is possible to write an analytical paper that also considers the work's context. After all, the text was not created in a vacuum. The author lived and wrote in a specific time period and in a specific cultural context and, like all of us, was shaped by that environment. Learning more about the historical and cultural circumstances that surround the author and the work can help illuminate a text and provide you with productive material for a paper. Remember, though, that when you write analytical papers, you should use the context to illuminate the text. Do not lose sight of your goal—to interpret the meaning of the literary work. Use historical or philosophical research as a tool to develop your textual evaluation.

Thoughtful readers often consider how history and culture affected the author's choice and treatment of his or her subject matter. Investigations into the history and context of a work could examine the work's relation to specific historical events, such as the Salem witch trials in 17th-century Massachusetts or the restoration of Charles II to the English throne in 1660. Historical context is not limited to politics and world events. While knowing about the Vietnam War is certainly helpful in interpreting much of Tim O'Brien's fiction, and some knowledge of the French Revolution clearly illuminates the dynamics of Charles Dickens's *A Tale of Two Cities*, historical context also entails the fabric of daily life. Examining a text in light of gender roles, race relations, class boundaries, or working conditions can give rise to thoughtful and compelling papers. Exploring the conditions of the working class in 19th-century England, for example, can provide a particularly effective avenue for writing about Dickens's *Hard Times*.

You can begin thinking about these issues by at first asking broad questions. What do you know about the time period and about the author? What does the editorial apparatus in your text tell you? These might be starting places. Similarly, when specific historical events or dynamics are particularly important to understanding a work but might be somewhat obscure to modern readers, textbooks usually provide notes to explain historical background. These are a good place to start. With this information, ask yourself how these historical facts and circumstances might have affected the author, the presentation of theme, and the presentation of character. How does knowing more about the work's specific historical context illuminate the work? To take a well-known example, understanding the complex attitudes toward slavery during the time Mark Twain wrote *Adventures of Huckleberry Finn* should help you begin to examine issues of race in the text. Additionally, you might compare these attitudes with those of the time in which the novel was set. How might this comparison affect your interpretation of a work written after the abolition of slavery but set before the Civil War?

WRITING ABOUT PHILOSOPHY AND IDEAS

Philosophical concerns are closely related to both historical context and thematic issues. Like historical investigation, philosophical research can provide a useful tool as you analyze a text. For example, an investigation into the working class in Dickens's England might lead you to a topic on the philosophical doctrine of utilitarianism in *Hard Times*. Many other works explore philosophies and ideas quite explicitly. Mary Shelley's famous novel *Frankenstein*, for example, explores John Locke's tabula rasa theory of human knowledge as she portrays the intellectual and emotional development of Victor Frankenstein's creature. As this example indicates, philosophical issues are somewhat more abstract than investigations of theme or historical context. Some other examples of philosophical issues include human free will, the formation of human identity, the nature of sin, or questions of ethics.

Writing about philosophy and ideas might require outside research, but usually the notes or other material in your text will provide you with basic information, and often footnotes and bibliographies suggest where you can read further about the subject. If you have identified a philosophical theme that runs through a text, you might ask yourself how the author develops this theme. Look at character development and the interactions of characters, for example. Similarly, you might examine whether the narrative voice in a work of fiction addresses the philosophical concerns of the text.

WRITING COMPARE AND CONTRAST ESSAYS

Finally, you might find that comparing and contrasting the works or techniques of an author provides a useful tool for literary analysis. A compare and contrast essay might compare two characters or themes in a single work, or it might compare the author's treatment of a theme in two works. It might also contrast methods of character development or analyze an author's differing treatment of a philosophical concern in two works. Writing compare and contrast essays, though, requires some special consideration. While they generally provide you with plenty of material to use, they also come with a built-in trap: the laundry list. These papers often become mere lists of connections between the works. As this chapter will discuss, a strong thesis must make an assertion that you want to prove or validate. A strong compare/contrast thesis, then, needs to comment on the significance of the similarities and differences you observe. It is not enough merely to assert that the works contain similarities and differences. You might, for example, assert why the similarities and differences are important and explain how they illuminate the works' treatment of theme. Remember, too, that a thesis should not be a statement of the obvious. A compare/contrast paper that focuses only on very obvious similarities or differences does little to illuminate the connections between the works. Often, an effective method of shaping a strong thesis and argument is to begin your paper by noting the similarities between the works but then to develop a thesis that asserts how these apparently similar elements are different. If, for example, you observe that Emily Dickinson wrote a number of poems about spiders, you might analyze how she uses spider imagery differently in two poems. Similarly, many scholars have noted that Nathaniel Hawthorne created many "mad scientist" characters so devoted to their science or their art that they lose perspective on all else. A good thesis comparing two of these characters—Aylmer of "The Birth-mark" and Dr. Rappaccini of "Rappaccini's Daughter," for example—might initially identify both characters as examples of Hawthorne's mad scientist type but then argue that their motivations for scientific experimentation differ. If you strive to analyze the similarities or differences, discuss significances, and move beyond the obvious, your paper should avoid the laundry list trap.

PREPARING TO WRITE

Armed with a clear sense of your task—illuminating the text—and with an understanding of theme, character, language, history, and philosophy, you are ready to approach the writing process. Remember that good writing is grounded in good reading and that close reading takes time, attention, and more than one reading of your text. Read for comprehension first. As you go back and review the work, mark the text to chart its details as well as your reactions. Highlight important passages, repeated words, and image patterns. "Converse" with the text through marginal notes. Mark turns in the plot, ask questions, and make observations about characters, themes, and language. If you are reading from a book that does not belong to you, keep a record of your reactions in a journal or notebook. If you have read a work of literature carefully, paying attention to both the text and the context of the work, you have a leg up on the writing process. Admittedly, your ideas are probably very broad and undefined at this point, but you have taken an important first step toward writing a strong paper.

Your next step is to focus, to take a broad, perhaps fuzzy, topic and define it more clearly. Even a topic provided by your instructor will need to be focused appropriately. Remember that good writers make the topic their own. You can use a number of strategies—often called "invention"—to develop your own focus. In one such strategy called *freewriting,* you spend 10 minutes or so just writing about your topic without referring to the text or your notes. Write whatever comes to mind; the important thing is just to keep writing. Often this process allows you to develop fresh ideas or approaches to your subject matter. You could also try *brainstorming*: Write down your topic, then list all the related points or ideas you can think of. Include questions, comments, words, important passages or events, and anything else that comes to mind. Let one idea lead to another. In the related technique of *clustering,* or *mapping,* write your topic on a sheet of paper and write related ideas around it. Then list related subpoints under each of these main ideas. Many people then draw arrows to show connections between points. This technique helps narrow your topic and can also help you organize your ideas. Similarly, asking journalistic questions—Who? What? Where? When? Why? and How?—can develop ideas for topic development.

Thesis Statements

Once you have developed a focused topic, you can begin to think about your thesis statement, the main point or purpose of your paper. It is imperative that you craft a strong thesis; otherwise, your paper will likely be little more than random, disorganized observations about the text. Think of your thesis statement as a kind of road map for your paper. It tells your reader where you are going and how you are going to get there.

To craft a good thesis, you must keep a number of things in mind. First, as the title of this subsection indicates, your paper's thesis should be a statement, an assertion about the text that you want to prove or validate. Beginning writers often formulate a question that they attempt to use as a thesis. For example, a writer exploring the theme of marriage in Austen's *Pride and Prejudice* might ask, Why does Charlotte Lucas's marriage inspire outrage in Elizabeth Bennet, but only complacency in the narrator? While a question like this is a good strategy to use in the invention process to help narrow your topic and find your thesis, it cannot serve as the thesis statement because it does not make any assertion about Charlotte Lucas's marriage or the reactions it inspires. You might shape this question into a thesis by instead proposing an answer to that question: Though Elizabeth refuses to believe it possible, *Pride and Prejudice* convinces us—through historical context, Charlotte Lucas's lucid opinions, and the narrator's own commentary—that the loveless Collins marriage is, in fact, an understandable, if costly, choice for Charlotte Lucas. That the choice is a good one is an implicit criticism of the social position of young women at this time. Notice that this thesis provides an initial plan or structure for the rest of the paper, and notice too that the thesis statement does not necessarily have to fit into one sentence. From this thesis the reader expects an argument that will analyze the relevant historical context, then show how Charlotte's opinions and choices are endorsed by the narrator. A final assessment of what the Collins marriage signifies to the novel overall would be an appropriate conclusion to this essay.

Second, remember that a good thesis makes an assertion that you need to support. In other words, a good thesis does not state the obvious. If you tried to formulate a thesis about marriage by simply saying, Elizabeth Bennet has strong feelings about marriage in *Pride and Prejudice*, you have done nothing but rephrase the obvious. Since Austen's novel is centered around Elizabeth and other young people of marriageable age who all seem to be looking for the right mate, there would be no point in spending three to six pages supporting that assertion. You might try to develop a thesis from that point by asking yourself some further questions: Why does Elizabeth Bennet consider marriage to Mr. Collins "impossible" (1: 22)? Does the novel seem to share Elizabeth's opinion or does it have a different opinion? Does the novel indicate that marriage for practical reasons is insupportable or worthwhile? Does it present women as needing marriage at all costs? Such a line of questioning might lead you to a more viable thesis, like the one in the preceding paragraph.

As the comparison with the road map also suggests, your thesis should appear near the beginning of the paper. In relatively short papers (three to six pages), the thesis almost always appears in the first paragraph. Some writers fall into the trap of saving their thesis for the end, trying to provide a surprise or a big moment of revelation, as if to say, TA-DA! I've just proved that in *Sense and Sensibility*, Austen uses the ruin of Eliza Williams and Eliza Brandon to symbolize the risks Marianne Dashwood is taking. Placing a thesis at the end of an essay can seriously mar its effectiveness. If you fail to define your essay's point and purpose clearly at the beginning, your reader will find it difficult to assess the clarity of your argument and understand the points you are making. When your argument comes as a surprise at the end, you force your reader to reread your essay in order to assess its logic and effectiveness.

Finally, you should avoid using the first person as you present your thesis. Though it is not strictly wrong to write in the first person, it is difficult to do so gracefully. While writing in the first person, beginning writers often fall into the trap of writing self-reflexive prose (writing *about* their paper *in* their paper). Often this leads to the most dreaded of opening lines—In this paper I am going to discuss. Not only does this self-reflexive voice make for very awkward prose, it frequently allows writers to announce a topic boldly while completely avoiding a thesis statement. An example follows: "In Austen's *Sense and Sensibility*, the tone of the novel changes when Colonel Brandon tells the sad stories of Eliza Brandon and Eliza Williams, two women destroyed by passion. In this essay I am going to discuss these fallen women." The author of this paper has done little more than announce a general topic for the paper (the ruined Elizas). Although the last sentence might be a thesis, the writer fails to present an opinion about the significance of the Eliza stories. To improve this "thesis," the writer would need to back up a couple of steps. First, the announced topic is too broad; it largely summarizes the events in the story without saying anything about its ideas. The writer should highlight what she considers the meaning of the story: What is the novel about? The writer might conclude that Colonel Brandon's stories reveal the risks particular to women of sensibility and, specifically, the risks that the passionate Marianne has been running. From here, the writer could identify the means by which Austen communicates these ideas and then begin to craft a specific thesis. A writer who chooses to explore the significance of the fallen women in the novel might, for example, craft a thesis that reads: Eliza Brandon and Eliza Williams, though they occupy little narrative space in *Sense and Sensibility*, loom large in their significance for the passionate Marianne Dashwood. The Elizas exemplify how, when paired with sensibility or passion, their fundamentally good natures are destroyed by unscrupulous men and social censure. Ultimately, their tales are cautionary and represent the fate that Marianne narrowly escapes.

Outlines

Though developing a strong, thoughtful thesis early in your writing process should help focus your paper, outlining provides an essential tool for logically shaping that paper. A good outline helps you see—and develop—the relationships among the points in your argument and assures you that your paper flows logically and coherently. Outlining not only helps place your points in a logical order but also helps you subordinate supporting points, weed out any irrelevant points, and decide whether any necessary points are missing from your argument. Most of us are familiar with formal outlines that use numerical and letter designations for each point. However, there are different types of outlines; you may find that an informal outline is a more useful tool for you. What is important, though, is that you spend the time to develop some sort of outline—formal or informal.

Remember that an outline is a tool to help you shape and write a strong paper. If you do not spend sufficient time planning your supporting points and shaping the arrangement of those points, you will most likely construct a vague, unfocused outline that provides little, if any, help with the writing of the paper. Consider the following example:

Thesis: The stories of Eliza Brandon and Eliza Williams exemplify how a woman's loving, but overly sensible nature can be destroyed by unscrupulous men and an unforgiving society. In *Sense and Sensibility*, the Eliza tales are cautionary and represent the fate that Marianne Dashwood narrowly escapes.

    I. Introduction and thesis

   II. Elizas are good, similar to Marianne
        A. Innocent
        B. Loving hearts
        C. Their lives are cautionary tales for Marianne
        D. Passionate (excessive sensibility)

  III. Society

   IV. Colonel Brandon's brother's depravity
        A. Sexual sins

    V. Conclusion
        A. Elizas' lives are examples of what happens to good women with bad men

This outline has a number of flaws. First, the major topics labeled with Roman numerals are not arranged in logical order. If the paper's aim is to show how the Eliza characters exemplify the risks of excessive sensibility, the writer should establish, first, how the Elizas are associated with sensibility. Similarly, the thesis makes no reference to society or to Colonel Brandon or his brother's depravity, but the writer includes each of these as major sections of the outline. As the sympathetic narrator of the Eliza stories, as well as the disappointed lover of Eliza Brandon and the distraught guardian of Eliza Williams, Colonel Brandon may well have a place in this paper, but the writer fails to provide details in the outline about his place in the argument. Society, too, though it contributes to the sufferings of the Elizas, does not logically merit a major section. The writer could, however, discuss social consequences of sensibility in another section of the essay. Third, the writer includes the idea of how the Elizas resemble Marianne as one of the lettered items in section II. Letters A, B, and D all refer to examples of the Elizas' goodness; the idea of their stories as cautionary tales does not belong in this list. The fact that the Eliza stories are cautionary tales is significant; this is not, however, an example of their goodness. A fourth problem is the inclusion of a section A in sections IV and VI. An outline should not include an A without a B, a 1 without a 2, and so forth. The final problem with this outline is its overall lack of detail. None of the sections provides much information about the content of the argument, and it seems likely that the writer has not given sufficient thought to the content of the paper. A better outline might be the following:

Thesis: The stories of Eliza Brandon and Eliza Williams exemplify how a woman's loving, but overly sensible nature can be destroyed by unscrupulous men and an unforgiving society. In *Sense and Sensibility*, the Eliza tales are cautionary, revealing the fate that Marianne Dashwood narrowly escapes.

I. Introduction and thesis

II. Qualities shared by Elizas and Marianne
    A. Passionate (governed by sensibility)
    B. Innocent

III. Elizas are destroyed by unscrupulous men
    A. Eliza Brandon destroyed by unscrupulous men
        i. Guardian exploits her fortune

             ii. Husband is cruel, doesn't love
                her
           iii. Lovers abandon her to her fate
       B. Eliza Williams destroyed by one man
             i. Willoughby impregnates her
            ii. Willoughby abandons her to her
                fate
       C. Both women social outcasts, isolated

IV. What the cautionary aspects of these stories
    reveal to Marianne and the reader
       A. Tragic consequences of passion
             i. death (Eliza Brandon)
            ii. social death (Eliza Williams)
       B. Willoughby's past actions and character
          flaws
       C. Dubious conduct of Willoughby with Marianne
          had potentially ruinous consequences

V. Conclusion

This new outline would prove much more helpful when it came time to write a paper. It could be shaped into an even more useful tool if the writer fleshed out the arguments by providing specific examples from the text to support each point. Once you have listed your main points and your supporting ideas, develop this raw material by listing related supporting ideas and examples under each main heading. From there, arrange the material in subsections and order it logically.

For an example of an outline that uses more specific examples, consider the thesis discussed previously: Though Elizabeth refuses to believe it possible, *Pride and Prejudice* convinces us with historical context, Charlotte's lucid opinions, and the narrator's own commentary that the loveless Collins marriage is, in fact, an understandable, if costly, choice for Charlotte Lucas. This thesis already gives you the beginning of an organization. Start by identifying the role of marriage for women at this time and then explain how the novel makes Charlotte's decision to wed Mr. Collins understandable. You could start your outline, then, with four topic headings: 1) historical context of marriage's role for women, 2) narrator's opinions about unromantic realities of marriage, 3) Charlotte's insights prove correct, 4) Charlotte's marriage benefits herself and her family, 5) personal costs of this kind of marriage. Under each heading you could then list ideas that support that particular point. Be sure to include references to parts of the text that help build your case.

An informal outline might look like this:

Thesis: Though Elizabeth refuses to believe it possible, *Pride and Prejudice* convinces us with historical context, Charlotte's lucid opinions, and the narrator's own commentary that entering the loveless Collins marriage is, in fact, an understandable, if costly, choice for Charlotte Lucas.

1. Historical context of marriage's role for women
   - Married women were at this time granted more social authority than single women
   - Charlotte, at age 27, is nearing the end of her marriageable years and wants to marry to escape being a dependent daughter
   - *Pride and Prejudice* quietly criticizes society's treatment of women in this social sphere by presenting
     o Young women trained to be wives (no other viable work option)
     o Precarious situation of unmarried young women like Charlotte is "fearful" (Polhemus 89)
   - Set up transition from historical context to novel itself with feminist scholarship that asserts Austen's novels show the author's discomfort with place of "women in patriarchy" (Gilbert and Gubar 112)

2. Novel candid about unromantic aspects of marriage
   - Narrator sympathetic to Charlotte's unromantic marriage goals
   - Narrator places Charlotte's decision within larger context of young women in society
     o Charlotte wants to marry but does not think "highly either of men or of matrimony"
     o Narrator asserts that marriage "however uncertain of giving happiness, must be a young woman's pleasantest preservative from want"
     o Narrator's ambivalence about marriage as a solution seen in the "must be" of quote above

3. Ways Charlotte's decision to marry shown to be beneficial
   - Charlotte's decision to wed beneficial to her family
     o Her parents "overjoyed" since they could offer little fortune and Charlotte now will be taken care of
     o Benefit to her brothers—they will not have to take care of a spinster sister
     o Benefit to her sisters—their eldest sister being married means that their own marriage pursuits can begin
   - Charlotte's decision to wed beneficial to herself
     o Narrator describes Charlotte's fulfillment of goal as "the pure and disinterested desire of an establishment"
     o Charlotte describes her own goals to Elizabeth as wanting a "comfortable home"

     o After marriage, she enjoys her home and belongings and being independent of her family, as seen in the repetition of "her": "Her home and her housekeeping, her parish and her poultry . . . had not yet lost their charms"

- Transition to how this choice is costly to Charlotte personally by noting that the narrator's comment about possessions "not yet" having "lost their charms" suggests that they will

4. Costs of beneficial marriage
   - One cost is personal to her character—the loss of intimacy with Elizabeth
     - Elizabeth, "whose friendship [Charlotte] *valued* beyond that of any other person" (italics added), is nearly lost by Charlotte's decision
     - Elizabeth believes that Charlotte "disgraces" herself with the marriage; one scholar proclaims that Elizabeth is describing "socially respectable prostitution" (Polhemus 89)
   - Another cost is Charlotte's silence and erasure of identity in the novel
     - After her marriage, the narrator no longer has access to Charlotte's excellent insights; the reader and the narrator must project meaning onto her, as Elizabeth does
     - After her marriage, she is silent at Rosings (probably to show deference to Lady Catherine de Bourgh, her husband's patroness)
     - Mr. Collins's belief that he and his wife are "of one mind" implies that

> Charlotte keeps her true opinions
> to herself

5. Conclusion
   - Though Elizabeth is not reconciled to Charlotte's marriage, the narrator is more understanding
   - The novel, in making a case for the merit of Charlotte's marriage, is lodging a criticism against society
   - Jane Austen, herself a lifelong dependent daughter, must surely have understood the decision that Charlotte makes
   - Charlotte's and Elizabeth's marriages contrast; while we understand Charlotte's philosophy of marriage, we cheer for Elizabeth's practice of love

You would set about writing a formal outline in a similar way, though in the final stages you would label the headings differently. A formal outline that argues the thesis discusssed above might look like this:

Thesis: The stories of Eliza Brandon and Eliza Williams exemplify how a woman's loving, but overly sensible nature can be destroyed by unscrupulous men and an unforgiving society. In *Sense and Sensibility*, the Eliza tales are cautionary, revealing the fate that Marianne Dashwood narrowly escapes.

I. Introduction and thesis

II. Resemblances shared by the Elizas and Marianne
   A. Passionate (governed by excessive sensibility)
      1. Eliza Brandon and Marianne: "same warmth of heart, the same eagerness of spirits"

    2. Marianne: "eager in every thing; her sorrows, her joys, could have no moderation"

    3. Eliza Williams and Marianne share identically passionate love for Willoughby

  B. Innocent of personal wrongdoing

    1. Eliza Brandon described by Colonel Brandon: "a mind so young, so lively, so inexperienced"

    2. Marianne shows both innocence and passion in her faith in Willoughby: "I felt myself . . . to be as solemnly engaged to him, as if the strictest legal covenant had bound us to each other"

    3. Brandon associates Eliza Williams with "youth and innocence," though this innocence is later called into question by Willoughby

III. Elizas repeatedly destroyed by unscrupulous men

  A. Eliza Brandon destroyed by multiple men (domino effect)

    1. Guardian (Brandon's father): marries Eliza Brandon to eldest son so that her fortune can save a "much encumbered family estate"

    2. Brother/husband: simply disregards her, offers none of the love that she needs: "his pleasures not what they ought to have been . . . from the first he treated her unkindly"

    3. Lover/father of daughter: unidentified, but we assume that he abandoned her to pregnancy, destitution, and illness

B. Eliza Williams destroyed by one man

1. Willoughby, with no thought of marrying her, seduces Eliza Williams and leaves her pregnant ("in a situation of utmost distress")

2. Willoughby abandons Eliza to her fate when he moves on to Marianne

   a. He promises that he will return and write: does not

   b. This echoes his actions with Marianne: shows pattern of irresponsibility in his conduct with women

IV. What the cautionary aspects of these stories reveal

A. Tragic consequences of passion without love

1. Eliza Brandon experiences social and actual death

   a. Divorces: rare, socially forbidden, financially ruinous for women

   b. Loses fortune: upon divorce, a woman's fortune becomes the property of her husband

   c. Has lovers and an illegitimate child

   d. Dies of consumption in abject poverty

2. Eliza Williams experiences social death

   a. Has an illegitimate child

   b. Is socially isolated/ostracized; Colonel Brandon has "removed her and her child into the country and there she remains"

B. Willoughby's character flaws and past actions

   1. Marianne feels the loss of his character more than the loss of his love

   2. His dangerously selfish actions, especially regarding his conduct with women

C. Dubious conduct of Willoughby with Marianne had potentially ruinous consequences

   1. In light of these stories, reader realizes how dangerous the relationship was between Marianne and Willoughby

     a. Colonel Brandon cryptically observes: "Who can tell what were [Willoughby's] designs on Marianne"

     b. Elinor imagines his designs nefarious, though when Willoughby makes his confession, she reassesses

   2. Two especially risky acts from Marianne's time with Willoughby

     a. Symbolic risk: letting Willoughby clip a lock of her hair (allusion to loss of virginity via *The Rape of the Lock*)

     b. Physical and symbolic risk: going unchaperoned to Allenham with Willoughby

V. Conclusion

  A. How the Eliza stories help us understand Elinor's concerns over her sister's conduct

      B. Willoughby's confession to Elinor makes
         understandable some of his actions, but
         does not absolve him of his conduct
      C. Benefits of these stories
         1. Marianne now sees Colonel Brandon
           as in possession of appealingly
           romantic tragic past
         2. Stories lead to Marianne's getting
           over Willoughby and her happy
           marriage to Colonel Brandon

As in the previous example outline, the thesis here provided the seeds of a structure, and the writer was careful to arrange the supporting points in a logical manner, showing the relationships among the ideas in the paper.

Body Paragraphs

Once your outline is complete, you can begin drafting your paper. Paragraphs, units of related sentences, are the building blocks of a good paper, and as you draft you should keep in mind both the function and the qualities of good paragraphs. Paragraphs help you chart and control the shape and content of your essay, and they help the reader see your organization and your logic. You should begin a new paragraph whenever you move from one major point to another. In longer, more complex essays you might use a group of related paragraphs to support major points. Remember that in addition to being adequately developed, a good paragraph is also unified and coherent.

Unified Paragraphs

Each paragraph must be centered around one idea or point, and a unified paragraph carefully focuses on and develops this central idea without including extraneous ideas or tangents. For beginning writers, the best way to ensure that you are constructing unified paragraphs is to include a topic sentence in each paragraph. This topic sentence should convey the main point of the paragraph, and every sentence in the paragraph should relate to that topic sentence. Any sentence that strays from the central topic does not belong in the paragraph and needs to be revised or deleted. Consider the following paragraph about the personal costs to Charlotte Lucas caused by her marriage. Notice how the paragraph veers away from the main point that in spite of the marriage's advantages, it also has serious drawbacks:

> The limited appeal of Charlotte's possessions and social advancement is a personal cost that results from her decision to marry Mr. Collins. The disadvantages to Charlotte are personal to her character and are shown symbolically within the novel. Many characters suffer because they do not properly love their spouses. Another character that marries for reasons other than love is Lydia Bennet, who marries solely for pleasure. Mr. and Mrs. Bennet themselves show that the suitability of a husband and wife is important. Mr. Bennet, though he is charming, shows his disrespect for his wife throughout the novel. The primary personal cost of Charlotte's marriage is her distance from Elizabeth, whose "friendship [Charlotte] *valued* beyond that of any other person" (1: 22; italics added). The absence of love in this match is what is particularly galling to Elizabeth, and she "could not have supposed it possible that when called into action, [Charlotte] would have sacrificed every better feeling to worldly advantage" (1: 22). For Elizabeth, a marriage for any reason other than love must be wrong, must be suspect, must even be depraved. That Elizabeth thinks Charlotte has "disgraced" herself by this union suggests that a marriage without love is, in the starkest assessment, a disgraceful exchange of body for money, a kind of "socially respectable prostitution" (Polhemus 89). In exchange for her wifely duties, Charlotte is compensated with a home and material possessions.

Although the paragraph begins solidly, and the second sentence provides the central idea of the paragraph, the author goes off on a tangent. If the purpose of the paragraph is to demonstrate that Charlotte suffers because of her decision, the sentences about the other marriages are irrelevant here. These statements and observations may find a place later in the paper, but they should be deleted from this paragraph.

Coherent Paragraphs

In addition to shaping unified paragraphs, you must also craft coherent paragraphs that develop their points logically with sentences that flow smoothly into one another. Coherence depends on the order of your sentences, but it is not strictly the order of the sentences that is important to paragraph coherence. You also need to craft your prose to help the reader see the relationship among the sentences.

Consider the following paragraph about the personal costs of Charlotte Lucas's decision to marry Mr. Collins in *Pride and Prejudice*. Notice how the writer uses the same ideas as those in the paragraph above but fails to help the reader see the relationships among the points:

> The limited appeal of Charlotte's possessions and social advancement is the personal cost that coincides with her decision to marry Mr. Collins. The disadvantages to Charlotte are personal to her character and are shown symbolically. A primary personal cost is that of alienation from Elizabeth, whose "friendship [Charlotte] *valued* beyond that of any other person" (1: 22; italics added). The narrator's sense of economic exchange, and of value, stands out here. The idea intensifies when she considers the exchange that Charlotte made. The absence of love in this match is galling to Elizabeth, and she "could not have supposed it possible that when called into action, [Charlotte] would have sacrificed every better feeling to worldly advantage" (1: 22). For Elizabeth, a marriage for any reason other than love must be wrong. Elizabeth thinks Charlotte has "disgraced" herself by this union and that this is a degrading exchange of body for money, a kind of "socially respectable prostitution" (Polhemus 89). In exchange for her wifely duties, Charlotte is compensated with a home and material possessions.

This paragraph demonstrates that unity alone does not guarantee the ideas will be effectively presented. The argument is hard to follow because the author fails both to show connections between the sentences and to indicate how they work to support the overall point.

A number of techniques are available to aid paragraph coherence. Careful use of transitional words and phrases is essential. You can use transitional flags to introduce an example or an illustration (*for example, for instance*), to amplify a point or add another phase of the same idea (*additionally, furthermore, next, similarly, finally, then*), to indicate a conclusion or result (*therefore, as a result, thus, in other words*), to signal a contrast or a qualification (*on the other hand, nevertheless, despite this, on the contrary, still, however, conversely*), to signal a comparison (*likewise, in comparison, similarly*), and to indicate a movement in time (*afterward, earlier, eventually, finally, later, subsequently, until*).

In addition to transitional flags, careful use of pronouns aids coherence and flow. If you were writing about *The Wizard of Oz*, you would not want to keep repeating the phrase *the witch* or the name *Dorothy*. Careful substitution of the pronoun *she* in these instances can aid coherence. A word of warning, though: When you substitute pronouns for proper names, be sure that your pronoun reference is clear. In a paragraph that discusses both Dorothy and the witch, substituting *she* could lead to confusion. Make sure that it is clear to whom the pronoun refers. Generally, the pronoun refers to the last proper noun you have used.

While repeating the same name over and over can lead to awkward, boring prose, it is possible to use repetition to help your paragraph's coherence. Careful repetition of important words or phrases can lend coherence to your paragraph by reminding readers of your key points. Admittedly, it takes some practice to use this technique effectively. You may find that reading your prose aloud can help you develop an ear for effective use of repetition.

To see how helpful transitional aids are, compare the paragraph below to the preceding paragraph about the costs of Charlotte Lucas's marriage in *Pride and Prejudice*. Notice how the author works with the same ideas and quotations but shapes them into a much more coherent paragraph whose point is clearer and easier to follow:

The transient appeal of possessions and social advancement suggests disappointment in the future, but the profound disappointments associated with Charlotte's marriage are more immediate and more personal. These costs to Charlotte are heavy ones. The most significant personal cost to Charlotte is alienation from Elizabeth, whose "friendship [Charlotte] *valued* beyond that of any other person" (1: 22; italics added). The narrator's use of economic language, of value, stands out here; it is in keeping with the novel's awareness of the economic and social circumstances that compel Charlotte's decision to marry without love. The notion of economic motivation is emphasized when Elizabeth considers the exchange that Charlotte has made. The absence of love in the Collins match is particularly galling to Elizabeth, and she "could not have supposed it possible that when called into action, [Charlotte] would have sacrificed every better feeling to worldly advantage" (1: 22). For the romantic Elizabeth, a marriage for any reason other than love must be wrong, and a marriage for "worldly advantage" must be suspect, must even be depraved. That Elizabeth thinks Charlotte has "disgraced" herself by this union further suggests that any marriage without love is, in the starkest assessment, a degrading exchange of body for money, a kind of "socially respectable prostitution" (Polhemus 89). Here, in exchange for her wifely duties, Charlotte is compensated with a home and material possessions. The ugly notion of this economic arrangement must certainly contribute to Elizabeth's feeling that her friend is "disgraced" by marrying Mr. Collins.

The following paragraph from a paper on the role of the Eliza stories in *Sense and Sensibility* also demonstrates both unity and coherence. In it, the author analyzes how Eliza Brandon is systematically destroyed by unscrupulous men.

Eliza Brandon and Eliza Williams are both portrayed as innocent of wrongdoing themselves; their fall into infamy is caused by the carelessness of unscrupulous men. Eliza Williams is ruined by one man—Willoughby—while Eliza Brandon is a victim of multiple men. Her destruction is initiated by her guardian, Colonel Brandon's father, who compels her marriage to the eldest Brandon son strictly to acquire her fortune, which will save his indebted family estate. Eliza's happiness and life, then, are effectively exchanged for money. The next unscrupulous male to perpetrate her destruction is her husband, who "did not . . . love her," disregards her, and "treat[ed] her unkindly." There is, in fact, a hint of abuse or even immorality when Brandon describes his brother's "pleasures" as "not what they ought to have been." Eliza's passionate nature, consequently, compels her to seek love beyond her marriage, and the scandalous divorce that follows requires that she forfeit her fortune. Eliza Brandon is now destitute, and we infer from the absence of her first lover that he, too, leaves her to her fate and to the raising of their illegitimate child. When Colonel Brandon finds his Eliza again, she is so ill and her ruin is so complete that he considers her death a blessed reprieve from her sufferings.

Introductions

Introductions present particular challenges for writers. Generally, your introduction should do two things: capture your reader's attention and explain the main point of your essay. In other words, your introduction should contain your thesis, but it needs to do a bit more than that. You are likely to find that starting your first paragraph is one of the most difficult parts of the paper. It is hard to face a blank page or screen, and as a result, many beginning writers, in desperation to start somewhere, start with overly broad, general statements. While it is often a good strategy to start with more general subject matter and narrow your focus, do not begin with sweeping statements such as this: Everyone likes to be creative and feel understood. Such sentences are nothing but filler. They begin to fill the blank page, but they do nothing to advance your argument. Instead, you should try to gain your readers' interest. Some writers like to begin with a pertinent quotation or with a relevant question. Or you might begin with an introduction of the topic you will discuss. If you are writing about Austen's use of the stories of Eliza Williams and Eliza Brandon in *Sense and Sensibility,* for instance, you might begin by talking about the notions of fate and tragedy. Another common trap to avoid is depending on your title to introduce the author and the text you are writing about. Always include the work's author and title in your opening paragraph.

Compare the effectiveness of the following introductions:

1) Since the beginning of time, people have told sad stories. Greek tragedies are sad, as anyone who has ever seen one can tell you. In this novel, we see women's lives made tragic by unscrupulous men.

2) In drama, a tragedy is as illuminating as it is inevitable. Classic Greek tragedies show how character determines fate: Individuals in tragedies can avoid neither their natures nor the miserable ends that the gods arrange. Though Jane Austen's characters are generally held to be in control of their actions, there is a measure of tragic inevitability in the stories of Eliza Brandon and Eliza Williams. The women's passionate natures, when left to the unscrupulous men who exploit them, result in ruin. In *Sense and Sensibility,* the stories of these two fallen women are cautionary; they reveal the fate that Marianne Dashwood only narrowly escapes.

The first introduction begins with a vague, overly broad sentence, cites unclear, undeveloped examples, and then moves abruptly to the thesis. Notice, too, how a reader deprived of the paper's title does not know the title of the novel that the paper will analyze. The second introduction works with the same material and thesis, but provides more detail and is, consequently, much more interesting. It begins by discussing the notion of tragedy as staged by the Greeks, gives some specific explanations about the relevant aspects of Greek tragedy, then identifies the Eliza characters as tragic ones. Next the paragraph mentions how unusual these characters are for an Austen novel. The paragraph ends with the thesis, which includes the title of the work to be discussed.

The paragraph below provides another example of an opening strategy. It begins by introducing the author and the text it will analyze, then it moves on to introduce relevant details of the story to set up a thesis:

> Of the many marriages in Jane Austen's *Pride and Prejudice*, that of Charlotte Lucas and Mr. Collins is the least romantic. Elizabeth Bennet considers it "unaccountable" that her close friend Charlotte could possibly marry the "conceited, pompous, narrow minded, [and] silly" Mr. Collins (2: 1). Elizabeth is not alone in seeing Mr. Collins's flaws. Charlotte herself considers Mr. Collins's company "irksome" and knows that he has no actual love for her, but in spite of these serious disadvantages, Charlotte skillfully orchestrates his offer of marriage (1: 22). Charlotte's hard-nosed philosophy of marriage is in clear contrast to Elizabeth's romantic feelings about love. One scholar asserts that the novel's fundamental ideas of marriage "are enacted in the juxtaposing of the two young women" (Gill and Gregory 134). Though Elizabeth refuses to believe it possible, *Pride and Prejudice* convinces us with historical context, Charlotte's lucid opinions, and the narrator's own commentary that entering the loveless Collins marriage is a good, if costly, choice for Charlotte Lucas.

Conclusions

Conclusions present another series of challenges for writers. No doubt you have heard the adage about writing papers: "Tell us what you are going to say, say it, and then tell us what you've said." While this formula does not necessarily result in bad papers, it does not often result in good ones, either. It will almost certainly result in boring papers (especially boring conclusions). If you have effectively established your points in the body of the paper, the reader already knows and understands your argument. There is no need merely to reiterate. Do not just summarize your main points in your conclusion. Such a boring, mechanical conclusion does nothing to advance your argument or interest your reader. Consider the following conclusion to a paper about the significance of the Eliza stories for *Sense and Sensibility*:

> In conclusion, Austen uses the stories of the fallen women to explain the risks of passion. Eliza Brandon is ruined by the corrupt men who take advantage of her. Eliza Williams is also ruined, and she is passionate. Marianne Dashwood, unlike the Elizas, is not ruined by an unscrupulous man, though it is a close call.

Besides starting with a mechanical transitional device, this conclusion does little more than summarize the main points of the outline (and it does not even touch on all of them). It is incomplete and uninteresting.

Instead, your conclusion should add something to your paper. A good tactic is to build upon the points you have been arguing. Asking "why?" often helps to draw further conclusions. For example, in the paper discussed above, you might speculate or explain how the stories of the Elizas help a contemporary reader to understand the society that the novel describes. Scholars often discuss these stories as a deviation from most Austen novels because they describe a world beyond the genteel drawing rooms of the country gentry. You could discuss whether these scandalous stories are presented as anomalous for the characters or whether, instead, the characters seem to accept that this immorality is an expected part of their world. Another method for successfully concluding a paper is to speculate on other directions in which to take your topic, by tying it to larger issues, or to other books by the same author.

The following conclusion could have connected the Eliza stories to the tales of scandalous romances referred to in *Northanger Abbey* or

Mansfield Park. It might also help your conclusion to envision your paper as just one section of a longer essay or work. Having established your points in this paper, how would you build on this argument? Where would you go next? In the following conclusion to the paper on *Sense and Sensibility,* the author reiterates some of the main points of the paper, but does so to amplify the discussion of the story's central events and themes:

The stories of Eliza Brandon and Eliza Williams are cautionary tales for Marianne Dashwood, but they also act as expository tales for a 21st-century reader. The Eliza tales explain to us why Marianne's conduct—such as her giddily unsupervised visit to Allenham—so alarmed Elinor. In fact, we see that in the society of Austen's novel a small mistake by a young woman could lead to far more tragic ones: For Eliza Williams, after all, a giddily unsupervised visit to Bath leads to a love affair, a seduction, abandonment, an illegitimate child, and social ostracism. Another important expository aspect of the Eliza tales within the novel is that of Willoughby's past. His conduct with Eliza Williams shows that his variety of romantic heroism is deplorable. Willoughby has an excessive passion that, for young women, is of a very destructive sort. His later confession to Elinor reveals that he had truly loved Marianne, but this does not change the flaws in his character. His selfishness— a criticism this book makes of sensibility—is evident in his confession, one that shows more rationalization and justification than true contrition. Ultimately, the stories of Eliza Brandon and Eliza Williams initiate two positive changes for Marianne. The first change is that with the revelations about Willoughby's conduct and his consequent fall in her esteem, Marianne is able to get over her love for him (2: 10). The second change is more interesting in terms of the novel's overall philosophy of sense and sensibility. This second change relates to Marianne's feelings for Colonel Brandon. His revealing the Eliza tales shows him to be in possession of a past that is, in Marianne's opinion, appealingly romantic. Of course, she grows to love and then marry Brandon, and since "she could never love by halves . . . her whole heart became, in time, as much devoted to her husband, as it had once been to Willoughby" (3: 14). Brandon and Marianne's union shows that the passion that so derailed the Elizas is, when met with an appreciative lover, a strength instead of a liability.

In the following ending to a paper on Charlotte Lucas's marriage in *Pride and Prejudice*, the author draws a conclusion about how the novel, in making understandable such a loveless marriage, is lodging a criticism at society. The conclusion also meditates on Austen's biography in light of her novel's representation of love and marriage:

Though Elizabeth is convinced that the Collins marriage is fundamentally wrong, the narrator is understanding of Charlotte's decision. In fact, the narrator presents convincing reasons for the marriage by explaining Charlotte's philosophies, her circumstances, and the social context in which she lives. The narrator's interest, if not outright endorsement, is seen in her showing how Charlotte manages to live with the flaws in her marriage. Charlotte Lucas's story illuminates a criticism that Pride and Prejudice makes about society's treatment of young women at this time. While a practical marriage offered a step up the social ladder for unmarried women, it was a chilling proposition nonetheless. It is difficult to avoid thinking that Jane Austen, herself unmarried and, up until the end of her life, dependent on her family, would have understood too well the decision that Charlotte makes. While writing this novel, it must have been a relief for Austen to move imaginatively from the Collins's loveless marriage to the marriage of Elizabeth and Darcy, a romantic union of love, affinity, desire, respect, and understanding.

In this novel full of marriages, we come to understand
Charlotte Lucas's philosophy of marriage, but we cheer
for Elizabeth Bennet's practice of love.

Citations and Formatting
Using Primary Sources

As the examples included in this chapter indicate, strong papers on literary texts incorporate quotations from the text in order to support their points. It is not enough for you to assert your interpretation without providing support or evidence from the text. Without well-chosen quotations to support your argument, you are, in effect, saying to the reader, "Take my word for it." It is important to use quotations thoughtfully and selectively. Remember that the paper presents *your* argument, so choose quotations that support *your* assertions. Do not let the author's voice overwhelm your own. With that caution in mind, you should follow some guidelines to ensure that you use quotations clearly and effectively.

Integrate Quotations

Quotations should always be integrated into your own prose. Do not just drop them into your paper without introduction or comment. Otherwise, it is unlikely your reader will see their function. You can integrate textual support easily and clearly with identifying tags, short phrases that identify the speaker. For example:

The narrator describes Edward Ferrars as "not handsome."

While this tag appears before the quotation, you can also use tags after or in the middle of the quoted text, as the following examples demonstrate:

"You may esteem him," says Elinor to her mother.

"It is yet too early in life," says Mrs. Dashwood, "to despair of such a happiness."

You can also use a colon to introduce a quotation formally:

> Marianne's passionate nature is evident in her assessment
> of Edward's reading style: "Oh! mama, how spiritless,
> how tame was Edward's manner in reading to us last
> night!"

When you quote brief sections of poems (three lines or fewer), use slash marks to indicate the line breaks in the poem:

> As the poem ends, Dickinson speaks of the power of the
> imagination: "The revery alone will do, / If bees are
> few."

Longer quotations (more than four lines of prose or three lines of poetry) should be set off from the rest of your paper in a block quotation. Double-space before you begin the passage, indent it 10 spaces from your left-hand margin, and double-space the passage itself. Because the indentation signals the inclusion of a quotation, do not use quotation marks around the cited passage. Use a colon to introduce the passage:

> Marianne's passionate good-bye to the family home
> reflects her emotional and lyrical way of speaking:
>
> > Oh! happy house, could you know what I suffer
> > in now viewing you from this spot, from whence
> > perhaps I may view you no more!—And you, ye well-
> > known trees!—but you will continue the same.—No
> > leaf will decay because we are removed, nor any
> > branch become motionless although we can observe
> > you no longer!—No; you will continue the same;
> > unconscious of the pleasure or the regret you
> > occasion, and insensible of any change in those
> > who walk under your shade!—But who will remain to
> > enjoy you?
>
> The exclamations, the dashes, the addresses to nature
> all testify to Marianne's associations with the

romantic movement's propensity for dramatic and lyrical expression.

The whole of Dickinson's poem speaks of the imagination:

> To make a prairie it takes a clover and one bee,
> One clover, and a bee,
> And revery.
> The revery alone will do,
> If bees are few.

Clearly, she argues for the creative power of the mind.

It is also important to interpret quotations after you introduce them and explain how they help advance your point. You cannot assume that your reader will interpret the quotations the same way that you do.

Quote Accurately

Always quote accurately. Anything within quotation marks must be the author's exact words. There are, however, some rules to follow if you need to modify the quotation to fit into your prose.

1. Use brackets to indicate any material that you have added to the author's exact wording. For example, if you need to add words to the quotation or alter it grammatically to allow it to fit into your prose, indicate your changes in brackets:

   > Marianne falls in love with Willoughby almost immediately. Soon his "society [becomes] gradually her most exquisite enjoyment."

2. Conversely, if you choose to omit any words from the quotation, use ellipses (three spaced periods) to indicate missing words or phrases:

> While Marianne has eyes only for Willoughby,
> Elinor is closely observing Colonel Brandon:
> "Colonel Brandon's partiality for Marianne . . .
> now first became perceptible to Elinor."

3. If you delete a sentence or more, use the ellipses after a period:

> On Willoughby's excessive gift of a horse to
> Marianne, "Elinor thought it wisest to touch
> that point no more. . . . Opposition on so
> tender a subject would only attach [Marianne]
> the more to her own opinion."

4. If you omit a line or more of poetry, or more than one paragraph of prose, use a single line of spaced periods to indicate the omission:

> To make a prairie it takes a clover and one bee,
> . . . .
> And revery.
> The revery alone will do,
> If bees are few.

Punctuate Properly

Punctuation of quotations often causes more trouble than it should. Once again, you just need to keep these simple rules in mind.

1. Periods and commas should be placed inside quotation marks, even if they are not part of the original quotation:

> Mrs. Jennings alludes to her daughter's pregnancy:
> "She expects to be confined in February."

The only exception to this rule is when the quotation is followed by a parenthetical reference. In this case, the period or comma goes after the citation (more on these later in this chapter):

```
Mrs.  Jennings  alludes  to  her  daughter's
pregnancy:  "She  expects  to  be  confined  in
February" (1: 19).
```

2. Other marks of punctuation—colons, semicolons, question marks, and exclamation points—go outside the quotation marks unless they are part of the original quotation:

```
What  does  Elinor  mean  when  she  says  that  when
"at  Barton  Park,  [she]  never  think[s]  of  tame
and quiet children with any abhorrence"?
```

```
    The  hopeless  Anne  Steele  once  again  talks
about  eligible  bachelors  in  conversation  with
the Dashwood sisters: "And had you a great many
smart beaux there?"
```

Documenting Primary Sources

Unless you are instructed otherwise, you should provide sufficient information for your reader to locate material you quote. Generally, literature papers follow the rules set forth by the Modern Language Association (MLA). These can be found in the *MLA Handbook for Writers of Research Papers* (sixth edition). You can find this book in the reference section of your library. Additionally, its rules for citing both primary and secondary sources are widely available from reputable online sources. One of these is the Online Writing Lab (OWL) at Purdue University. OWL's guide to MLA style is available at http://owl.english.purdue.edu/owl/ resource/557/01/. The Modern Language Association also offers answers to frequently asked questions about MLA style on this helpful Web page: http://www.mla.org/style_faq. Generally, when you are citing from literary works in papers, you should keep a few guidelines in mind.

Parenthetical Citations

MLA asks for parenthetical references in your text after quotations. When you are working with prose (short stories, novels, or essays), include page numbers in the parentheses. Note that many of Jane Austen's novels are organized by their original three-volume arrangement. If working with an Austen novel, you may cite either the page number or the volume and chapter numbers (separating the volume and chapter numbers by a colon and a space):

> The narrator describes the sad state of the Bennet marriage. After Mr. Bennet realizes the "weak understanding and illiberal mind" of his wife, "[r]espect, esteem, and confidence . . . vanished for ever; and all his views of domestic happiness were overthrown" (155).

Or,

> ". . . were overthrown" (2: 19).

When you are quoting poetry, include line numbers:

> Dickinson's speaker tells of the arrival of a fly: "There interposed a Fly— / With Blue—uncertain stumbling Buzz— / Between the light—and Me—" (12-14).

Works Cited Page

These parenthetical citations are linked to a separate works cited page at the end of the paper. The works cited page lists works alphabetically by authors' last names. An entry for the above reference to Austen's *Sense and Sensibility* would read as follows:

> Austen, Jane. *Sense and Sensibility*. Peterborough, Ontario: Broadview Press, 2001.

The *MLA Handbook* includes a full listing of sample entries, as do many of the online explanations of MLA style.

Documenting Secondary Sources

To ensure that your paper is built entirely on your own ideas and analysis, instructors often ask that you write interpretative papers without any outside research. If, on the other hand, your paper requires research, you must document any secondary sources you use. You need to document direct quotations, summaries or paraphrases of others' ideas, and factual information that is not common knowledge. Follow the guidelines above for quoting primary sources when you use direct quotations from secondary sources. Keep in mind that MLA style also includes specific guidelines for citing electronic sources. OWL's Web site provides a good summary: http://owl.english.purdue. edu/owl/resource/557/09/.

Parenthetical Citations

As with the documentation of primary sources, described above, MLA guidelines require in-text parenthetical references to your secondary sources. Unlike the research papers you might write for a history class, literary research papers following MLA style do not use footnotes as a means of documenting sources. Instead, after a quotation, you should cite the author's last name and the page number:

> "The barriers which have to be broken down between Elizabeth and Darcy are social as well as personal" (Pinion 95).

If you include the name of the author in your prose, then you would include only the page number in your citation. For example:

> According to F. B. Pinion, "The barriers which have to be broken down between Elizabeth and Darcy are social as well as personal" (95).

If you are including more than one work by the same author, the parenthetical citation should include a shortened yet identifiable version of the title to indicate which of the author's works you cite. For example:

> In Ian Watt's estimation of *Sense and Sensibility*, "Elinor is good and nice, but she is only intermittently interesting. Yet her general functions in the narrative are clear enough, and some of them have occasionally been overlooked" (*Essays* 39).

Similarly, and just as important, if you summarize or paraphrase the particular ideas of your source, you must provide documentation:

> In *Sense and Sensibility,* the character of Elinor is morally sound and pleasant company, but not always interesting to read. Still, she serves important functions in the novel (Watt, *Essays* 48).

Works Cited Page

Like the primary sources discussed above, the parenthetical references to secondary sources are keyed to a separate works cited page at the end of your paper. Here is an example of a works cited page that uses the examples cited above. Note that when two or more works by the same author are listed, you should use three hypens followed by a period in the subsequent entries. You can find a complete list of sample entries in the *MLA Handbook* or from a reputable online summary of MLA style.

WORKS CITED

Pinion, F. P. *A Jane Austen Companion: A Critical Survey and Reference Book.* London: Macmillan, 1973.

Watt, Ian. "*On Sense and Sensibility.*" *Jane Austen: A Collection of Critical Essays.* Ed. Ian Watt. Englewood Cliffs, NJ: Prentice-Hall, Inc., 1963. 41–51.

———. *The Rise of the Novel.* Berkeley: University of California Press, 1957.

Plagiarism

Failure to document carefully and thoroughly can leave you open to charges of stealing the ideas of others, an act which is known as plagiarism. This is a very serious matter. Remember that it is important to include quotation marks when you use language from your source, even if you use just one or two words. For example, if you wrote, The barriers between Elizabeth and Darcy are social as well as personal, you would be guilty of plagiarism, since you used Pinion's distinct language without acknowledging him as the source. Instead, you should write: There are "social as well as personal" impediments to Elizabeth and Darcy's relationship (Pinion 95). In this case, you have properly credited Pinion.

Neither summarizing the ideas of an author nor changing or omitting just a few words means that you can omit a citation. The remainder of this section demonstrates how to properly cite a section of Claire Tomalin's biography of Jane Austen. In the following passage, Tomalin discusses three of Austen's early novels, *Sense and Sensibility, Pride and Prejudice,* and *Northanger Abbey:*

> The first striking thing about these three early novels is that each approaches its subject in a radically different way. *Sense and Sensibility* is—roughly speaking—a debate, *Pride and Prejudice* a romance, and *Northanger Abbey* a satire, a novel about novels and novel reading. You might expect a young writer to keep working within the same formula several times, learning as she goes. Not so with Jane Austen. She was too inventive and too interested in the techniques of fiction to settle in any one mode, and she tackled the problems of three such diverse forms with astonishing skill.

Below are two examples of passages that plagiarize Tomalin:

> Austen was a curious and courageous young writer. Three early novels testify to her desire to experiment with different literary forms. Austen used the form of a debate for *Sense and Sensibility,* a romance for *Pride and Prejudice,* and a satire for *Northanger Abbey.*

> Austen was too inventive and innovative to settle for a single literary form and return to it for future works. Consider three early novels and notice how each approaches its subject in a different way: *Sense and*

> *Sensibility* is a debate, *Pride and Prejudice* is a romance, and *Northanger Abbey* is a satire (Tomalin 157).

While the first passage does not use Tomalin's exact language, it does list the same ideas she proposes as the literary forms of three of Austen's novels, and it does not cite Tomalin's work. The second passage has condensed some of the ideas, changed some wording, and included a citation, but some of the phrasing is Tomalin's. The first passage could be fixed with a parenthetical citation. Because some of the wording remains the same, though, the second would require the use of quotation marks in addition to a parenthetical citation. The passage below represents an honestly and adequately documented use of the original passage:

> Claire Tomalin notes Jane Austen's technical skill and innovation and points to three of Austen's early novels—*Sense and Sensibility, Pride and Prejudice,* and *Northanger Abbey*—as examples of "radically different" approaches to storytelling. Tomalin observes that "*Sense and Sensibility* is—roughly speaking—a debate, *Pride and Prejudice* a romance, and *Northanger Abbey* a satire, a novel about novels and novel reading" (157). What is even more remarkable, according to Tomalin, is how skillfully Austen "tackled the problems of three such diverse forms" (157).

This passage acknowledges that this interpretation is derived from Tomalin while appropriately using quotations to indicate her precise language.

Although it is not necessary to document well-known facts, often referred to as "common knowledge," any ideas or language that you take from someone else must be properly documented. Common knowledge generally includes the birth and death dates of authors or other well-documented facts of their lives. An often-cited guideline is: if you can find the information in three sources, it is common knowledge. Despite this guideline, it is, admittedly, often difficult to know whether the facts you uncover are common knowledge. When in doubt, document your source.

Sample Essay

Ruby Dalton
Mr. Delgado
English 200
July 7, 2009

THE CASE FOR THE LOVELESS MARRIAGE OF
CHARLOTTE LUCAS IN *PRIDE AND PREJUDICE*

Of the many marriages in Jane Austen's *Pride and Prejudice,* that of Charlotte Lucas and Mr. Collins is the least romantic. Elizabeth Bennet considers it "unaccountable" that her closest friend, Charlotte, could possibly marry the "conceited, pompous, narrow minded, [and] silly" Mr. Collins (2: 1). Elizabeth is not alone in seeing Mr. Collins's flaws. Charlotte herself considers Mr. Collins's company "irksome" and knows that he has no actual love for her, but in spite of these serious impediments, Charlotte skillfully orchestrates his offer of marriage (1: 22). Charlotte's hard-nosed philosophy about marriage is in clear contrast to Elizabeth's romantic feelings about love. One scholar asserts that the novel's fundamental ideas of marriage "are enacted in the juxtaposing of the two young women" (Gill and Gregory 134). Though Elizabeth refuses to believe it possible, *Pride and Prejudice* convinces us through historical context, Charlotte's lucid opinions, and the narrator's own commentary that the loveless Collins marriage is a good, if costly, choice for Charlotte Lucas.

The novel's historical context informs and influences Charlotte's decision. She is a "sensible, intelligent young woman . . . [of] about 27," an age that was then considered advanced to be unmarried, and she is eager to become married, though not because she is driven by love (1: 5). She desires marriage because it is a step up from her position as a dependent daughter. Marriage, curiously, permitted young women such as Charlotte a variety of independence in that it offered more financial and domestic autonomy than that of an unmarried woman. This independence is, however, more symbolic than actual: Until the Married Women's Property Act (1882), married women were the material and legal property of their husbands (Brown 72). Austen does not criticize outright the society that keeps in limbo capable and intelligent women like the Bennet sisters, Caroline Bingley, and Charlotte Lucas—women who are educated and trained to become wives—but Charlotte's story shows that there are very good practical reasons to escape the "fearful" situation of unmarried women at this time (Polhemus 89). Another compelling reason for marriage was its long-term benefits. Even widows, as women who were married at one time, enjoyed more social authority and autonomy, and often financial security, than unmarried women did. Austen's novels, according to feminist scholars Gilbert and Gubar, show discomfort with "the tight place assigned women in patriarchy," a place that demands women labor for husbands in order to acquire some parity within "the economics of sexual exploitation" (112). *Pride and Prejudice* certainly reveals anxieties about the options for survival available to young women in society.

The narrator of *Pride and Prejudice* is forthright about the unromantic aspects of the institution of marriage. The narrator is sympathetic to Charlotte's very practical goal and places that goal within the larger conditions of young women and society: "Without thinking highly either of men or of matrimony, marriage had always been [Charlotte's] object; it was the only honourable [sic] provision for well-educated young women of small fortune, and however uncertain of giving happiness, must be their pleasantest preservative from want" (1: 22). The narrator is here explaining that "for well-educated young women of small fortune," marriage is the only means by which to ensure financial security within a social class that rarely allowed women to work to support themselves. The narrator's qualification that marriage "must be" the young women's "pleasantest preservative from want" further suggests that the narrator is not deceived into thinking that marriage is a sure solution. The narrator's ambivalence about marriage guaranteeing sustenance, let alone felicity, is echoed by Charlotte, who believes that "Happiness in marriage is entirely a matter of chance" (1: 6). Charlotte and the narrator both believe in the pervasiveness of marriage's less romantic manifestations.

Once Charlotte attains her matrimonial objective, she has time to reflect on her accomplishment and the benefits it will provide her and her family. The Lucas family is "properly overjoyed" at the engagement, not least because they "could give very little fortune" to Charlotte; for her parents, this engagement means that Charlotte will be provided for; for her brothers this engagement means they will not have to worry about later supporting a spinster sister; for her sisters, this engagement means that they will now be able to come out into society and begin their own marriage pursuits (1: 22). The entire Lucas family enjoys a windfall because of Charlotte's success with the "irksome" Mr. Collins. Charlotte's ambition for the marriage is described by the narrator as "the pure and disinterested desire of an establishment," while Charlotte herself describes her hopes more prosaically as being for a "comfortable home" (1: 22). Once married, Charlotte manages to retain the benefits of marriage by diligently lessening the annoyances of her husband's company; she "wisely" does not hear what he says and encourages, as "much as possible," his working in the garden and away from her (2: 5). Though the narrator does not give us access to Charlotte's thoughts once she is married, Elizabeth tries to imagine how one might tolerate Mr. Collins. Elizabeth comments on the atmosphere of the house: "When Mr. Collins could be forgotten, there was really a great air of comfort throughout, and by Charlotte's evident enjoyment of it, Elizabeth supposed he must be often forgotten" (2: 5). Another concession that Elizabeth makes to Charlotte's choice is one that Charlotte would surely admit to: her material advancement. We see this in the repetition of the possessive "her" in the survey of Charlotte's possessions: "Her home and her housekeeping, her parish and her poultry, and all their dependent concerns, had not yet lost their charms" (2: 26). That qualifying "not yet," of course, suggests that whatever boons Charlotte has gained by her marriage will eventually be overcome by the deficiencies in her mate. The narrator here suggests that Charlotte's personal satisfaction with these material and social advancements will soon give way beneath the titanic irritations of her husband's company.

The transient appeal of possessions and social advancement suggests disappointment in the future, but the profound disappointments associated with Charlotte's marriage are more immediate and more personal. These costs to Charlotte are heavy ones. The most significant personal cost to Charlotte is alienation from Elizabeth, whose "friendship [Charlotte] *valued* beyond that of any other person" (1: 22; italics added). The narrator's use of economic language, of value, stands out here; it is in keeping with the novel's awareness of the economic and social circumstances that compel Charlotte's decision to marry without love. The notion of economic motivation is also emphasized when Elizabeth considers the exchange that Charlotte has made. The absence of love in the Collins match is particularly galling to Elizabeth, and she "could not have supposed it possible that when called into action, [Charlotte] would have sacrificed every better feeling to worldly advantage" (1: 22). For the romantic Elizabeth, a marriage for any reason other than love must be wrong, and a marriage for "worldly advantage" must be suspect, must even be depraved. That

Elizabeth thinks Charlotte has "disgraced" herself by this union suggests that any marriage without love is, in the starkest assessment, a degrading exchange of body for money, a kind of "socially respectable prostitution" (Polhemus 89). Here, in exchange for her wifely duties, Charlotte is compensated with a home and material possessions. The ugly notion of this economic arrangement must certainly contribute to Elizabeth's feeling that her friend is "disgraced" by marrying Mr. Collins.

The costs to Charlotte, in the loss of her friend's respect and, perhaps, in her own, are shown in the novel in a significantly quiet way: Charlotte is, after her marriage, effectively silent. We are no longer given access to Charlotte's valuable and lucid thoughts; like Elizabeth, we and the narrator have to project significances onto Charlotte. Charlotte's silence, at least in drawing room conversations at Rosings, is an expression of deference to the socially higher-ranking and domineering Lady Catherine de Bourgh, the Collinses's patroness. One symbolic reading of this silence is that Charlotte's identity is, by social necessity, erased by her marriage. Mr. Collins inadvertently remarks on this erasure of his wife's individual identity when he gloats to his cousin, "My dear Charlotte and I have but one mind and one way of thinking" (2: 16). Since we are well acquainted with both Collinses, we can easily deduce from this assertion that Charlotte keeps her true opinions to herself.

Though Elizabeth is convinced that the Collins marriage is fundamentally wrong, the narrator is understanding of Charlotte's decision. The narrator presents convincing reasons for the marriage by explaining Charlotte's philosophies, her circumstances, and the social context in which she lives. The narrator's interest, if not outright endorsement, is seen in her showing how Charlotte manages to live with the flaws in her marriage. Charlotte Lucas's story illuminates a criticism that *Pride and Prejudice* makes about society's treatment of young women at this time. While a practical marriage offered a step up the social ladder for unmarried women, it was a chilling proposition nonetheless. It is difficult to avoid thinking that Jane Austen, herself unmarried and, until the end of her life, dependent on her family, would have understood too well the decision that Charlotte makes. While writing this novel, it must have been a relief to Austen to move imaginatively from the Collinses' loveless marriage to the marriage of Elizabeth and Darcy, a romantic union of love, affinity, desire, respect, and understanding. In this novel full of marriages, we come to understand Charlotte Lucas's philosophy of marriage, but we cheer for Elizabeth Bennet's practice of love.

WORKS CITED

Austen, Jane. *Pride and Prejudice*. Norton Critical Edition. 3rd edition. New York: Norton, 2001.

Brown, Julia Prewitt. *A Reader's Guide to the Nineteenth-Century English Novel*. New York: Macmillan Publishing Company, 1985.

Gilbert, Sandra A., and Susan Gubar. "Shut Up in Prose: Austen's Juvenilia." *The Madwoman in the Attic: The Woman Writer and the Nineteenth-Century Literary Imagination*. New Haven, CT: Yale UP, 1979. 107–45.

Gill, Richard, and Susan Gregory. "*Sense and Sensibility*." *Mastering the Novels of Jane Austen*. New York: Palgrave-Macmillan, 2003. 63–119.

Polhemus, Robert M. "The Fortunate Fall: Jane Austen's *Pride and Prejudice*." *Jane Austen's* Pride and Prejudice: A Sourcebook. Ed. Robert Morrison. Routledge Guides to Literature. New York: Routledge, 2005. 88–90.

HOW TO WRITE
ABOUT JANE AUSTEN

AN OVERVIEW
Austen's Legacy

JANE AUSTEN'S six finished novels have had a remarkable effect on both literary and popular cultures. Austen's cultural impact resonates every time a new film based on one of her novels is released, which in the last 20 years has been happening with seemingly greater frequency and to varied effects. To take two popular examples, *Clueless* (1995) translates *Emma* (1816) onto the campus of a Southern California high school, while *Bride and Prejudice* (2004) borrows the dramatic situation of *Pride and Prejudice* (1813) to create a Bollywood-style musical comedy. Librarians can also testify to the spell that Austen's books have cast. Bookshelves are full of novels that tap into Austen's popularity. There are prequels and sequels about the lives of Elizabeth Bennet, Mr. Darcy, and their fictional counterparts from other novels. Jane Austen has herself become fictionalized, solving crimes in mysteries and having scenes from her life acted out in films. With all of these creations and re-creations, it should not perhaps surprise us that there are even books about books about Jane Austen. Scholars, too, needless to say, have also been busy with Austen.

What is most astonishing about Austen's novels is how durable her stories of English provincial families have proved to be for both popular and scholarly audiences. Looking solely at the characters (young women and men, clergymen and naval officers, flirts and gadflies) and their situations (growing up and into the right marriage), one would not expect the novels to have seen such high traffic in adaptations, but there is hardly any sign of slackening interest. Literary cults can be distracting; as a literary scholar, your focus should not be on Austen's iconography, but on Austen's work. What you will find is that her masterfully ironic stories, as well as her accomplishments in narrative, character, and literary realism, all merit the dominant position she holds in the canon.

The intimate feeling of Austen's novels is, in many ways, a direct result of her narrative style. The voice of her narrators is familiar, wry, knowing, and amused: They are philosophers of her characters and friends to the reader. An example of this is seen in *Emma* when the narrator unambiguously suggests the illegitimate birth of Harriet Smith: "Harriet Smith was the *natural* daughter of *somebody. Somebody* had placed her, several years back, at Mrs. Goddard's school, and *somebody* had lately raised her from the condition of scholar to that of parlour-boarder. This was all that was generally known of her history" (1: 3; italics added). The word *natural* was at that time a euphemism for illegitimate, and by using it the narrator is already drawing us into somewhat scandalous territory; the perverse repetition of "somebody" transforms that mysterious personage into a kind of character, a figure to be speculated about among friends. Austen's intimate narration takes a more ironic tone and form in the first line of her most popular novel, *Pride and Prejudice*: "It is a truth universally acknowledged, that a single man in possession of a good fortune, must be in want of a wife." The ironies in this sentence are many (and will be explored at greater length in the chapter on that novel): With its utilization of a heavy-handed declaration of a "truth universally acknowledged," we are then witness to a claim about wealthy men that is so obviously spurious that we, as readers, are given the opportunity to enjoy the delicious task of taking down a peg the hyperbolic proclamation. Our eyebrows rise at the assertion, but while reading the sentence in its entirety we become attuned to the narrator's sense of humor and the droll witness she bears to the provincial world that she is about to show us. The style and tenor of the voice ensure that, while the characters themselves are presented with their follies, the reader is customarily travelling shotgun with the opining narrator: We, along for the ride, are treated to the foibles of the characters in a way that allows us to feel privy to the jokes of a smart, funny, and invaluable friend.

In addition to the narration, the characters themselves represent another one of Austen's legacies. Some of the first accolades of Austen's work focused on characterization, and in the years following her death, her achievements in characterization drew comparisons to those of Shakespeare (Watt 5). In 1830, the novelist Thomas Henry Lister discussed Austen's characterization as her particular talent: she "possessed the rare and difficult art of making her readers intimately acquainted with the character[s] . . . she describes. We feel as if we had lived among them; and yet she employs no elaborate description—no metaphysical analysis—no antithetical balance of their good and bad qualities. She scarcely does more than make them act and talk, and we know them directly" (Trickett 165).

A good example of what Lister describes, Austen's ability to let her characters' words establish who they are, is illustrated in *Emma* in a monologue Mrs. Elton delivers at a picnic. At this point in the novel, Mrs. Elton has already distinguished herself as a self-important know-it-all, and if we needed any reminders of her persona, we learn that she has been disappointed in her scheme to bring picturesque accessories (a donkey and a parasol) to this informal outing. Notice how Mrs. Elton demonstrates her own overbearing foolishness in this outlined speech that takes place while picking strawberries:

> The Best fruit in England—every body's favourite—always whole-some—These the finest beds and finest sorts.—Delightful to gather for one's self—the only way of really enjoying them.—Morning decidedly the best time—never tired—every sort good—hautboy infinitely superior—no comparison—the others hardly eatable—hautboys very scarce—Chili preferred—white wood finest flavour of all—price of strawberries in London—abundance about Bristol—Maple Grove—cultivation—beds when to be renewed—gardeners thinking exactly different—no general rule—gardeners never to be put out of their way—delicious fruit—only too rich to be eaten much of—inferior to cherries—currants more refreshing—only objection to gathering strawberries the stooping—glaring sun—tired to death—could bear it no longer—must go and sit in the shade. (*Emma* 3: 6)

In this speech, Mrs. Elton is unconsciously eloquent about her character flaws. She begins in a flurry of energy, since she is "never tired," and she praises strawberries, "every body's favourite," but soon, as her exertions are felt, she begins to think of strawberries' disadvantages, such as their "price . . . in London," the fact that some varieties are "hardly eatable," "the stooping" one must do to pick them, the "glaring sun" that makes one "tired to death." She also reveals her snobbery; she transforms even something as innocuous as fruit picking into an opportunity to be competitive about which is better and which is less preferable—strawberries are, after all, "inferior to cherries," and "currants [are] more refreshing." Mrs. Elton's arrogance also slips out when she implies that gardeners do not know as much as she does about gardening. In the characterization of self-important fools like Mrs. Elton, Austen simply allows them to talk. The narrator pulls back, and the characters tell us all we need to know about them.

All of Austen's talents, for narration, for dialogue, and for characterization, work together to contribute the sense of realism to her works. Realism is rendered by Austen's ability to create characters who feel familiar and a narrator who feels like a close friend, and by her limiting the scope of events to fathomable ones. She is credited with transforming the English novel by keeping her focus on the everyday and the unremarkable. The English novel, before Austen, had largely been the realm of melodramatic stories of bigger-than-life romantic figures and villains. Throughout much of the 17th century, popular novels tended toward the grandiose and exotic, often featuring sensationalized gothic or sentimental situations. Some of the most popular novels featured antiheroes—thieves, murderers, prostitutes—who narrated their scandalous life stories in a "confession of exploits," sometimes on their way to the gallows (Irvine 17). Jane Austen's novels, taking place as they do within an ordinary world, expanded the possibilities of what a novel could be. Sir Walter Scott's favorable review of *Emma* in *Edinburgh Magazine* (1818) remarked on the realism that Austen brought to fiction (Grey 282). In his private journal Scott expounded on her talent after reading, "for the third time at least," *Pride and Prejudice*:

> That young lady had a talent for describing the involvements and feelings and characters of ordinary life, which is to me the most wonderful I ever met with. The Big Bow-wow strain I can do myself like any now going; but the exquisite touch, which renders ordinary commonplace things and characters interesting . . . is denied to me. (quoted in Watt 3)

Scott was the hugely popular author of historical, romantic, and other "Big Bow-wow" novels. That he envied Austen's ability to render "ordinary commonplace things and characters interesting" says a great deal not only about his understanding of his own work but also his vision of what art could be: regular, middle-class, murder-free, and mundane. What Scott recognized in Austen's realistic novels was that life itself is art; art, then, need not be grander than life to captivate us.

Austen's Influences

Jane Austen was born and raised in the English countryside village of Steventon, and it is in provincial settings that the most felicitous moments of her novels are set. Bath and London also make appearances in Austen's works, but they are generally characterized as chaotic, the stomping grounds of mountebanks—characters set on deceit, deception, and appearances. Austen knew these urban places well, and her family connections ensured that she was apprised of the cosmopolitan world, but her heart was in neither fashion nor society. She did not love the hectic pulse of a city street. Her personal preference was for comfortable rooms and expansive grounds, such as those she writes about at Mansfield Park, Pemberley, and Longbourn. While a gravel walk in Bath will satisfy her lovers in search of solitude, it is the countrysides' rolling hills, hedgerows, paths, and avenues that get Austen's more frequent attention and endorsement.

As integral as these landscapes were to Austen's imagination, it is the characters themselves that are central to the action. About Austen's novels, Virginia Woolf remarked, "Always the stress is laid upon character" (139). It is on characters that Austen's focus rests. Her personal life must have set this in motion: She was one of eight children, and in addition to this brood, boys boarded at the Austen house as pupils of her clergyman father. The teaching was, in addition to the farming and the preaching, a way for the well-educated but not wealthy family to support itself. Mrs. Austen and her two daughters, Cassandra and Jane, would have been busy tending the garden and running the household (Tomalin 63). Though Austen and her sister, Cassandra, never married, their lives were never empty; time was filled with parents, nieces, nephews, siblings, in-laws, neighbors, and servants (families of even meager means employed servants to help with the many household tasks). With all this activity, it is impressive that Austen got anything written at all, but she clearly distilled from the volume of her acquaintance the resources for deft characterization. The complications of big families are also conveyed in her novels. In *Sense and Sensibility*, Fanny Dashwood's swooping in like a raptor on the home of her grieving in-laws is an example of how an entire family is affected by one ill-chosen spouse. With a relation like her, we cannot help but see Mr. Woodhouse's point in *Emma* about marriages being tragic events. The social life of the Austens was a rich one, and Jane Austen's masterly examples of dialogue suggest that she was listening the whole time. We see how quickly she drew characters when, in a letter to her sister, Austen described the people she met at a ball: "I had long wanted to see Dr. Britton, & his wife amuses me very much with her affected refinement & elegance—Miss Lee I found very conversible; she admires Crabbe [the poet] as she ought" (Parrish 329–330).

As Austen's brothers grew up, went to sea, joined the clergy or the army, got married, had children, buried wives, and remarried, the scope of the young writer's imagination and knowledge grew exponentially. The era was one of profound disruptions, both philosophical and political. Even from its seemingly remote Hampshire location, the Austen family experienced the tumult of the times. A close cousin's husband is guillotined in France, a casualty of the Revolution; two brothers are fighting Napoléon's forces on myriad seas; another brother opens (and later loses) a bank in London; Warren Hastings, a family connection and former governor of India, is on trial for corruption; across England, revolutionary talk and sympathy with France drives neighbors to spy on one another. From the letters exchanged with her brothers and the stories they told when they were home, Austen would have gleaned insights into the lives of men when they are away from the strict controls imposed by a supervising society. The very notion of freedom and independence, such as these men knew, would have sent a young woman's imagination spinning. Austen's pride and patriotism for the Royal Navy is clear in both *Mansfield Park* and *Persuasion*. Sometimes erroneously believed to be ahistorical, Austen's works feature persistent reminders of how larger historical forces shape individual destinies. You get the sense from her novels that middle-class English families recognized how the larger world affected their lives. The empire, slavery, and military threats matter to these people, even while—for the Austens, at least—their days were busy with laundry and farming.

Jane Austen and her family were representative of their time, but they were unusual in many ways too. A highly literary group, all were immensely fond of good stories, and even Mrs. Austen wrote comic verse in her personal letters. The Austen patriarch, Reverend George Austen, was also unusual for an Anglican clergyman, particularly in his support of his daughter's often irreverent writings. He was surely one of her first fans, as well as serving as an important mentor. A scholar in addition to a clergyman, farmer, and teacher, he read long novels aloud to his children; later, as they grew older, they staged plays for him (Grey 279). One of Jane Austen's surviving notebooks bears her father's inscription: "Effusions of Fancy by a very Young Lady Consisting of Tales in a Style entirely new" (Tomalin 69). Paper was very expensive at that time, but even more dear to Austen must have been the encouragement that such a gift would signify to a budding writer.

In her father's library—quite large and always open to his children—Jane Austen settled down with Shakespeare, Samuel Richardson, Dr. Johnson, Henry Fielding, Fanny Burney, Maria Edgeworth, and many other popular novelists, dramatists, and essayists (Tomalin 69–70). Some of this material is intellectually sophisticated, and from it Austen would have learned the rhetorical style of moral instruction, which she would later ape in *Northanger Abbey*. In addition to the moral tomes, there were worldly novels that featured such risqué subjects as children born out of wedlock, sexual impropriety, drunkenness, and vice in general. Some of these scandalous situations materialize in her own novels. In *Sense and Sensibility*, for instance, Willoughby marries for money a woman whom he wishes were dead; he also impregnates and thereby ruins the life of another innocent young woman (whose respectability he questions); he is consequently involved in a duel; he drinks to excess. His is the plotline of a picaresque hero, such as that in *Tom Jones*. Austen was well aware of society's thirst for scandal. Her narrator points to this when neighbors are characterized in *Pride and Prejudice* as disappointed that Lydia Bennet married the man with whom she eloped. "To be sure," the narrator informs us, "it would have been more for the advantage of conversation" if Lydia had instead pursued the course expected for fictional characters in her situation by getting pregnant and later becoming a prostitute (3: 8).

The deft insertion of picaresque details into an otherwise realistic novel such as *Pride and Prejudice* marks a talent gleaned from Austen's years of attentive reading and writing. She had the skill and confidence to make fun of literature. Austen must have gained confidence as she shared her writings with her parents and siblings. We assume that they were a receptive audience, and having such a literary family must have served as one of the most important influences in the genesis of Jane Austen, the writer. She would have amused them with lampoons such as her *A History of England by a Partial, Prejudiced, and Ignorant Historian,* written at age 15 and dedicated to (and illustrated by) her sister. The joking continued with other works of juvenilia, much of which roundly mock the clichéd dramatic conflict of an innocent heroine beset by villains. Austen's early *Lady Susan* (c. 1796) so overturns the didactic rules of a sentimental novel that it features a heroine who acts more like a villain in her ruthless sexual pursuits.

Since Austen's family was her first audience and she relied on their feedback, they also functioned as her editors. Later, when she had completed novels ready for publication, her father's approval of her efforts was such that in 1797 he acted as her agent and sent to a publisher the novel that would later be *Pride and Prejudice.* This effort was rebuffed, but Austen's diligence about her writing did not wane. Around this time she had three novels in complete form, and for the remainder of her life she worked on multiple books simultaneously (Leavis 185). Later, her brother Henry would act as her agent (women did not customarily conduct such business). Even years later, after the men in her family were scattered across the country, they sent their commentary in letters. Feedback from acquaintances was also important to Austen, and she kept a journal of the opinions she heard from neighbors and friends about *Mansfield Park* and *Emma* (Tomalin 239). These journals—which include both accolades from friends and criticisms from people who did not realize they were expostulating on the defects of a novel in the author's presence—show that Austen took seriously her authorship and the publication of her works. Part of her desire to publish was driven by poverty: Austen was, after all, always dependent on others for her income, and the meager earnings she later received from her novels were both needed and validating. Sometimes thought of as a writer who dashed off novels between social calls, Austen was in fact a committed artist.

Over the influences of her family and her favorite books, above the din of her eventful era, we recognize the creative genius of Jane Austen herself. Her innovations for the English novel include her unusual narration and her focus on realistic stories. Her masterfully crafted, singular, yet familiar characters—Mr. Collins, Elizabeth Bennet, Emma, Miss Bates, Marianne Dashwood, Wickham—still resonate, down to the present day.

All the discussion of her literary legacy and the enduring fascination with her work must be only a prelude to the main event—reading Austen. Once you sit down with one of Austen's novels you will generate your own ideas about her stories, the characters that populate them, and the way they are constructed. This volume aims to guide your talents in literary analysis and enrich both your reading of and your writing about Jane Austen's novels.

TOPICS AND STRATEGIES

The sample topics provided below are designed to suggest how you might approach writing an essay about a work, or a number of works, by Jane Austen. The subsequent chapters describe analytical approaches to single works by Austen; the remainder of this chapter focuses on broader approaches to her works. Many of the sample topics will give you the titles of possible works to focus on. Be mindful of the length of your essay when you are deciding which works, and how many of them, to include in an essay. Make sure that you have adequate space to give a thorough treatment to each work you analyze. You are free as well to select works not mentioned in the sample topics. If you choose multiple texts, it is important to have a rationale for grouping those texts in your essay. For example, you might select novels that register a change in Austen's writing approach, or novels that explore similar themes. The following section offers topics to consider and also discusses some of the notable elements of Austen's work: the patterns in her use of themes, her construction of character, the history and context of her writing, the philosophical ideas that circulate in her novels, the way she designed her stories, and her use of symbolism and language. Finally, this chapter will discuss the best ways to make comparative analyses of Austen's novels.

Theme

Austen's novels are rooted in the English countryside and center on the education of women in the years leading up to their marriage. Within this narrow dramatic scope, Austen worked with a wide variety of themes. Some of these include broad social themes, such as those related to socioeconomic class, marriage, and the social situation of women.

Women's social situation and the restrictions that limited their lives are clearly illustrated in works such as *Emma,* where Miss Bates and her mother uncomplainingly abide their poverty and social insignificance. Jane Fairfax also exemplifies the desperate straits of destitute single women. That middle-class women were trained only to be wives is elucidated in all of Austen's novels, but the fact that these novels end in marriage should in no way suggest an endorsement of this practice. You might explore how the novels reveal Austen's ambivalences about marriage as an institution.

Socioeconomic class is another broad social theme that courses through her works. Austen's criticism of the status quo is readily recognized. She was writing at a time when there was considerable mobility within the English class structure, and her novels show that one's class position and social consequence were often fiercely defended. *Pride and Prejudice* offers many examples of the anxieties related to social position. The Bingley sisters, for instance, display their insecurities about the newness of their money when they volubly criticize actions that suggest a humbler class association (for example, Elizabeth Bennet's walking outdoors). Lady Catherine de Bourgh vigilantly protects her family's social position, as when she orders Elizabeth to entertain no ideas about marrying her aristocratic nephew, Darcy. Socioeconomic class is also a central theme in *Persuasion,* where the established gentry position is yielding, by their own degeneracy and lassitude, to the more active and deserving naval officers, who have returned triumphant from their battles against Napoléon. What Austen's novel suggests here is rather radical: That the old social order is overdue for an overhaul.

A theme and individual quality that all her novels celebrate is merit. An essay might explore what, exactly, constitutes merit in Austen's work. In the case of *Persuasion,* the merit of the naval officers is evident in their kindness, generosity, and constancy. Mr. Darcy's merit in *Pride and Prejudice* is not initially evident, but he works to be worthy of Elizabeth Bennet's good opinion. Merit in the morally minded *Mansfield Park* is more unabashedly presented. You might also explore in an essay on this or another novel whether merit is represented as innate or learned.

Another theme that recurs in Austen's novels is related to the coming-of-age dynamic: the theme of education. The education that many of Austen's heroines undergo has to do with understanding both themselves and their place in the world. Emma Woodhouse, Elizabeth Bennet, and Catherine Morland, as different as these heroines are from one another, all undergo profound educations. Their illusions—about themselves, their families, and their acquaintances—are replaced by understanding.

Sample Topics:

1. **Education:** Education is an important aspect of every Austen novel. What kind of education do her characters undergo?

   Every Austen novel shows the importance of education. Emma Woodhouse in *Emma* is one character whose self-awareness is stunted for an individual who so prides herself on her insight. Elizabeth Bennet in *Pride and Prejudice* is far more worldly and wise than Emma, but even Elizabeth must suffer for faulty perception before recognizing that even she has flaws. Marianne Dashwood in *Sense and Sensibility* undergoes perhaps the most pronounced education since she transforms from a spirited, passionate young woman to the wiser, and perhaps sadder, wife of Colonel Brandon at the end of the book. Catherine Morland in *Northanger Abbey* also learns hard lessons before she can distinguish between her illusions and the real world. In an essay, you might choose two or more novels and focus on how the heroine is educated about her flaws, or how she changes her conduct or herself. Another essay might instead explore how a heroine must gain an understanding of the world before she is able to become a part of it: Catherine Morland and Marianne Dashwood would be interesting characters in this regard. Another essay on education might look to heroines who seem to do more teaching than learning, such as Anne Elliot in *Persuasion*, Elinor Dashwood in *Sense and Sensibility*, and Fanny Price in *Mansfield Park*. How do these characters effectively educate the individuals around them?

2. **Merit:** How is merit characterized in Austen's oeuvre?

All of Austen's novels meditate on what constitutes merit, but three particularly good novels to examine are *Sense and Sensibility, Mansfield Park,* and *Persuasion.* One approach to this topic might focus on two novels and identify individuals within them who represent merit. How, for instance, does Elinor Dashwood puzzle out Edward Ferrars's merit? Are there times when she doubts it? *Mansfield Park* is especially aware of morality, so discussions of merit run throughout the novel. According to these discussions and the narrator's commentary, how is merit gained? Is it innate or learned? Another approach to an essay on merit in Austen's works might discuss the character traits associated with merit. With this approach, you might discuss how kindness, intelligence, self-sacrifice, and generosity are represented as meritorious. Other discussions of merit in Austen's work could consider whether merit is rewarded and whether merit is more important than socioeconomic position.

3. **Home:** What do Austen's works tell us about the theme of home?

For an author whose works seem largely domestic, it is perhaps surprising how frequently homeless Austen's heroines are. The themes of home and homelessness dramatize the precarious position of young women. Anxieties about home pervade *Pride and Prejudice*; for the Bennet women, their home belongs to them only for the duration of Mr. Bennet's life. With Mr. Bennet's death, the home will go to Mr. Collins, the nearest male heir to the estate. In *Sense and Sensibility,* the dual tragedies of a father's death and the women's subsequent displacement from their home are further complicated by a brother's withholding of financial support. For this topic, you will want to choose one or more novels and explore how both the acquisition and the loss of a home prove to be central concerns for the female characters. How do we see that the desire for a home is important to these women? Though she had previously criticized Charlotte Lucas's single-minded focus in acquiring a home, Elizabeth Bennet's own desire for a home is revealed when she realizes her love for Darcy after first seeing his estate (the home she will eventually occupy).

Character

Partly because of their flaws, Austen's characters draw us in. Her heroes, heroines, chatterboxes, hypochondriacs, sycophants, opportunists, pedants, flibbertigibbets, flirts, and rakes engage us and vitalize her stories. Austen's characters are variously driven by motivations that are familiar and palpable: fear, conviction, passion, reason, ambition, and a desire for security and true love. On this last desire—that for true love—Austen's novels bestow their benevolent attention, but also their skepticism. Many individuals, her narratives show, betray their greater motivations for lesser drives such as lust, greed, or even inertia.

Austen's deft touch with characters is best seen in her heroines who tend toward the brainy, the quirky, and the unconventional. Elizabeth Bennet stands as the quintessential Austen heroine because she is the most outspoken. She is confident of her reason, she is a true believer in love, she never abandons her individuality, and best of all, she becomes aware of her flaws. When she realizes that she was as taken in by Wickham as everyone else, she upbraids herself willingly. Austen's first novel completed for publication, *Northanger Abbey*, shows that she was already experimenting with what a heroine could be. At the outset the narrator announces: "No one who had ever seen Catherine Morland in her infancy, would have supposed her born to be a heroine" (1: 1). An interesting essay could consider how Austen's unconventionally imperfect heroines operate in their stories.

Even Austen's minor characters offer considerable analytical opportunities. You might focus on the antagonists and discuss how their character traits help us understand the protagonists. Another approach would be to focus on Austen's depictions of character types, such as rakes or snobs, both of whom pose threats to the protagonists. Studying Austen's fools is likewise informative; an essay might fruitfully examine how they contribute to the plot or our understanding of the protagonists.

Sample Topics:

1. **Heroines:** What, in Austen's works, constitutes a heroine?

Austen's heroines make up an eclectic collection of female characters. To address this topic you will focus on two or three heroines and record as much as you can about their behaviors and characteristics. Your notes will lead you to ask questions about differences among them. You might consider analyzing two especially contrasting heroines and examine how their characterizations help articulate the ideas in their respective novels. What is the effect on a novel with a retiring heroine, such as Anne Elliot, Fanny Price, or even Elinor Dashwood? What is the effect on a novel of an outspoken heroine, such as Elizabeth Bennet or Emma Woodhouse? Your essay should reach a conclusion about the effects Austen creates with her experimentations with heroines.

2. **Antagonists:** Analyze and evaluate the role of antagonists in Austen's works.

An essay on this topic could explore antagonist figures in two or more works by Austen. You might examine how socially ambitious characters—such as Mrs. Clay or Mr. Elliot in *Persuasion,* Mr. Collins in *Pride and Prejudice,* or Lucy Steele in *Sense and Sensibility*—threaten the felicity of the protagonists. You might also explore how their mercenary values are antithetical to those of the protagonists, a fact that is also true of the socially arrogant, such as Lady Russell and Sir Walter Elliot in *Persuasion* or Lady Catherine de Bourgh in *Pride and Prejudice.* Another approach to this topic could explore more traditionally villainous characters, such as Aunt Norris in *Mansfield Park.* The rakes or charming scoundrels—Wickham, Willoughby, Henry Crawford, and Mr. Elliot—form another kind of threat to the protagonists. An essay focusing on one or more of these characters could discuss how charm often masks duplicity in Austen's works. Whatever approach you take to this topic, your essay should reach a conclusion about how the antagonists help us better understand the protagonists or the novel overall.

3. **Fools:** What is the role of fools in Austen's novels?

Some of Austen's most memorable characters are addled, misguided, neurotic, dim, or simply stupid. Promising books for a discussion of fools include *Pride and Prejudice* (Mr. Collins, Lydia Bennet), *Emma* (Miss Bates, Harriet Smith, Mr. Woodhouse), *Sense and Sensibility* (Sir John Middleton, Robert Ferrars), *Mansfield Park* (Mr. Rushworth, Lady Bertram), or *Northanger Abbey* (Catherine Morland, Mrs. Allan). One approach to this essay is to consider how your chosen fools compare with one another. How is their foolishness made clear to us? Is it declared by the narrator or exhibited in their words and actions? How are your selected characters significant within their respective novel(s)? Do they serve only as contrasts to the sophistication of other characters? Might they reveal truths that other characters are simply more skilled at concealing? The fools in *Emma* perform an especially pronounced symbolic function. Their treatment at the hands of others illuminates who is sympathetic or unsympathetic. Both Emma and Mr. Knightley, for instance, are generally kind to foolish characters, while Frank Churchill is prone to teasing them. The case of Catherine Morland is special because she is the heroine of a novel and, while her naïveté often borders on simple-mindedness, the plot would not work with a sophisticated heroine. How might Catherine's foolishness be necessary for the satire in *Northanger Abbey*?

History and Context

In *Pride and Prejudice,* an army regiment is stationed nearby in preparation for a French invasion. In *Mansfield Park,* anxieties over the abolition movement silence a dinner conversation. In *Persuasion,* the end of the Napoleonic Wars brings home naval officers and their newly minted fortunes. Clearly, Jane Austen's novels show that national and international events affected everyone. There are a number of ways in which you can approach essays on history and context in Austen's work.

One approach to an essay on the context of Austen's novels would be to focus on the military events mentioned in the novels. Though she was at a safe remove, war was a constant fact of life for Austen. She was born during the French Revolution and the Britain of her day was either worried about or battling with France until Austen's late thirties. A reference work on British history will help you understand these events and assess how the English responded to the French Revolution and the Napoleonic Wars. We see evidence of the wars in many Austen novels. In *Northanger Abbey*, General Tilney is described as reading pamphlets to ferret out signs of subversive voices, and you could research how the general's efforts remind us of the government's attempts to suppress dissent; these efforts followed the Anti-Treason and Seditious Meeting Acts in 1795. Because the wartime atmosphere is so evident in Austen's novels, evaluating how it affects characters would be a worthy pursuit for an essay.

Another interesting context to consider would be the state of the institution of marriage at the time Austen was writing. As her books establish marriage as the collective goal of her heroines, researching the reasons women married would help illuminate your understanding of the plots and characters. *Emma* contains some especially intriguing discussions of marriage. Emma, after all, makes a good case for why, as a wealthy woman, marriage is unappealing. In contrast to Emma's secure situation is that of Miss Bates; the older woman's experience as a spinster implicitly directs us to consider the social and economic consequences of not being married. *Pride and Prejudice* also meditates on the practical advantages of marriage when Charlotte Lucas decides that they are worth the cost of a lifetime spent with Mr. Collins.

Jane Austen herself is a historical figure, and studying her life would enrich your understanding of her books and her reputation. You could study her biography in light of a single novel. For instance, you might research the feedback she received and recorded about *Emma* and *Mansfield Park*. Do you see signs that she responded to that feedback when she wrote *Persuasion,* her next novel? Austen's reactions to reviews published during her lifetime would also be interesting, and you could look to her surviving letters for her own impressions of her work. How did she discuss her writing with her siblings or others? Another essay on Austen as a historical figure could research how the presentation of her life has changed over the years.

Sample Topics:

1. **Military context:** How is Austen's wartime era presented in her novels?

A number of Austen's novels refer to the wartime era in which she wrote, and you could choose one or more books to analyze. *Pride and Prejudice, Mansfield Park,* and *Persuasion* are all good choices for this topic. You would want to do some research on English reactions to the French Revolution and the Napoleonic Wars; a reference work on Britain during the Regency era would provide that. How did military events create social instability in a book such as *Pride and Prejudice*? How does this atmosphere enable a rake such as George Wickham to succeed? The more philosophical aspects of the wartime context are also interesting. In *Persuasion,* for instance, there is considerable discussion of how the exigencies of wartime preempt peacetime social practices, such as courtship and marriage. Ultimately, your essay should show the significance of the military context for your chosen novel(s).

2. **Marriage:** Why is marriage so important to the women in Austen's novels?

To answer this topic, you should research the social situation of women during the era. Julia Prewitt-Brown's *A Reader's Guide to the Nineteenth-century Novel* is one source that discusses marriage, and a number of other books on women's history in Britain would also be useful. After gaining a sense of the social and legal advantages offered by marriage, you could analyze one or more of the novels and discuss how this sociohistorical context underlies the decisions that female characters make regarding marriage. One approach to an essay would be to reconsider the husband-hunting women in the novels and consider why, in light of the social context, they might be so mercenary. Good examples of this character type are found in *Persuasion* (Mrs. Clay and Miss Elliot), *Mansfield Park* (Mary Crawford), *Northanger Abbey* (Isabella Thorpe), and *Sense and Sensibility* (Lucy Steele).

After learning about women's legal status and the advantages marriage offered, do these women seem less objectionable? Do the heroines seem more heroic for transcending these considerations? Another approach to an essay on this topic could focus on the female characters who are effectively out of the marriage market. After your research on the legal status of widows, for instance, is it any wonder that so many did not remarry?

3. **Jane Austen as a historical figure:** How does Jane Austen's biography or her letters help illuminate her books?

To have a complete sense of Jane Austen's literature and life, it would be worthwhile to read her personal writings. Though some interesting letters remain, many of Austen's personal writings were censored or destroyed by her family in a short-sighted desire to protect her privacy. There are two fondly written biographical works by close family members: her brother Henry's biographical note, which was included with the posthumous publication of *Persuasion* and *Northanger Abbey* (1818), and her nephew James Edward Austen-Leigh's *A Memoir of Jane Austen* (1870). One interesting approach to an essay on Austen as a historical figure could research these family-penned biographies to assess how they represent her writing process or her values. Henry Austen's short biographical essay focuses on his sister's piety but does not mention her irreverent wit. You might look for ways that one of her novels argues against such a depiction of her. A similar approach might look to how Austen-Leigh's biography—written during the Victorian era, when female modesty was revered—also downplays the sharpness of Austen's critiques of the status quo. More recent works, such as Claire Tomalin's biography, are more apt to identify the bold assertions and portrayals in Austen's novels. Reading such a biography would provide a contrast to the depictions of Jane Austen in the works by her brother and her nephew. You might compare her letters to biographies: Does Jane Austen's voice differ from her family's impressions and representations of her? Another approach to this topic would be to read Austen's collected letters and research how she discusses one or more of her books. Do her opinions of her novels conflict with your own? What do her letters reveal are her primary concerns about her writing?

Philosophy and Ideas

Jane Austen's era was one of fierce debates about morality and political philosophy. Many of these debates were sparked by the revolutions in the United States and France; both events upset ideological beliefs in security and the old order, while also galvanizing a long-standing English francophobia. While some in Britain supported the ideals of the French Revolution, British conservatives believed that staunching the flow of revolutionary ideas into England was the only way to prevent bloodshed and wholesale ruin. Austen and her family were conservative, though her novels show sympathy for the liberal causes of the day. Later in the 19th century, the ideas of the French Revolution would foster the aesthetic movement we know as romanticism. Austen predates the romantics, but there are a number of ways in which the values of the romantics were circulating during Austen's life and appeared in her books. In *Sense and Sensibility,* for instance, the passionate, honest, and iconoclastic Marianne is very much a romantic figure. Austen's last complete novel, *Persuasion,* includes a romantic heroine, Anne Elliot. In an essay you could explore how romantic ideals appear in Austen's novels.

Another liberal notion debated during Austen's era was the situation and legal status of women. Culturally, women were expected to be quiet, modest, and domestic. Women were, for instance, thought not able to sustain the rigors of a classical education, and so were educated instead in less taxing subjects: Romance languages, dancing, music, literature, and needlework. New voices were starting to be heard, however, and they insisted that the relegation of women to life's quietest margins was misguided, insulting, and unjust. The radical activist and writer Mary Wollstonecraft maintained that women were intelligent creatures prevented by society from reaching their full potential as adult human beings. Austen did not consider herself remotely radical, yet her novels reveal an affinity with Wollstonecraft's ideas. Anne Elliot in *Persuasion,* for example, is an especially outspoken critic of the traditions that historically barred women from self-expression. When Captain Harville, arguing for women's inconstancy in love and for evidence of "woman's fickleness," cites examples from literature, Anne responds that since "Men have had every advantage of us in telling their own story," she "will not allow books to prove any thing" (2: 23). An essay could analyze any of Austen's novels for their commentary on the debates concerning the situation of women.

Sample Topics:

1. **Romanticism:** How are the values of romanticism presented in Austen's novels?

To answer this question, you would need to gain a working knowledge of romanticism, and any good literary dictionary will provide you with one. *Sense and Sensibility* and *Persuasion* are Austen's novels most associated with romanticism, but *Mansfield Park* and even *Northanger Abbey* also include ruminations on the transcendent power of nature, a particularly romantic notion. Once you have a sense of where Austen includes ideas about romanticism, you can explore how her novels treat romanticism. Many scholars maintain that she criticizes romanticism in *Sense and Sensibility,* but are there ways in which the narrator seems to applaud Marianne's honesty and passion?

2. **The situation of women:** Using a selection of her novels, analyze Austen's position on the situation of women.

Austen's narrators do not directly disagree with the patriarchy that kept women poor, dependent, and powerless, but it is clear that she understood how women's lives were "not . . . very enviable" (*Persuasion,* 2: 23). Women's lives were negatively affected by primogeniture—the inheritance laws that kept property in the hands of men (as is shown in *Sense and Sensibility* and *Pride and Prejudice*). Women's lives were controlled by their fathers, sometimes unjustly (as in *Northanger Abbey, Persuasion,* and *Mansfield Park*). Women were utterly dependent on their male relatives or a husband for their survival; without male patronage, life could be grim, as we see in the example of Miss Bates in *Emma*. To write this essay, you could choose two or more novels and analyze how they contain an implicit criticism of the situation of women. You might, for instance, show how primogeniture negatively affects female characters in two novels. Do your chosen novels present these inheritances as just or unjust? Another approach might explore how women's lives are presented as detrimentally affected by figures who have control and authority over them. *Northanger Abbey, Persuasion,* and *Pride and Prejudice* all present parent figures making bad decisions that the younger women must accept. Another approach to an essay on this topic might analyze how some of Austen's female characters exert control. How do they gain and maintain their power?

Form and Genre

Austen is well and deservedly known for the technical accomplishments of her novels, for their innovations in the genre of realism and the form of narrative. Both of these provide ample material to discuss in an essay. Her narrative style is now referred to as free indirect speech or discourse and is best understood as a novelistic style where the narrator periodically adopts the voice of one (or more) of her characters. Free indirect speech blurs the line between narrator and character and gives readers access to both a character's subjective experience and the narrator's objective appraisal of that experience (Irvine 97). Free indirect speech is evident when the narrator lodges an assertion that is clearly that of a character. *Emma* offers many examples of this. When Emma decides to adopt Harriet Smith as a protégée, and thereby "improve" the younger woman, Emma reasons that Harriet "would be loved as one to whom [Emma] could be useful" (1: 4). The term *useful*, articulated in this line by the narrator and not directly attributed to Emma, captures Emma's point of view. Because of the narrative form, we simultaneously recognize Emma's good intentions and what Mr. Knightley thinks of as her condescending interference. Another aspect of form and genre that you might explore is Austen's comedy. What techniques does she use to construct the humor in her novels? How is Austen's famous irony deployed?

Sample Topics:

1. **Narrative style:** How does free indirect speech function in Austen's novels?

Before your analysis, consider how our understanding of characters would be affected had Austen used a more traditional third-person narration, or had the novel been related in the first person from, for example, Elizabeth Bennet's or Anne Elliot's point of view. This consideration will help prepare you to discuss how Austen's narrative style affects her novels. An essay on this topic needs to show how free indirect speech, as defined above, operates in one or more novel(s). Your essay should give examples of this style of narration and, in your close readings of those examples, show how the style contributes a particular atmosphere or familiarity with characters. How, for instance, does free indirect speech enable us to understand the fervent passion residing within the quiet Anne Elliot in *Persuasion*? How does the narrative style enable us to sympathize with Emma Woodhouse, a character who might otherwise be unsympathetic? How does the narrative's silence on Jane Fairfax lead us to misinterpret her, as Emma does? If you focus on multiple novels, you will want to show how free indirect speech is significant to each story, while also registering any varieties you see in the narrative form across different novels.

2. **Comic effects:** How does Austen make her novels so amusing? Analyze some of her comic techniques.

This broad question asks you to survey and analyze the means by which Austen achieves her comic effects. You could choose a single form or technique—such as satire, parody, understatement, hyperbole, caricature, burlesque, or irony—and track its use in two or three novels. A literary handbook, such as Cuddon's *A Dictionary of Literary Terms,* provides definitions so that you may knowledgeably discuss these techniques. Depending on the length of your essay, you could select two or more techniques and analyze how they operate together. It would also be worthwhile to consider the overall use of humor in your chosen novels. Is the humorous tone suspended in places? Are there sections where irony yields to earnestness? How does the cessation of humor help us understand a novel's values?

Language, Symbol, and Imagery

Austen's novels rarely rely on figurative language, such as similes or metaphors, but instead use crisp, deliberate diction and careful punctuation to convey her ideas. As the discussions above about her use of characterization and narration imply, Austen's language is principally presented in her characters' dialogue and in the narration. We understand characters by their own utilization of language and the motifs within their dialogue. Mr. Collins's sycophancy is made clear in *Pride and Prejudice* by the servile way in which he defers to his patroness, Lady Catherine de Bourgh. In *Mansfield Park,* Mary Crawford's inappropriate sexuality is revealed in her flirtations and knowing dialogue. Willoughby demonstrates his inability to be truly contrite during his confession to Elinor at the end of *Sense and Sensibility* when he repeatedly catalogues the injustices he has suffered. Particularly in his repetition of "I" and "me," we are made aware that Willoughby's ego rejects his complicity in his unhappiness. An essay on language and style might look at how characterization is established through motifs—sycophancy, sexuality, and egoism—in dialogue.

One of the few ways in which Austen uses modified symbolism is in her depictions of places. These places—regions, landscapes, and houses—are extensions of character. An essay might analyze how places either symbolize or help us understand character.

Sample Topics:

1. **Language style:** What do characters' communication styles tell us?

   This topic is related to characterization and involves looking at how different individuals express themselves. You could select two or more characters from a single novel or instead focus on characters in two or more novels. Any of Austen's novels are appropriate for this topic, and you might narrow your focus by considering characters that share connections. You could, for instance, look at the ostensible antagonists in two novels to ascertain whether they share tendencies in their language style. Another way to approach this topic is to look for distinctive motifs in dialogue. In *Sense and Sensibility*, Anne Steele's agenda is easy to discern since she so repeatedly refers to handsome young men. Mrs. Elton's motifs in *Emma* all relate to money, so we understand that she is materialistic and likely insecure about her own class position. For evidence in addition to dialogue, you should closely read any letters written by characters.

2. **Places:** How are places symbolic in Austen's work?

This topic could encompass a variety of cities, villages, resort towns, and domiciles. If you concentrate on place of origin, you might compare how London is represented in some novels as a source of disorder. This is especially true in *Mansfield Park* and *Emma*. Resort towns also prove dangerous, particularly for young women, as we see in *Pride and Prejudice*, *Sense and Sensibility*, and *Northanger Abbey*. Your essay might explore how towns are characterized in relation to villages. Another approach to a topic on places could focus on houses and what they tell us about characters. For Elizabeth Bennet Pemberley helps communicate unspoken messages about Mr. Darcy's character. The dark and cacophonous Portsmouth home of the Prices in *Mansfield Park* stands in contrast to Fanny Price's less excitable nature. Kellynch Hall in *Persuasion* is another house worth investigating for its larger symbolic significance. What does it mean that its owner is not as worthy of the estate as the intended Admiral Croft?

Comparison and Contrast

Analyzing the different elements of literature to determine their similarities and differences can lead to strong, compelling essays. You might choose to look at two similar elements and focus on their distinguishing characteristics. How, for instance, does the individualism of Emma Woodhouse compare with that of Elizabeth Bennet? You might select two dissimilar elements and examine them for underlying similarities.

An essay could explore how Mr. Knightley and Elinor Dashwood, characters from two different novels, both perform similar functions; they serve as the voices of reason in their respective stories. Instead of looking at similar elements in a novel or selection of novels, you might instead focus on contrasts, such as those between the Westons in *Emma* and the Palmers in *Sense and Sensibility*. How do these different marriages help us understand how important compatibility is? You might choose elements from within a single work, elements in two or more works by the same author, or elements in works by different authors. Instructors assign comparison-and-contrast essay topics not only to guide you toward identifying differences and similarities, but also to see how you assess and select meaningful elements and interpret them. By paying special attention to the significances of similarities and differences, your essay will amount to much more than a catalogue. Readers will appreciate your analytical syntheses of the similarities and differences between and among literary elements and texts.

Sample Topics:

1. **Austen's early work versus her later work:** How did Austen's work change during her life? What elements are consistent over the course of her career?

   This topic could take any number of approaches. One approach might examine an idea—such as love or socioeconomic class—and assess its presentation in an early and a later work. *Sense and Sensibility* and *Persuasion* are good choices for this approach. If you are interested in researching Austen's juvenilia, you might look to *Love and Friendship* or *Lady Susan*, then compare it to a later work to assess whether her writing changed. To help you focus, you might read for a particular writing technique, such as narration, characterization, or form. Many of Austen's early efforts were novels composed entirely of letters. You might read one of these epistolary novels and discuss why you think she moved away from that form. How did it limit her ability to create and represent a narrative voice? *Sense and Sensibility* was originally an epistolary novel, and you might find vestiges of that initial form in the published novel.

2. **Compare with a contemporaneous novel:** Read a popular novel from Austen's era and draw comparisons between it and one of Austen's novels. Consider, especially, choosing a novel from one of the genres that Austen ironically aped, such as the sentimental or the gothic novel.

You will need to dedicate time to writing this topic, since many of Austen's contemporaries wrote quite long novels. As you read your selection, take note of particular points of comparison. You might discuss how the heroines are characterized differently or perform different functions in the novels. Or you might instead discuss how the tone or the narration of the novels is distinctive. If you are interested in reading a gothic novel, you might read *Northanger Abbey* in conjunction with one of Ann Radcliffe's thrillers, such as *The Italian* (1797) or the one that so captivates Catherine Morland, *The Mysteries of Udolpho* (1794). If you are interested in the sentimental novel, consider reading Fanny Burney's *Camilla* (1796) or Maria Edgeworth's *Belinda* (1801). To assess how Austen's work differs in moral sensibility or characterization, you could read your selected sentimental novel along with *Sense and Sensibility*, *Mansfield Park*, or *Emma*.

Bibliography and Online Sources

Auerbach, Emily. *Searching for Jane Austen*. Madison, WI: Wisconsin UP, 2004.

Austen, Henry. "Biographical Notice of the Author." Preface. *Northanger Abbey and Persuasion*. In *Persuasion*. Norton Critical Edition. Ed. Patricia Meyer Spacks. New York: Norton, 1995. 191–96.

Austen-Leigh, James Edward. *A Memoir of Jane Austen and Other Family Recollections* (1870). Ed. Kathryn Sutherland. Oxford: Oxford UP, 2002.

Brown, Julia Prewitt. *A Reader's Guide to the Nineteenth-Century English Novel*. New York: Macmillan Publishing Company, 1985.

Cuddon, J. A. *A Dictionary of Literary Terms*. London: Penguin Books, 1979.

Gilbert, Sandra M., and Susan Gubar. *The Madwoman in the Attic: The Woman Writer and the Nineteenth-Century Literary Imagination*. New Haven, CT: Yale UP, 1984.

Grey, J. David. "Military (Army and Navy)." *The Jane Austen Companion with a Dictionary of Jane Austen's Life and Works.* Ed. J. David Grey. New York: Macmillan, 1986. 307–31.

———. "Life of Jane Austen." *The Jane Austen Companion with a Dictionary of Jane Austen's Life and Works.* Ed. J. David Grey. New York: Macmillan, 1986. 279–82.

Honan, Park. "Bibliographies." *The Jane Austen Companion with a Dictionary of Jane Austen's Life and Works.* Ed. J. David Grey. New York: Macmillan, 1986. 18–23.

Irvine, Robert. *Jane Austen.* Routledge Guide to Literature. New York: Routledge, 2005.

Kelly, Gary. "Jane Austen Biography." Retrieved 24 July 2007. <http://people. brandeis.edu/~teuber/austenbio.html>.

Leavis, Q. D. "Not an Inspired Amateur." Excerpt from "A Critical Theory of Jane Austen's Writings." *Scrutiny* 10.1 (1942): 61–66; 68–71. Rpt. in *Northanger Abbey.* Ed. Susan Fraiman. New York: Norton, 2004. 182–90.

Monaghan, David. "Austen's Women in a Conservative Society." *Readings on Jane Austen.* Ed. Clarice Swisher. San Diego: Greenhaven Press, Inc., 1997. 42–50.

Pinion, F. B. *A Jane Austen Companion: A Critical Survey and Reference Book.* London: Macmillan, 1973.

Tomalin, Claire. *Jane Austen: A Life.* New York: Vintage Books, 1999.

Trickett, Rachel. "Jane Austen's Comedy and the Nineteenth Century." *Critical Essays on Jane Austen.* Ed. B. C. Southam. London: Routledge. 162–81.

Watt, Ian. Introduction. *Jane Austen: A Collection of Critical Essays.* Englewood Cliffs, NJ: Prentice-Hall, 1963. 1–14.

Woolf, Virginia. "Jane Austen." *The Common Reader.* Ed. Andrew McNeillie. San Diego: Harvest-Harcourt, 1925. 134–45.

NORTHANGER ABBEY

READERS COMING to Jane Austen for the first time may discover that *Northanger Abbey* (1817) is a surprisingly welcoming read, with its modern style of comic irreverence. The novel pokes fun at itself and literature in general, but the primary focus of its satire is the highly stylized gothic novel, a genre ripe for lampooning. Because gothic fiction, a subset of the sentimental novel, was tremendously popular in the 1790s, it is not surprising that it was at the gothic that Austen directed her comic talents for what would have been her first published novel (*Northanger Abbey* was bought, but not published, in 1803). *Northanger Abbey* reveals an author so confident of her skills that her narrator trades barbs with the literary world. Ostensibly about a young woman's coming of age, *Northanger Abbey* also opines about literature—essays, novels, conduct books, histories—with all the firebrand conviction of a veteran writer. It seems fitting that the first novel Austen prepared for publication would include such an engaged discussion of the English novel, a form of storytelling that she would later be credited with transforming. Scholars disagree about the achievement of *Northanger Abbey*—some believe it should be considered an example of her juvenilia—but all agree that its comedy is accomplished.

From the start of *Northanger Abbey,* Austen's satire targets the gothic and sentimental novels' overwrought style. The novel's atypical heroine is not beautiful, intelligent, and talented, but instead "almost pretty," "often stupid," and utterly lacking in artistic accomplishments. Catherine's situation is also atypical of the gothic genre. Instead of being kidnapped and taken to a dangerous and exotic locale, Catherine is cordially invited to Bath by a trusted family friend. Once in Bath, Catherine makes friends, learns about society through her acquaintances, and falls in love. A regular young woman at a regular English resort—such a figure in such a scenario both disarms dramatic conflict and waters down the rich flavor of gothic novels. With its emphasis on the familiar and mundane, *Northanger Abbey* offers an ironic and realistic counterstory to the bizarre stories of gothic fiction. The clever twist that Austen crafts in this novel is not that threats do not exist for a regular English woman in realistic circumstances, but that many threats to her happiness do. These threats, however, come in familiar forms, principally from strangers who are unkind, ambitious, or false.

Northanger Abbey feels modern because of its irreverence and also because of its self-referential elements. Self-referentiality is a literary technique in which the narrator refers to herself as a creation, or directly refers to the fiction that is being enacted in the novel. The narrator in *Northanger Abbey* describes her characters as literary creations and also discusses literature. The characters devoutly read novels that were best sellers in the 1790s; in one scene, the action of *Northanger Abbey* ceases while the heroine sits down with Ann Radcliffe's *The Mysteries of Udolpho* (1: 7). Postmodern literary critics have deemed this kind of novel metafiction, a variety of self-referential text that highlights its own artifice. Though not an example of postmodern literature, *Northanger Abbey* uses some of the same techniques as those utilized by postmodern authors.

Before analyzing the form, themes, and other literary elements of *Northanger Abbey,* you must examine the particulars of Austen's language. This section gives an example of close reading, a skill that, once acquired, will help you generate the analysis and find the evidence for writing an essay.

Close reading any work of literature requires concentration on the significances of passages: You should pay particular attention to word choice, ideas mentioned by characters, and narrative opinion. One example of both self-referencing and narrative opinion is registered after Catherine Morland laments a social error that she was unwittingly compelled to commit. The narrator ends the scene by observing, "And now I may dismiss my heroine to a sleepless couch, which is the true heroine's portion; to a pillow strewed with thorns and wet with tears. And lucky may she think herself, if she gets another good night's rest in the course of the next three months" (1: 11). A close reading of this passage shows how the narrator emphasizes the conventions within which she is writing. When the narrator calls Catherine "my heroine," we are reminded that we are reading a literary creation. Even more specifically, the possessive "my" reminds us of the narrator's presence in the book, while "heroine" reminds us that this is a piece of fiction that has certain conventions (such as heroes, villains, conflicts, and resolutions). The narrator satirizes what the conventional heroine of a sentimental novel can expect from her lot by declaring that a "true heroine's portion" is a "sleepless couch . . . wet with tears." That such a heroine is likely to remain sleepless for the "next three months" satirizes the romances and the romantic pining that are customary events in sentimental novels. The narrator's reference to Catherine Morland as "my heroine" furthermore implies a fond ownership of her character.

The narrator's bemused fondness is established in the opening lines of the novel, when she marvels at how unlike a literary heroine Catherine Morland is:

> No one who had ever seen Catherine Morland in her infancy, would have supposed her born to be an heroine. Her situation in life, the character of her father and mother, her own person and disposition, were all equally against her. Her father was a clergyman, without being neglected, or poor . . . he had never been handsome . . . and he was not in the least addicted to locking up his daughters. Her mother was a woman of useful plain sense, with a good temper, and what is more remarkable, with a good constitution. She had three sons before Catherine was born; and instead of dying in bringing the latter into the world, as any body might expect, she still lived on—lived to have six children more . . . and to enjoy excellent health. (1:1)

A close reading reveals that these first lines establish salient elements of plot, character, narrative style, and themes. The narrator, in arguing for what Catherine is not, is also outlining for the reader the conventions of a literary heroine. The narrator could have simply asserted that Catherine had a normal childhood and two kind, healthy parents, but such an assertion would convey none of the comic impact of the quoted passage. As it is, we gain by inference an education in the conventions of a sentimental heroine. For instance, the description of Catherine's father, who is "not in the least addicted to locking up his daughters," tells us that the fathers of other heroines frequently do so. That Catherine's mother is kind and unaffected, and manages routinely to give birth safely, tells us that mothers of heroines customarily die (with routine self-sacrifice, usually while giving birth to the heroine herself). The passage also uses the technique of deflation—by which the amplified expectations of a heroine are systematically deflated by the description of a regular and rather ordinary life. The narrator's implication that the Morland family is ordinary also suggests a distinction between real life and life in literature: The former is mundane, the latter is unbelievable.

The most arresting aspect of this passage is its implicit assertion about the theme of heroism: Though Catherine Morland does not fulfill our expectations of a literary heroine, we are assured by her introduction that she will be the heroine of this story. An essay might explore how Catherine, an unheroic protagonist heroine, becomes a heroine. Another essay might explore how *Northanger Abbey* is a rallying cry for the heroism of all young women. Might this novel, with its mundane characters and realistic situations, be arguing that all of us are heroic? No matter what analytical approach you eventually take to this novel, a slow and careful reading of *Northanger Abbey*'s language will enable you to recognize the novel's patterns and ideas. Reading slowly and taking notes makes for a rich understanding of the novel and will enable you to gather the evidence you need to write a strong essay.

TOPICS AND STRATEGIES

This section of the chapter discusses several possible topics for essays on *Northanger Abbey*, as well as general approaches to those topics. The material below will help guide your own approach to an essay, but it is not an exhaustive master key. Use this material to generate your own analysis of *Northanger Abbey*. Every topic discussed here could lead to a variety of good papers.

Theme

Northanger Abbey deals with many themes—ideas and concepts that organize and emphasize the importance of the events in the novel. Themes that run through the novel include those related to the heroism previously discussed, as well as romance, danger, and common life. Writers analyzing the novel often begin by identifying a central theme and then determine—through an essay—what the novel is saying about that theme. You can identify themes by noting the ideas, symbols, words, or events that repeat in the story. Interpretation of this novel is made a bit more challenging by its ironic tone, but an attentive reader will become attuned to how the novel presents different themes.

The ordinary traits of the heroine, discussed above, as well as the novel's depiction of reality, suggest a theme the narrator terms "common life." The Morlands are representative of the common life: busy, healthy people who have no time and little leisure to imagine the melodramatic threats so central to gothic fiction. The Morlands have no "presentiments of evil" about Catherine's going to Bath, and they help her with practical preparations for her journey "with a degree of moderation and composure, which seemed rather consistent with the common feelings of *common life*, than with the refined susceptibilities, the tender emotions which the first separation of a heroine from her family ought always to excite" (1: 2; italics added). The narrator here points out the disparity between the behavior associated with everyday life and behavior more often seen in fiction. The narrator's diction in describing those things associated with the ordinary life—"moderation" and "composure"—are complementary, while the diction related to the fictional, literary world—"refined," "susceptibilities," "tender"—suggests vanity and weakness. Mrs. Morland's health and practical intelligence is particularly representative of the common life qualities of which the narrator approves. That the family of a heroine "ought always" fear separation suggests, by its ironic hyperbole, that the family should not fear it at all. An essay could explore how *Northanger Abbey* celebrates the "plain sense" of Mrs. Morland and those like her over the extravagant fancies of other characters. Other themes could be approached in similar ways: You could approach the theme of heroism by analyzing how the unlikely Catherine is, in fact, a heroine. The real dangers that she faces would furnish another interesting topic for an essay.

Sample Topics:

1. **Common life:** The narrator distinguishes "common life" from the extraordinary lives portrayed in gothic and sentimental novels. How is this common life characterized?

To discuss this topic it would be necessary to locate those passages where the narrator is describing the everyday world and to analyze how the narrator presents this life. Is the novel suggesting that everyday concerns are ridiculous by nature, or that the fictive world is ridiculous by its disparity from the everyday world? Mrs. Morland's practical perception of the world makes her a good character to analyze closely. An example of her outlook is when she declares that General Tilney's unexplained expulsion of her daughter from Northanger Abbey is, simply, "a strange business . . . something not at all worth understanding." Is Mrs. Morland's decisive, even uninterested philosophy approved of by the narrator? Consider, too, what significance there is in the fact that the Morland household situates the beginning and end of the novel. Your essay on common life might also consider how explicable common life events invariably explain away Catherine Morland's delusions of gothic grandeur at Northanger Abbey.

2. **Heroism:** What is the significance of this novel's heroine being described as so unconventional? What kind of commentary is this novel thereby making about heroism?

The narrator discusses archetypes of heroism when Catherine Morland is introduced as the unlikely heroine for a novel. In spite of her atypical characteristics, however, the narrator continually refers to her as a heroine. Are we to deduce from this that Catherine is actually a heroine, and if so, what are we to make of her ordinariness? One approach to an essay on this topic might consider how Catherine fulfills the duties of a heroine: What challenges does she meet and triumph over? What strength of character does she display? Another approach might examine how Austen uses Catherine's ordinariness as a way to celebrate implicitly the ordinary heroism of all women.

3. **Danger:** When Catherine imagines threats, they tend to be in keeping with those she has read about in gothic thrillers:

malevolent husbands, ghosts, and dungeons. Instead of these fantastic fears, what does the novel present as being truly threatening to Catherine Morland?

To address this topic, consider what threats Catherine faces. Those presented by the Thorpes, for instance, include the social consequences of deceit and rudeness. How do these seemingly mundane events have serious consequences for Catherine's life? That these faux pas are potentially catastrophic is intuitively understood by Catherine, who actively seeks to repair the damage that the Thorpes wreak. Another threat is posed by General Tilney, who imagines that Catherine is an heiress and, as such, an attractive prospect for his younger son, as well as his estate. General Tilney is a character that most closely approximates the gothic villain. You might focus on the novel's presentation of his villainy.

4. **Romance:** Does the narrator's unsentimental presentation of courtship and romance in *Northanger Abbey* undermine the project of love that is so important to Catherine's coming of age?

This topic makes an assertion about the narrator's presentation of romance, and the first step in an essay on this topic would be to verify whether the assertion is true. You might read closely the sections on Isabella's approaches to romance and how she treats the men that she meets and pursues. Is Isabella's artifice at odds or in keeping with romance? Does the narrator present her actions as appropriate? Once you establish the narrator's presentation of courtship and romance, you can analyze what bearing this presentation has on love. You will certainly want to include the final sections of the novel, in which the narrator sums up Catherine's final steps to the altar. What are we to make of the narrator's "confess[ion] that [Henry Tilney's] affection [for Catherine] originated in nothing better than gratitude"? Does *Northanger Abbey* make a case for the simple utility of love? Ultimately, is the narrator of *Northanger Abbey* mocking or celebrating love?

Character

Much of *Northanger Abbey* focuses on the conduct and manners of its characters. Looking at characters is a productive means of analyzing the novel. Essays can focus on questions of character development (such as how Austen distinguishes Eleanor Tilney from Isabella Thorpe by their respective approaches to marriage), means of characterization (such as the way the reader understands General Tilney's character by his chilling effect on his children and Catherine); or interpretations of changes in a character as the novel proceeds (such as the shift from innocence to experience in Catherine herself).

To write an essay on character, you need to assess the novel by questioning how readers come to know various characters. How, for instance, does Austen distinguish a character's behavior? John Thorpe's vulgarity is seen in his epithet-dependent monologues that center on horses, hunting, drinking, and dogs. Mrs. Morland's "useful plain sense" (1: 1) is demonstrated in her advice to Catherine before she leaves for Bath, when she encourages her daughter to wear a scarf "around her neck" and keep a budget (1: 2). Isabella's inconstancy and disingenuousness are seen in her dialogue, her letters, and her actions, such as when she indiscriminately pursues men. In spite of decrying women's shortcomings, Henry Tilney's ability to discuss fabrics, dresses, and novels suggests that he is genuinely interested in women. Eleanor Tilney's intelligence and kindness are demonstrated by her relaxed and confident conduct with her brother and her erudition on many subjects.

To an extent, you are instructed by the narrative as to what to expect from characters. If you pay attention to the narrator's editorial comments about individuals, you will understand what the characters signify in the novel. We are apprised of the flaws in John Thorpe's character when he is first introduced: He seemed "fearful of being . . . too much like a gentleman unless he were easy [informal] where he ought to be civil, and impudent where he might be allowed to be easy" (1: 7). The narrator's description of him prepares us for a man who will be both rude and impudent—and so he is. The narrator also announces the defining characteristics of Catherine Morland—our unheroic heroine—who "was fond of all boys' plays, and greatly preferred cricket not merely to dolls, but to the more heroic enjoyments of infancy, nursing a dormouse, feeding a canary-bird, or watering a rose bush" (1: 1). That Catherine grows into an "almost pretty" girl is just one of the many changes that take place in her character. She later, the narrator wryly informs us, trains to be a heroine by reading books appropriate to that vocation (1: 1). That *Northanger Abbey* tracks the growth of Catherine Morland is just one of the ways in which the work is a bildungsroman, or novel of education. An essay might explore how Catherine's character is affected by her education over the course of the book. To analyze questions of character development, look closely for distinguishing traits of language, action, or interactions with other characters. Tracking the ways characters behave with one another helps the reader not only understand the means by which characters are created but also determine what characters signify and represent for the story overall.

Sample Topics:

1. **The education of Catherine Morland:** In many ways, this is a novel of education. How does Catherine Morland's character change as a result of her education? What and how does she learn?

This topic asks you to analyze changes in Catherine's character by focusing specifically on her education. You might consider the lessons of her education. One source of her education is novels. Explore what kinds of lessons she receives from reading. For instance, though they do not prepare her for how modern Northanger Abbey is, novels do alert her to the fact that strange men (such as the Tilney patriarch) can be threatening. Another way that Catherine receives an education is through teaching, either by direct instruction or by example. Both Henry and Eleanor Tilney are important mentors to Catherine, especially Henry. What does he teach Catherine about reality and fantasy, about landscape, about the proper reading of novels? For negative examples of teaching, you might also consider what Catherine learns from the Thorpes or, more broadly, from her time in Bath. An essay might also discuss what Catherine does and does not learn. You will certainly want to include Catherine's finally transformed understanding of Isabella. How does Isabella's duplicitous letter teach Catherine that people are a "mixture of good and bad"?

2. **Isabella as a character:** The reader is aware long before Catherine that Isabella is flighty, fickle, and duplicitous. Her excessive intimacy, compliments, and teasing provocations are just a few of the traits that reveal the true nature of Isabella Thorpe. A conniving flirt, Isabella does serve a serious purpose in the story in relation to Catherine Morland. Analyze Isabella's character as she illuminates Catherine's character. What might Isabella represent to Catherine and her family?

This topic requires that you look less at Isabella's character and more at what her character represents for the heroine. You might consider how Isabella contrasts with Catherine concerning moral values, personality, and behavior. Are there other ways in which we come to understand Catherine in contrast to Isabella? Are there ways in which Henry Tilney comes to understand Catherine better because of Isabella's actions? You might also consider how Isabella seems to embody Bath. How are her values and behaviors—her love of fashion, flirtation, and artifice—representative of Bath as it is depicted in *Northanger Abbey*? You might also consider what Isabella represents to the Morland family: In what ways does she pose a threat to their provincial world?

3. **Character development in general:** What techniques does the novel use to present character to the reader? Are characters transparent or somewhat concealed?

A paper on this topic would look at how Austen gives insight into character. A possible approach would be to look carefully at a pair of characters or a set of techniques and attempt to show their effects. A paper could examine how social conventions, such as conversation, reveal character. Henry Tilney, for example, makes fun of the niceties of a clichéd chitchat when he first speaks to Catherine. By contrast, Mrs. Allen and Mrs.

Thorpe unironically employ the clichés of such a conversation when they are reunited in Bath. Another social convention, dancing, is also revealing in the novel. While John Thorpe breaks every rule about the practice, Henry Tilney is acutely alert to its rules and implications. Another paper could analyze how reading reveals character. The Thorpe siblings and the Tilney siblings juxtapose flawed and admirable ways of reading, respectively.

4. **Mrs. Morland as a character:** Mrs. Morland is characterized as markedly ordinary. What is the effect of this regular, mundane, and steady character on this novel?

Mrs. Morland is a minor character. Her presence does, however, bookend the events of the novel, and she is an important character because so many of her opinions are endorsed by the narrator. It is Mrs. Morland, after all, who recognizes that General Tilney's treatment of her daughter is "strange," but she does not waste time dwelling on this. At the end of the novel, Mrs. Morland again shows her practical side when she suggests to her melancholy daughter more activity, more essay reading, and less thinking about disappointments. Read her character closely and consider the parallels between her and the narrator. How do they agree on the topics of villainy, life, and love?

History and Context

Another suitable approach to the analysis of *Northanger Abbey* is through history and context. Even a small amount of historical research into the world in which this novel is set will yield great returns in both understanding and analytical possibilities. Another reason to do research into the historical context of *Northanger Abbey* is that it will enable you to understand better the humor of the novel. Some of its irony depends on the reader's being aware of the literary world that the novel is lampooning. The novel refers to many timely debates in literature, including those around novels, histories, periodicals, and controversies triggered by the growing number of female authors and readers. At one point, the narrator actually steps away from describing the events of her story to take part in these debates; in this and other sections, she defends novels and, by extension, women who write, and denounces those who criticize or dismiss novels. Austen's narrator gives the names of actual novels by and about women—"Cecilia, or Camilla, or Belinda"—to assert then their value: "some work in which the greatest powers of the mind are displayed, in which the most thorough knowledge of human nature, the happiest delineation of its varieties, the liveliest effusions of wit and humor are conveyed to the world in the best chosen language" (1: 5). The narrator's convictions about novels are inherently defensive; she is obviously responding to public criticism. A challenge for this essay would be to focus on the literary-historical context. You might write about how varieties of writing were gendered or deemed appropriate for men or women. Or you might explore how Catherine Morland's dislike of history is paralleled in Austen's own juvenilia in *The History of England*. You could instead research the context of conduct books, manuals that instructed young people in proper behavior. In *Northanger Abbey*, Austen's assertions run counter to the conduct books that insisted women be so modest that they became nearly invisible. All of the suggested topics below are related to the literary-historical context in which the novel is deeply embedded.

Sample Topics:

1. **Debates about novels:** How does *Northanger Abbey* show that the novel was a disputed genre at this time? How was a genre believed to be the lowly provenance of women actually celebrated in *Northanger Abbey*? How is the narrator participating in a debate about novels?

   To discuss this topic you would need to do research into the literary world of the late 18th century, an era that saw the rise of female readership and authorship. That to be a woman writer was a dubious distinction is attested to by the fact that so many women wrote under pseudonyms or anonymously. Exceptions to this rule, such as Frances Burney, were rare. One of the reasons that novels were dismissed was that their authorship did not require the classical education from which women were overwhelmingly excluded. After researching this topic, you will need to decide how to focus your approach. One method would be to analyze *Northanger Abbey* to show how it engages the debate about novels. How does Austen's narrator valorize the genre? Another related approach might be to discuss how you see the debate about authorship and gender materializing in *Northanger Abbey*. What do the narrator and the characters (principally, Henry Tilney) have to say about the writings of women and men? Henry argues for what he sees as the sloppy but vigorous writing of women found in journals, letters, and novels. *Northanger Abbey*'s discussions of history and essays (in *The Rambler* and *The Spectator*, two periodicals of the day) show that these were considered the serious writings of serious individuals who were, customarily, men.

2. **Representations of history:** Catherine Morland dislikes histories, and she tells the Tilneys that there is nothing in history books that does not either "vex or weary" her. The narrator complains that while novels are disparaged, "the nine-hundredth abridger of the History of England . . . [is] eulogized by a thousand pens." Is this dismissing of 18th-century histories justified?

To discuss this topic, you could research how histories at the time were written. During Austen's lifetime, history books were more narrative and lyrically composed than ones of today. *The History of England* by Oliver Goldsmith, for instance, featured many of the fictions (quotes and speeches, for instance, attributed to historical figures) that Catherine Morland takes exception to. Austen had earlier satirized Goldsmith's style by writing a contrastingly short, incomplete, and highly opinionated history in an adolescent work that even aped the title of his four-volume behemoth, *The History of England*. It would be worthwhile (and fun) to read sections of it during your research. From your analysis of Catherine's comments and Austen's representations of history in her own juvenilia, what aspect of history as a genre would you argue Austen takes exception to? What is Austen suggesting about the exalted reputation history enjoyed or, more interestingly, about its content? The final question this topic asks you to theorize about is whether you think Austen's lampooning of history is justified. Base your conclusions on your own research of examples of historical writings that Austen would have known.

3. **Conduct books:** *Northanger Abbey* accounts for the coming of age of a young woman entering society. It alludes to the conduct books that were written to teach young women how to behave. What aspects of these very popular conduct books does Austen's narrator criticize?

Considered anachronistic now, conduct books were popular in Austen's time, though if you have read *The Boy Scout Handbook,* you have some familiarity with the genre. These books instructed young people on the rules of society and personal conduct. We see Austen's narrator utilizing the didactic language and demeaning advice of conduct books when she proclaims: "A woman especially, if she have the misfortune of knowing any thing, should conceal it as well as she can" (1: 14). To explore this topic you would need to research 18th-century conduct books. The *Norton Critical Edition of Northanger Abbey,* for instance, gives an abridged example of a conduct book. Once you have gained knowledge of how these books generally instructed girls to act, you will be able to discuss in what ways Austen's novel alludes to and then argues against them. What kind of femininity did these conduct books try to foster? Is Catherine Morland a response to this kind of femininity?

Form and Genre

Form and genre provide instructive ways of thinking about literature. Form is the shape and structure of a literary work; genre is the kind, or classification, of a literary work. *Northanger Abbey* is a novel. This may seem like a facile observation, but it could provide the basis for an essay on form. An essay might observe how the symmetrical form of the plot, commencing and concluding with scenes set in the Morland home, speaks to the neoclassical value of formal symmetry. A true gothic novel plot would be rambling and convoluted, and the fact that *Northanger Abbey* does not adopt a gothic shape is another way that it counters the gothic novel. This form of the novel also contributes to the sense of overall stability in the world that the novel describes. Though its heroine experiences reversals and anxiety, she is consistently restored to a realistic middle-class England, and the novel's structure reiterates the sense of this world's order and control.

The genre, or variety of this novel, is a trickier category to fix: Scholars have deemed it a burlesque, a satire, a coming-of-age story, and a comedy. It is all of these. An essay could explore how the novel fulfills the requirements of all these genres, but that would probably be too broad a topic: It is more advisable to consider at greater length how the novel relates to one or two genres. This chapter has already begun a discussion of the gothic fiction that *Northanger Abbey* satirizes. In addition to being a satire of gothic fiction, this novel also uses many of the elements of the sentimental novel, the genre of which gothic novels are a subset. In sentimental novels, the young, innocent heroine successfully repels attacks on her honor; these attacks were often posed by guardians or employers (Cuddon 616). The end of a sentimental novel sees the heroine rewarded for her virtue. Novels such as Samuel Richardson's *Pamela* (1740) and *Clarissa* (1748) belong to this genre. Austen's first title for this novel was also a woman's name, *Susan,* so certainly she had the sentimental novel in mind when writing it.

The satirical energy for this novel revolves around the gothic thrillers that Catherine adores, and it is worth taking a moment here to discuss the genre briefly. Austen's era in England saw a revival of Gothic architecture; the atmospherics associated with the Gothic style complemented the romanticism that infused English aesthetics. In fiction, the gothic novel placed the heroine of the sentimental novel in an exotic and thereby more threatening scenario. Invariably set in a remote and isolated Continental locale, gothic novels unfolded within the decaying walls of mansions or castles that featured secret passageways, the ghostly reminders of suspiciously deceased innocents, sexually threatening guardian figures, and inexplicably animated draperies, furniture, and tapestries. These novels were tremendously popular among English middle-class readers, such as Henry Tilney. A writer who explores the gothic elements of *Northanger Abbey* should certainly refer to a literary dictionary to gain a greater sense of the genre. He or she might also read one of the novels that Isabella Thorpe recommends to Catherine (1: 6). Committed devotees of Austen read all the gothic thrillers mentioned in *Northanger Abbey*, but for the purposes of an essay, reading just one would suffice. Another approach to an essay on form and genre might explore the narrator's prominent role in this novel. What is the effect of so present a narrator?

Sample Topics:

1. **The gothic:** How is the gothic important to this novel? What aspects of the gothic novel does it retool? To what end does it use the genre?

   This topic on genre requires you to research gothic novels. Finding a definition in a literary dictionary or reading one of the novels from Isabella Thorpe's recommended list would certainly familiarize you with the salient aspects of the gothic form. After you discuss the traits of the form, you will be able to discuss knowledgeably how the novel uses aspects of the form. You might think about how some of the character types or events symptomatic of the gothic novel are reworked in *Northanger Abbey.* Instead of a gothic abduction, for instance, this novel offers an expulsion. Instead of inexplicable events, all-too-ordinary ones predominate. Instead of a mad and murderous guardian, Austen presents a rude one. Your essay could also include discussions of writing style, character types, or even architectural references.

2. **Satire:** Why are gothic novels the object of Austen's satire in this novel?

   For this topic you would need the same familiarity with gothic novels that the previous topic demands. In addition, you would need to research satire. Satire, like parody, often mocks for corrective purposes. Your essay for this topic should analyze what corrective *Northanger Abbey* might be offering. What fundamental aspects of gothic fiction, for instance, are implied to be in need of correction? Another approach could argue against the corrective theory and instead analyze how the gothic, though sometimes absurd, is instructive for Catherine Morland. If you pursue this line of inquiry, you should show how the novel satirizes the atmospherics but preserves the essential lessons of a gothic novel. What lessons do gothic novels offer Catherine? How do they prepare her for the Thorpes or General Tilney?

3. **The narrator:** Analyze the narrator and her prominent role in this novel.

This topic directs you to an analysis of the narrator, a shrewd, amused, and pronounced presence throughout *Northanger Abbey*. One approach to an essay on this topic could analyze the characterization of the narrator. You could discuss what she applauds and disparages, and from this you could deduce her values. Examining the narrator's comments at the beginning and the end of the novel, where her opinions are particularly pronounced, could prove especially helpful. Another approach is to consider the effect of such a prominent narrator on the story. How does the narrator's opinions of characters change our perception of them? Where does the commentary withhold facts? You might consider how complete information on General Tilney's motivations, for instance, is withheld. Another approach to an essay about the narrator is more connected to form: What is the effect of such an attendant narrator? You might consider how the narrator seems to confide in the reader, such as when she alludes to a socially inappropriate correspondence between our hero and heroine. The narrator also digresses in a way that seems to engender confidence in the reader, such as when she describes her opinions on topics related to morality or literature. Does the intimate tone of the narration, in your opinion, interfere with or enhance the reader's relationship with the characters and story?

4. **Metafiction and the self-referential:** How does *Northanger Abbey* use some of the techniques of metafiction? Analyze the effects of these metafictive techniques on the book.

To discuss this topic, you must first locate definitions of metafiction and self-referentiality in a literary handbook. Once you have a sense of their meaning, you would then locate places in *Northanger Abbey* where both techniques are used. You might, for instance, analyze a section in which the narrator discusses literary conventions. An example of a convention is the ending of a novel that, the narrator tells us, usually offers a moral. How does the moral offered in this book overturn the usual expectations of a novel? Does this change the way you interpret the events in *Northanger Abbey*? Another example of a metafictive moment is when the narrator steps out of the story to discourse on literature. Metafiction is sometimes presented by postmodern critics as actively resisting a general aesthetic philosophy that argues that art should be more lifelike, more committed to verisimilitude. While it is unlikely that Austen sought to redress literature radically in *Northanger Abbey*, it is interesting to analyze how the novel's many examples of self-reference affect the reading experience. To address this part of the topic, you might include some of the questions posed above in the topic on the narrator. For instance, does the novel's self-referencing technique—calling attention to itself as a novel and to its characters as characters— interfere with the reading of the novel or enhance it?

Language, Symbols, and Imagery

Language, symbols, and imagery are some of the creative means by which authors convey certain feelings or ideas that would, if simply declared, be enfeebled in terms of their imaginative and evocative power. All writers, and those of fiction especially, use language deliberately, and they choose words based on their connotative meanings. As you read fiction in preparation for writing about it, be alert to the connotative meanings of words, even as you register the surface meaning of language in order to follow the plot itself. Symbols, usually used in conjunction with imagery, are objects, either animate or inanimate, that writers also use to convey ideas. Jane Austen's writing does not use a great deal of overt imagery; similes, metaphors, and outright symbols are rare. There are, however, objects in the story that the characters themselves invest with symbolic meaning. Consider, for instance, the symbolic power that Northanger Abbey holds for Catherine's fervent fantasies. She anticipates and hopes for the gothic interiors that the idea of an abbey holds for her, and she is disappointed by the modernity of the house. She thinks of the windows:

> To be sure, the pointed arch was preserved—the form of them was Gothic—they might be even casements—but every pane was so large, so clear, so light! To an imagination which had hoped for the smallest divisions, and the heaviest stone-work, for painted glass, dirt and cobwebs, the difference was very distressing. (2: 5)

An essay could explore how Catherine's desire for a fantastically Gothic house is gradually replaced by the features of the Tilney home. Catherine's realization about the speciousness of gothic novels coincides with her realization that Northanger Abbey is, simply, a house. When her suspicions about the general's nefarious deeds prove false, the narrator tells us that for Catherine "The visions of romance were over" (2: 10). While her naive romantic notions dissipate at Northanger Abbey, their cessation permits a real romance to begin. Another essay could explore Northanger Abbey as an extension of General Tilney's characterization. He also sees his house symbolically, as an expression of his importance. In many ways, his obsession with his house and its gardens proves to show—even before his actions do—that he is driven by greed and self-importance, two qualities that the novel criticizes. The best essays on symbolism look at imagery and analyze it in conjunction with the novel's larger ideas. When you are asked to discuss symbolism, you are being asked to discuss what something signifies, means, and represents in light of the entire work.

Sample Topics

1. **Northanger Abbey:** Analyze the symbolism of Northanger Abbey for Catherine or General Tilney.

   As soon as Catherine receives an invitation to stay at Northanger Abbey, she imagines its gothic features: "long, damp passages . . . narrow cells and a ruined chapel . . . some awful memorials of an injured and ill-fated nun." One approach to an essay on this topic could analyze how Catherine's understanding of the home changes during her stay. You could explore how her desire for a fantastical reality battles, and is eventually replaced by, the reality of the house. How does Northanger Abbey itself represent a kind of education for Catherine Morland? Another approach to an essay on this topic could analyze how the house represents General Tilney's character. The gardens especially reveal an owner who takes pleasure in control and power. His desire to grow pineapples, for instance, seems driven not out of a particular fondness for his "pinery," but out of a compulsion to both compete with his neighbors and triumph over nature. The general's characteristic severity and control are on vivid display when he is at home; that his control over his children is deleterious is repeatedly demonstrated by uncomfortable interactions while he is home, and the levity that occurs when he is away. Whatever approach you take to this topic, you will want to reach a conclusion about what Northanger Abbey means to either Catherine or General Tilney.

2. **Bath:** The principal action of the first half of *Northanger Abbey* takes place in the fashionable resort town of Bath. How is life there characterized, and what does it represent for Catherine Morland?

To write about this topic, you would first need to locate sections of the novel where the narrator comments on Bath. The narrator's representation of the city as a frivolous place is seen in the description of Cheap-street, where, we learn, it is so busy and "impertinent" a street that "a day never passes in which parties of ladies, however important their business, whether in quest of pastry, millinery, or even (as in the present case) of young men, are not detained on one side or other." Further distinguishing traits of Bath are found in descriptions of its social events—such as visiting the Assembly Rooms or the Pump Room, or going to a ball or the theater. One character associated with Bath is Isabella Thorpe, whose shopping savvy and rapacious dating practices mark her as a true denizen of

Bath in the narrator's conception. After analyzing how Bath is characterized in the novel, you must then reach a conclusion about what the city represents to Catherine. Your essay might explore how the city's greater anonymity and social fluidity creates opportunities but also challenges for Catherine. Given virtually free rein because of Mrs. Allen's obtuse inattention, Catherine struggles to learn how to conduct herself. How do Catherine's experiences in Bath exemplify the growth she experiences there?

Comparison and Contrast

Comparing components of a novel in order to explain and analyze the similarities or differences among them is a useful approach to writing an essay. Remember to avoid simply creating a list of similarities or differences in a work; instead, you must analyze the significance of your observations. To begin a comparison/contrast essay, you might compare characters with each other: How does Isabella Thorpe compare to Eleanor Tilney? To Catherine Morland? How does Henry Tilney compare to John Thorpe? You could also compare characters (or other elements of the story, such as themes or events) across different Austen novels. For example, how do the love interests compare with one another in *Mansfield Park* and *Northanger Abbey*? How is romance depicted differently in *Pride and Prejudice* and *Northanger Abbey*? The challenge of this kind of essay is to decide what the similarities or differences you identify might mean. These questions make essays compelling and will yield different answers for each writer. To get to these questions, you might find it helpful to consider what kinds of effects Austen achieves by producing either similarities or differences among the elements of her stories. How, for example, does Emma Woodhouse's education in *Emma* compare with that of Catherine Morland's in *Northanger Abbey*?

Sample Topics:

1. **Contrasting examples of masculinity:** John Thorpe and Henry Tilney offer two different representations of young men. How do these characterizations implicitly invite a discussion of masculine gender identity?

To write an essay on this topic, you would first need to analyze how different are the modes of masculinity demonstrated by John Thorpe and Henry Tilney. Thorpe's is an extreme form of masculinity: He is motivated by competition and most interested in horses, dogs, drinking, hunting, and driving. His conduct with Catherine and his sisters shows that he is not remotely intrigued by the world of women. Henry, on the other hand, is well versed in the world of women, a fact that is evident in his knowledge of fabrics, novels, the rules and expectations of dancing, hosting meals, letter writing, and polite conversation. Though he often pokes fun at some of these conventionally feminine social practices, he is nonetheless able to find room for himself among the women. What does your analysis of Henry Tilney and John Thorpe suggest about the varieties of masculinity in *Northanger Abbey*?

2. **Contrasting the Morland and Thorpe families:** Though they are nearly united by marriage ties, the Morlands and the Thorpes are stark contrasts. How do the families contrast in terms of values, temperament, and the way they treat each other?

   Our initial encounter with James Morland shows that he is similar to his sister: without guile and without a clue about the vacuousness of Isabella Thorpe. Both Morlands are also genuinely fond of each other, a quality not shared by the Thorpe siblings. An example of this unkindness is when we learn that John Thorpe refuses to ride in a carriage with one of his sisters because she has "thick ancles" [*sic*]. Your essay should reach a conclusion about how the families are represented as being of a distinct type. What are these types? An effective essay would analyze how the families contrast with each other in terms of their values and behavior.

3. **Comparing the educations of Emma Woodhouse and Catherine Morland:** Both Emma and Catherine transform during their respective stories. What prompts their changing insights and how do their lessons compare?

This topic asks you to consider the educations of the protagonists of *Emma* and *Northanger Abbey*. Your essay should analyze how their educations are brought about. For instance, a common element for both protagonists is that they have a mentor who later becomes a love interest. You might also explore how much learning they do themselves: Is one character more self-aware when compared with the other? Your essay should also discuss what lessons these two protagonists learn. Emma, for instance, realizes that Mr. Knightley is an ideal mate for her: He is accepting of her father and in love with her. What does Catherine Morland, in comparison, realize about herself or about Henry Tilney?

Bibliography and Online Resources for *Northanger Abbey*

Austen, Jane. *"The History of England: By a Partial, Prejudiced, and Ignorant Historian."* Chapel Hill, NC: Algonquin Books, 1993.

Cuddon, J. A. *A Dictionary of Literary Terms.* London: Penguin Books, 1979.

Fraiman, Susan. Introduction. *Northanger Abbey.* Jane Austen. Ed. Susan Fraiman. Norton Critical Edition. New York: Norton, 2004. 7–14.

Leavis, Q. D. "Not an Inspired Amateur." Excerpt from "A Critical Theory of Jane Austen's Writings." *Scrutiny* 10.1 (1942): 61–66; 68–71. Rpt. in *Northanger Abbey.* Ed. Susan Fraiman. New York: Norton, 2004. 182–90.

Litz, A. Walton. "[Regulated Sympathy in *Northanger Abbey*]." Excerpt from *Jane Austen: A Study of Her Artistic Development.* New York: Oxford UP, 1965. 53–71 Rpt. in *Northanger Abbey.* Ed. Susan Fraiman. New York: Norton, 2004. 264–77.

Neill, Edward. "The Secret of *Northanger Abbey.*" *Essays in Criticism* 47: 1 (January 1997): 13–33. Electronic. Literature Resource Center. Berkeley Public Library. 24 August 2007.

Pinion, F. B. *"Northanger Abbey." A Jane Austen Companion: A Critical Survey and Reference Book.* London: Macmillan, 1973. 76–83.

SENSE AND
SENSIBILITY

For *Sense and Sensibility* (1811), her first published novel, Jane Austen adopted the form of the popular contrast novel, a style that juxtaposed two dissimilar characters to thereby illustrate a moral lesson. Though Austen's artistry and wit make *Sense and Sensibility* less didactic and more entertaining than other examples of contrast novels, she did observe the conventions of this form by orchestrating many oppositions in the story. Protagonists Elinor and Marianne Dashwood are sisters who, respectively, contrast the qualities of sense (reason) and sensibility (passionate feeling). Other contrasting characters include matriarchs (Mrs. Jennings and Mrs. Ferrars), suitors (Willoughby and Edward Ferrars), and spouses (Sir John and Lady Middleton). Still more contrasts exist in parallel events, such as disappointments in love, dispossessions of inheritance, and irregular engagements. As you track these contrasts in your reading, be sure to identify which element of the contrast is presented in the more favorable light. More illuminating still is noting where the lines between contrasts blur: when, for instance, we see a character acting more like his or her antithetical contrast.

Many characters are associated with either sense or sensibility, and while the novel favors the moderation and selflessness associated with sense, *Sense and Sensibility* is no absolutist morality play. The views expressed by the novel are complex and even ambiguous at times. In these ambiguities rest opportunities for your literary analysis. No matter what analytical approach you take to the novel, you must first grapple with Austen's language. This section of the chapter will demonstrate how to do a close reading of two early passages from *Sense and Sensibility* to prepare for writing an essay.

The initial chapters establish the two protagonists and the conflicts they face. The challenges are of two related losses: the death of their father and consequent dispossession of their home. The characterizations of Elinor and Marianne demonstrate their opposed approaches to challenges and suggest the narrator's opinions of their moderate and immoderate, respectively, expressions of woe. Elinor is described with approbation: "She had an excellent heart;—her disposition was affectionate, and her feelings were strong; but she knew how to govern them" (1: 1). It is noteworthy that the narrator asserts the strength of Elinor's sensibility or feelings; though Elinor is quickly revealed to be the character of sense or reason, she is not, we here learn, apathetic. Marianne, unlike her sister, is "eager in everything; her sorrows, her joys." She is also "generous, amiable, interesting; she was every thing [*sic*] but prudent." The narrator approves of Marianne in every respect save that of her immoderate approach to feeling. So though these two young women are contrasts in terms of their restraint, the narrator is quick to point out the many positive qualities that they share; these overlaps that occur early on in the narrative hint that Austen's novel is fundamentally more complicated than a conventional contrast novel.

The differences in their characters, while not absolute, are presented in high relief when the narrator describes their individual reactions to the loss of their beloved father. Mrs. Dashwood is, like Marianne, a creature of feeling. Marianne and her mother

> encouraged each other now in the violence of their affliction. The agony of grief which overpowered them at first, was voluntarily renewed, was sought for, was created again and again. They gave themselves up wholly to their sorrow, seeking increase of wretchedness in every reflection that could afford it, and resolved against ever admitting consolation in future. Elinor, too, was deeply afflicted; but still she could struggle, she could exert herself. (1: 1)

Marianne's and Mrs. Dashwood's overwhelming grief is described with diction that suggests reckless and willful abandon. Their sorrow is "voluntarily renewed, was sought for," and they pursued "increase of wretchedness in every reflection that could afford it." The narrator acknowledges Elinor's deep feeling but committed fortitude, and so implies that Elinor's is the more heroic response to tragedy. Pay attention to these shades of meaning as you read.

Pose questions as you are reading any text in preparation for writing about it. In *Sense and Sensibility*, you might ask, what is the effect of not moderating one's feelings? How does immoderate sensibility affect the individual and, more broadly, the family? How do the events in the novel reflect the choices that characters make? These kinds of questions can become the core of an essay. Exploring these questions could, for instance, lead to an essay that explores the notion of conduct in the novel.

A slow and careful reading of *Sense and Sensibility* will better allow you to recognize its patterns, issues, and ideas. Reading slowly and taking notes will make for a rich understanding of the story, while also enabling you to gather the evidence for a strong essay.

TOPICS AND STRATEGIES

This section discusses various possible topics for essays on *Sense and Sensibility* and general approaches to those topics. The material below is only a starting point, not an exhaustive master key. Use this material to generate your own analysis. Every topic discussed here could encompass a variety of good papers.

Themes

Sense and Sensibility deals with many themes—ideas or concepts that organize and underscore the importance of the events in the novel. The section above examined some of these: loss, moderation, and conduct, among others. The novel also considers the ideas and practices associated with sense, sensibility, prudence, family, duty, and honor. Writers analyzing the novel often begin by identifying a central theme they see as important and then determine what the story says about that theme. You can identify themes by noticing the ideas, symbols, or words that recur in the story. In the initial chapters you will observe various examples of conduct following a tragic turn of events. This will not be the first challenge the heroines face, and as the novel progresses you should observe how they conduct themselves and what kinds of challenges they meet.

The next step in an essay on conduct would be to decide what the novel is saying about that theme. Details such as the way Marianne disregards rules of decorum for unmarried ladies when out in public with Willoughby might lead to an analysis of other moments in the novel where convention is flouted, such as when Willoughby bestows on Marianne an inappropriately extravagant gift, a horse. Other themes could be approached in similar ways. The theme of marriage could be undertaken by looking at the story's depiction of the many unsatisfactory marriages and thinking about what the novel is saying about this institution. A cautioning word on the eponymous themes of sense and sensibility seems useful here: The concepts treated together are vast enough to undermine the focus of a good essay. Though their complexities play out in tandem in the novel, in an essay of shorter length the concepts are most ably analyzed with an emphasis on one or the other concept, and so the sample topics present them here.

Sample Topics:

1. **Sense:** Which definition of sense does this novel promote? What varieties of sense does this novel critique?

   This topic asks you to identify the novel's varieties of sense. Some critics assert that sense in this novel means moderation, while others argue that it means rational understanding. To reach your own conclusion about sense as used in this novel, consider under what conditions the narrator approves of sense. Where does the narrator privilege sense over the passions associated with sensibility? You might consider, for example, how Elinor reacts with composure to Lucy Steele's revelation of her engagement to Edward Ferrars. The second part of the topic invites you to consider improper or otherwise dishonorable uses of sense. An example of this occurs early in the novel when Fanny uses adept reasoning to talk her husband out of providing for his deserving, and now destitute, sisters. Fanny's conduct provides many often humorous examples of unkindly employed sense. Ultimately, you will want to reach a conclusion about how the varieties of sense operate and decide which meaning of sense is the most celebrated in this novel.

2. **Sensibility:** How is sensibility shown to be the motivating force of a novel that appears to promote its antithetical value of sense?

Although this novel may seem to be a cautionary tale against sensibility, there is a case to be made that *Sense and Sensibility*, in fact, promotes the strong feelings customarily associated with sensibility. This topic guides you to scenes where the narrator applauds feeling and passion. Consider, for example, Elinor's passionate unburdening of herself to her sister or Marianne's heartfelt defense of Elinor in the face of Mrs. Ferrars's rudeness. A paper could also address this topic by focusing solely on how sensibility operates in Elinor's character. Elinor's reaction to Willoughby's confession is an intriguing moment for registering how her feelings of mercy and forgiveness are generated by her consideration of his regret and apparent unhappiness. Ultimately, this topic asks you to reach a conclusion about the laudatory aspects of sensibility.

3. **Marriage:** Though the novel ends with the agreeable marriages of both Elinor and Marianne, there are many examples of marriages that are tragic, ruinous, or simply unhappy. What does this novel say about the institution of marriage?

Some of Austen's most scathing depictions here are of marriages, yet marriage is the hoped-for goal of both heroines. To answer this topic, look to commentary that the narrator makes about marriage. The negative effects on a spouse are, for example, proclaimed for John Dashwood: "Had he married a more amiable woman, he might have been made still more respectable than he was." What are we to make of the discord in the marriages of the Palmers and the Willougbys or in the disparate natures of the Middletons? One approach to this topic would be to focus on the purposes of marriage, such as the creation of children. Why do you think children are so consistently characterized in the novel as spoiled and obnoxious? As a related point, consider why we never hear children speak.

4. **Fallen women:** Analyze what the stories of Eliza and her daughter (also named Eliza) contribute to our understanding of the events in the novel.

Colonel Brandon tells the sad stories of Eliza (his first love) and her illegitimate daughter, Eliza Williams, who has recently had an illegitimate child herself. These stories are a dramatic departure from the genteel drawing rooms and woodsy rambles of the majority of the novel. In fact, the stories of this pair of disgraced women can be analyzed as representative of the tragedy that might await immoderate females in this society. For this topic you could analyze how the stories of these women help us understand Elinor's fear for her sister's conduct. You would want to find scenes that demonstrate Elinor's anxieties about her sister's improper behavior, as when it is revealed that Marianne has visited Willoughby's house unchaperoned. Ultimately, you would want to discuss the social and personal consequences of behavior considered indecorous in an unmarried female.

5. **Civility:** In *Sense and Sensibility,* civility, the practice of courtesy and politeness, is a sign not only of good behavior, but also of good character. Where in this novel does civility slip? Are bad manners always a bad thing? What is the significance of false civility?

This topic asks you to analyze civility and the significance of its expression in good and bad manners. Manners were very important to the society that Austen writes about, and they were thought to communicate breeding, character, and dignity. Bad manners also communicate much in this novel. One approach to this topic is to consider how manners align with character. Consider, for instance, the manners of Robert Ferrars: How do his manners reveal his ill nature? Manners also reveal the insincerity of some, such as Lucy Steele, who exceeds the flattery customary to good manners to further her own aims. Excessive and insincere flattery is practiced by both

Steele sisters when they fawn over the distasteful Middleton children. Analyzing the goals and effects of false civility would be another way to approach this topic. Still another way to approach the subject would be to focus on when incivility is practiced by good characters and consider how this seeming incivility is represented in the novel. Does the narrator chastise or quietly cheer Marianne's upbraiding of Mrs. Ferrars? In other places Marianne's incivility seems more a matter of social protest than bad behavior. Whatever approach you take, you will want to reach a final conclusion about civility in the novel. Does it present civility as a true mark of character or a mask that covers true character?

Character

Because so much of the novel focuses on the conduct and manners of its characters, essays that look at character are a productive way to analyze *Sense and Sensibility*. In the world that Jane Austen depicted, character and manners were of paramount importance, especially for young women whose marriageability and thereby social and material survival depended on how well they understood and followed social rules.

There are various approaches to essays on character. You could concentrate on character development (such as how Austen distinguishes Elinor from her mother by their specific reactions to challenges), means of characterization (such as the way the reader learns about Mrs. Jennings from her words and later her generous actions), or interpretations of changes in a character as the novel proceeds (such as the profound shifts from selfishness to selflessness in Marianne).

To write an essay on character, you would need to question how readers come to know various characters. How, for instance, does Austen distinguish a character's behavior? Charlotte Palmer's ridiculousness is underscored by her inability to stop laughing, no matter what the circumstances. Fanny Dashwood's insensitivity is demonstrated by how quickly she arrives at Norland and displaces her sisters-in-law after their father's death. To an extent, the narrator instructs you what to expect from characters, and if you pay attention to the narrator's editorial comments about individuals, you will understand what the characters signify in the novel. When introducing John Dashwood, for instance, the narrator wryly castigates his character: "He was not an ill-disposed young man, unless to be rather cold hearted, and rather selfish, is to be ill-disposed" (1: 1). The narrator's initial assertion, that John Dashwood "was not an ill-disposed young man," is immediately counteracted by his being "rather cold hearted and rather selfish." The narrator's irony here tells us that John is coldhearted and selfish, but the implication is that, socially speaking, these shortcomings do not necessarily mark a man as "ill-disposed." The narrator goes on to relate that John "was, in general, well respected; for he conducted himself with propriety in the discharge of his ordinary duties." Note that the narrator's assessment of John Dashwood's character is clearly linked to a commentary on society; the implication here is that if society approves of John Dashwood, society is, to borrow a damning qualifier from Austen, rather flawed. To analyze questions of character development, look for distinguishing traits of language, action, or interactions with other characters. The ways characters behave with one another help readers not only understand how characters are created, but also assess what characters signify for the story overall.

Sample Topics:

1. **Marianne's character development:** How does Marianne change over the course of the novel? What is the significance of these changes?

   To write an essay on this topic, you should decide not only what types of changes Marianne undergoes, but also establish her initial behaviors. Before her metamorphosis, she demonstrates a tendency to indulge her grief over both her father's death and the loss of Willoughby. In the latter example, the narrator tells us that Marianne "courted . . . misery." How does this pattern of behavior undergo significant transformation following her illness? Why does her illness so profoundly change her? After you assess the substance of Marianne's changes, you should also identify any of her traits that remain unaltered. Is there a way that her character remains the same, though the direction of her energies adjusts? A strong essay will assess how Marianne's growth connects to the novel's larger themes.

2. **Willoughby as a character:** Willoughby storms into the story like the hero of a romance novel. Although his conduct is often dubious, the novel gives him an opportunity to redeem himself with a confession to Elinor. Do you think that the reader is supposed to sympathize with Willoughby? If so, what does that signify for the story's themes?

It is curious, perhaps, that while Willoughby drops out of the main action of the novel with his quick run to London and fortune, he remains an important character. This topic asks you to consider the conduct of Willoughby and to assess whether he earns the approval of the reader and/or narrator at the end of the novel. Pay particular attention to the drunken disclosures he makes to Elinor at Cleveland. One element that merits close reading is the number of times he uses the words "I" and "me" and to determine what bearing this has on his confession, contrition, and redemption. To ascertain the level of sympathy we are supposed to have for him, look to Elinor's and Marianne's reactions to his confession. More generally, why do you think Austen included his confession?

3. **Character development in general:** How does the novel present character to the reader? What techniques does it use? Are characters transparent or somewhat concealed?

A paper on this topic would consider how Austen gives insight into character. A possible approach would be to look carefully at a pair of characters or a set of techniques and attempt to show what effects they have. For instance, a paper could examine how social conventions, such as polite conversation, reveal character. Marianne is incapable of idle conversation, while Lucy Steele has mastered empty flattery in the pursuit of her ambitions. Another paper could analyze how letters—

their content, their style, and their very exchange—reveal a great deal about characters.

4. **Selfish/ambitious characters:** Elinor identifies selfishness as the fundamental flaw in Willoughby's character (3: 11). Analyze how other selfish or ambitious characters illuminate the novel's values.

To expand on this topic you would need to focus on a small number of selfish characters. You could choose from among Willoughby, Lucy Steele, Fanny Dashwood, John Dashwood, Mrs. Ferrars, Robert Ferrars, or Marianne. How does their selfishness motivate their actions? How does the narrator's opinion of these characters reveal itself? Robert Ferrars's conceit and self-centered manner is marked, and both the narrator and Elinor dismiss him as a pompous fool. How is it significant that Lucy Steele can so adeptly capitalize on his high opinion of himself? Ultimately, you want to reach a conclusion about what the novel says about the selfishness of your chosen characters: Does society reward or punish the selfish and ambitious? A different approach to this topic would be to examine how the novel treats the selfless and generous.

History and Context

Another suitable approach to the analysis of *Sense and Sensibility* is through history and context. Even a modest amount of historical research into the novel's world will yield great returns in both understanding and analytical opportunities. *Sense and Sensibility* reflects its time frame: England's Regency period straddled, historically speaking, the order and conservatism of the Age of Enlightenment and the experimentation and progressive spirit of the romantic era. Austen's generation was fascinated by the conflicts over conduct and morality of both individuals and larger groups, such as nations. Europe was reeling from the passions that boiled around the French and American Revolutions and the figurative and actual eradications of traditional authority in those countries. Though the novel makes no explicit reference to political circumstances on national stages, the revolutions certainly underlie the context of the novel. Romanticism, a mode of thought that found expression in art and politics and was the spirit that fueled the violence and liberalism of the revolutions, is a primary source of dramatic conflict in the novel. Marianne and Willoughby proclaim and exhibit sometimes absurdly untenable adherences to romantic practices. Some traits and proclivities endorsed by these characters include emotional extremes, individualism, tempestuous weather, a fondness for the rustic and quaint, the sublime, and iconoclasm. Assessing how romantic qualities are presented in this novel would be a useful approach to an essay on the historical context of *Sense and Sensibility*. Another element that could be discussed in terms of its historical context is its implicit meditations on the role of women. People were at this time questioning women's lack of power; for example, women forfeited their money and legal autonomy upon marriage. If found guilty of adultery, women sometimes forfeited their children, too. Though Austen herself was politically conservative, there are many indications in the novel that she disagreed with society's restrictions on women. A good paper could also explore how the novel reflects the era's sense of feminine modesty.

Sample Topics:

1. **Romanticism:** How does the novel present some of the precepts of romanticism? What does romanticism signify in this novel?

   This topic would need to investigate definitions and expressions of the romantic movement of this time period. A good encyclopedia will help you understand what romanticism encompasses. Once you appreciate the breadth of romanticism, you will appreciate how important it is to limit the scope of this topic. You could limit your approach to a single character, such as Willoughby, and analyze how he is associated with romanticism. Why do you think Austen drew a character with such romantic associations? What do his behavior and beliefs suggest about the romanticism with which he is associated? Another approach could be literary. You might explore Marianne's references to specific authors. Or you might note how Marianne's experience demonstrates the risks that conventionally romantic heroines must run.

2. *Sense and Sensibility* **and** *A Vindication of the Rights of Women*: Austen would not have considered herself a radical, yet her novel shares many of the same opinions as those of her radical contemporary Mary Wollstonecraft. How do Austen's novel and Wollstonecraft's treatise resonate with each other?

A contemporary of Austen, Mary Wollstonecraft was considered a dangerously intelligent and free-spirited woman. She led a public life, traveled to France to view the Revolution in action, had scandalous love affairs and a child out of wedlock, and, most important, authored a work—*A Vindication of the Rights of Women* (1792)—that argued for the abilities and reasoning power of her fellow women. In spite of their personal contrasts, Austen's and Wollstonecraft's works mirror each other in their respective outlooks on women. This topic asks you to research Wollstonecraft's treatise and identify ideas it shares with the novel. *Sense and Sensibility* is an especially apt amplification of Wollstonecraft's criticism of sensibility for its own sake; for example, *A Vindication* asserts that women encouraged to be overly sensible are "prey to their senses." How is that liability demonstrated in Austen's novel? Another point of comparison would be to reflect on how Wollstonecraft's ideas regarding the education of women are made manifest in the novel.

3. **Modesty of/in the novel:** It seems odd to us today that Jane Austen used the pen name "By a Lady" when she published *Sense and Sensibility*, but that anonymity was the custom at that time. It was considered scandalous for a woman to step out of the domestic shadows and into the public limelight by acknowledging that she had written a novel that might reveal personal facts or expose her to public discussion. How does this cultural modesty extend to the book itself? What kinds of things not mentioned in the narrative would it have been improper for an unmarried woman to have firsthand knowledge of?

To explore this topic you should know something about the manners of the time. You can gain such knowledge by reading about courtship practices for the middle classes in the Regency period. After identifying the mores of proper behavior, you will be able to locate scenes in the novel in which the author's modesty prevents her describing scenes of physical or emotional intimacy. Which scenes do we hear only second- or even thirdhand? Consider, for example, the moment of Elinor and Edward's engagement and marriage or Willoughby's taking the lock of hair from Marianne. Colonel Brandon's stories of the Elizas' fates are also examples of secondhand tales. Explore in your essay what these hearsay moments tell us about the era in which Austen's story is set.

4. **Economic context:** In what ways do we observe the economic awareness of this novel? What are the signs that it is a product of a mercantile society?

This is a broad topic, and you could answer the questions in the prompt in a number of ways. First, of course, you will do some background reading on England's economic history at this time; such information can be found in a general guide to Austen's era. One approach to this topic would be to assess the references to the particulars of financial practices that were a part of everyday life. You might look at inheritance laws and their associated annuities, settlements, and trusts. You might instead concentrate on the financial matters related to marriage. Your essay could consider how one or a number of these financial practices reverberates in the novel. Another approach could track how economic motivation propels the actions of many of the characters in *Sense and Sensibility*. How does the narrator represent economic considerations? As acceptable? Despicable?

Philosophy and Ideas

Another approach to forming an argument about the novel is to explore the many philosophical ideas in the novel. This approach is related to the thematic approach described above in that it tracks an idea in the story, but the result of this kind of essay would demonstrate how you see the story commenting on the idea in its more general form.

Austen was of an age that debated the morality—the rightness and wrongness—of actions and beliefs, and many of the ideas in this novel have moral connotations: honor, self-command, reason, pride, imprudence, as well as, of course, the title's sense and sensibility. In *Sense and Sensibility* the characters themselves discourse on ideas and personal adherence to morality. Even Marianne, the most iconoclastic of the principal characters, wonders at her lover's conduct in moral terms and at one point asks her sister: "can he be justified?" The characters' discussions of what is and is not justified behavior can form the basis for an essay on honor. Another philosophical approach could study how characters understand the world around them. Marianne, for example, uses intuition and feeling to guide her actions. Elinor, on the other hand, uses reason and empirical deduction to guide her actions and make sense of her feelings. Another idea that circulates in the novel is that of the proper understanding and use of the outdoors. By tracking the questions that the characters ask of themselves and each other, you can identify the ideas that are most important to the society in this novel and gather the evidence you need to write a strong essay.

Sample Topics:

1. **Honor:** In the initial description of John Dashwood, we are told that he is well respected, but we soon observe that he does not act with honor regarding his sisters. How does this novel define honor? What other examples are there of honor's employment or neglect?

   This kind of essay needs to assess how honor is defined by the characters and the narrator. Respectability is a gauge of how society rates an individual, while honor suggests an adherence, sometimes heroic, to morally proper behavior. For this essay, you might consider comparing the seemingly disparate conduct of Edward Ferrars and John Willoughby; there are, after all, many dishonorable similarities in their courtships of Elinor and Marianne. How do the outcomes of those courtships reveal the novel's contentions about conduct and honor? Does it suggest that honor is innate or learned behavior? Other characters whose understanding of honor is illuminating include

Colonel Brandon and Mrs. Jennings. Ultimately, what does the novel suggest are the consequences of dishonorable actions? Why, in short, is honor so important to this world? An ambitious essay might consider problems with honor. Would honor have been morally justified had it permitted the success of the dishonorable Lucy Steele and the misery of the honorable Edward and Elinor?

2. **Modes of understanding:** How do the protagonists make sense of their worlds and experiences? What does the novel say about the ways that Elinor and Marianne understand characters and events?

This topic requires that you analyze the modes of understanding that Elinor and Marianne employ. The narrator emphasizes Elinor's point of view, and so we can observe how she uses reason and logic to think through challenges. Marianne's point of view is less articulated by the narrator, but she is such an honest and outspoken character that she declares how she uses intuition and emotions to guide her. Good places to compare the sisters' disparate modes of understanding are the scenes following either the death of their father or their respective heartbreaks. Consider also whether one character learns the other's method of reasoning. Using the observations of the narrator, the events in the story, and the comments of the characters, you can reach a conclusion about which of the two forms of logic the book favors.

3. **Landscape:** Though much of *Sense and Sensibility* takes place indoors, landscape does crop up as an important and revealing idea. What is this book's philosophy of the outdoors?

To answer this topic, consider where the landscape is discussed or interacted with. One approach to an essay on this topic would be to discuss the aesthetics of landscape. Edward Ferrars is half-teasing Marianne when he says he knows nothing of the picturesque—a romantic concept of the outdoors that would be useful to define in your essay. Edward argues for the necessity of utility over aesthetics in landscape, but John Dashwood, the narrator implies, takes utility too far with his ambitions for increasing the enclosed farmland of Norland. Enclosure—a landholder's building walls around open and communal grazing lands—was a controversial practice of the time. Another approach to the topic would focus solely on the relationship between Marianne and the landscape that proves so pivotal to her character. How, for instance, does the landscape serve as a projection of her romantic nature? What does it mean that she is so often caught outside by storms?

Form and Genre

Form and genre provide useful ways of thinking about and describing different literary works. In the case of *Sense and Sensibility* the genre is fiction and, more specifically, a novel. Critics have debated how to categorize this novel even more specifically: It has been deemed a contrast novel, a didactic novel, and a moral debate. The discussion about the definitive categorization of this novel provides opportunities for your analytical participation. You might, for instance, analyze how the novel does not fit one of the categories listed. The contrast novel discussion is an especially fruitful one to join. To write an essay on genre, you might research what a contrast novel was expected to do and then locate ways that *Sense and Sensibility* does not fully conform to those expectations. When Austen wrote the first draft of this novel, 17 years before its publication, it was as an epistolary novel, a popular style composed entirely of letters between characters. Knowing this fact allows another approach to genre that tracks vestiges of the epistolary form in *Sense and Sensibility*. Another good approach to an essay on form and genre might look to one of the formal elements in the novel. The ending of this story, for instance, features intriguing resolutions: felicity for the heroes and modified felicity for the villains. You might, then, analyze the significance of the novel's lack of conventional poetic justice.

Sample Topics:

1. ***Sense and Sensibility* as contrast novel:** How does this novel both adopt and reject the conventions of the contrast novel? Why do you think it does not fit neatly into that generic category?

This topic requires a consideration of *Sense and Sensibility* as a contrast novel, and it guides you to examine how the book does not wholly conform to that category. One way to approach this topic would be to study the beginning and ending of the novel and assess whether the contrasting characters still represent the quality that they initially did. For instance, at the end, is Elinor so entirely motivated by sense? Are there not signs that she is also now motivated by emotion? Scholars contend that Austen brought a refreshing realism to the English novel. Is it her sense of realism that pushes against the contrast novel form?

2. ***Sense and Sensibility* and the epistolary form:** We know that an earlier draft of this novel was in the epistolary form. How is the epistolary genre still evident in this later version?

This topic gives you a fact and asks you to analyze the novel in terms of that fact. To build a thesis for an essay like this, you need to discuss the ways the epistolary form remains relevant to this novel. You can look to speeches, such as Willoughby's confession, that might have originally been given in the form of a letter. You might consider discussing the different challenges and opportunities for characterization that exist in a letter versus those that are generated by dialogue. Why do you think Austen ultimately dispensed with the epistolary form for this novel? Another approach would be to analyze how letters in the novel remain important elements of the narrative. How do the letters broaden the scope of voices that we hear?

3. **Poetic justice:** Some critics have noted that there is no dramatically clear poetic justice in the novel, but there is a degree of just desserts. Do characters get what they deserve in *Sense and Sensibility*?

Poetic justice is found in folk tales where the good are rewarded and the bad are punished. The contrast novel genre also depended on poetic justice to illustrate its moral message. This topic suggests you consider whether characters get what they deserve. Mrs. Ferrars is a worthwhile character to discuss because, although she does seem to be punished for her cruelty and snobbery, she is soon reconciled to her children by the clever stratagems of Lucy Steele. Willoughby is another character who, in a folk tale, would have suffered for his sins. In this work, however, the narrator tells us at the end that he "lived to exert, and frequently to enjoy himself." Does this novel mete out justice? Does it reward or punish the villainous? Another approach to this topic would be to examine how the novel treats the selfless and generous.

Language, Symbols, and Imagery

Language, symbols, and imagery are some of the creative means by which an author conveys certain feelings or ideas that would, if simply stated, be undermined in terms of their suggestive power. All writers, and those of imaginative fiction especially, use language deliberately and they choose words based on their connotative meanings. In Jane Austen's work, language is especially meaningful. She deliberately uses the words and even the patterns of language—such as sentence structure—to convey information about characters and situations. Character development, as discussed above in the section on character, is partly constructed by what that individual says. This is particularly true for Austen's characters. Communication style—either in conversation or by letter—conveys character. *Sense and Sensibility* is lauded for how deftly dialogue establishes both Dashwood sisters' personas. One scene that distinguishes their characterizations is when they discuss their former home. It is autumn, and Elinor observes with complacency how Norland "probably looks much as it always does at this time of the year. The woods and walks thickly covered with dead leaves" (1: 15). Marianne, reminded of autumn leaves and home, rhapsodizes:

> Oh! . . . with what transporting sensation have I formerly seen them fall! How have I delighted, as I walked, to see them driven in showers about me by the wind! What feelings have they, the season, the air altogether inspired! Now there is no one to regard them. They are seen

only as a nuisance, swept hastily off, and driven as much as possible from the sight.

Marianne's effusive emotions are evident in both the content of her speech and in its form. The feelings here are presented in a shape that approximates the romantic poetry to which she is devoted. Notice that her speech begins with the interjection "oh"—suggesting an emotional outburst that is too fervent for words. The high drama of Marianne's emotions are also communicated by the punctuation: There are many exclamation marks, many commas, and many clauses trailing off incomplete as the next idea overtakes her. In these moments of emotional transport, Marianne's diction, syntax, and overall form of expression communicate her understanding of herself and the world around her as romantic subjects. Marianne's hyperbolic voice is contrasted with Elinor's, who responds to her sister's speech with understated deadpan humor: "It is not every one . . . who has your passion for dead leaves."

Symbols, usually used in conjunction with imagery, are objects, either animate or inanimate, that writers also use to convey ideas. Jane Austen does not employ much overt imagery. Similes, metaphors, and outright symbols are infrequently encountered. There are, however, objects in the story that the characters invest with symbolic meaning. Consider, for instance, the outdoors. As the above discussion suggests, Marianne's poetic soul is often attracted to the outdoors. To her, nature provides solace, communion, and—the narrator suggests—a projection of her emotions onto the landscape. An essay on the symbolism of nature for Marianne might explore why she is drawn to the most inhospitable versions of nature available to her. The days preceding her nearly fatal illness, after all, are spent taking "twilight walks . . . all over the grounds, and especially in the most distant parts of them, where there was something more of wildness than the rest, where the trees were oldest, and the grass was the longest and wettest" (3: 7). In an essay on Marianne and nature, you might consider why she is drawn to a form of nature characterized by such superlative language (for example, oldest, longest, most distant, wettest). The best essays on symbolism analyze imagery in relation to a novel's larger ideas. When you are asked to discuss symbolism, you are expected to discuss what something signifies, means, and represents in light of the entire work.

Sample Topics:

1. **Communication styles:** An important dynamic in *Sense and Sensibility* is the different philosophies and modes of conduct that Elinor and Marianne embody. How do their communication styles also emphasize their opposed characterizations? How do their styles of expression adjust as their characters change?

   To answer this topic, you need to identify passages that illustrate Elinor's and Marianne's different speaking styles. Elinor's steady temperament is reflected in her use of few adjectives and adverbs. Marianne's passionate personality is seen in her reliance on all manner of descriptive language, as well as rhetorical questions and exclamations. Consider, for instance, Marianne's dramatic reaction to Elinor's measured revelation that she "likes" and "esteems" Edward Ferrars: "Esteem him! Like him! Cold-hearted Elinor! Oh! Worse than cold-hearted! Ashamed of being otherwise!" Your essay should track how their styles of expression adjust as their characters change. Marianne's severe illness inspires a change of heart, and her expression follows suit. This transformed style of expression is evident when Marianne speaks with equanimity about her earlier conduct: "I saw that my own feelings had prepared my sufferings, and that my want of fortitude under them had almost led me to the grave." One scene that reflects the changing of character and expression is Elinor's passionate defense of her conduct and feelings regarding Edward to Marianne. As the novel progresses, does each sister sound incrementally more like the other?

2. **Illness:** In what ways does Marianne's illness function as a symbol in this novel? What does it symbolize?

   This topic asks you to consider how an event—Marianne's near-fatal illness—serves a symbolic purpose. The story presents the illness as keyed to Marianne's emotional excesses. Your essay could analyze how they are presented as causing her illness. In addition to observing the contributing factors for Marianne's illness, you should also analyze the consequences of this event. For Marianne, her illness seems to function as a catharsis: It cleanses her of an untenably passionate life. Is her illness, then, revitalizing? Marianne's illness clearly means a great deal to Elinor as well. How does Marianne's illness change Elinor and her perception of the world?

Comparison and Contrast

Comparing components of a story in order to explain and analyze the similarities or differences among them is a useful approach to writing an essay. Avoid merely creating a list of similarities or differences; instead, take the necessary step of commenting on these observations. To begin a comparison/contrast essay, you might compare characters with each other: How does Mrs. Ferrars compare with Mrs. Dashwood? To Mrs. Jennings? How does Colonel Brandon compare with Marianne? You could also compare characters (or other elements of the story such as themes or events) across different Austen novels. For example, how do depictions of emotion compare in *Sense and Sensibility* and *Northanger Abbey*? The challenge of this kind of essay is to decide what the similarities or differences you identify might mean. These questions make essays compelling and will have different answers for each writer. To answer these questions, you might find it helpful to think about what kinds of effects Austen achieves by producing either similarities or differences between elements of her stories. How, for example, do Elizabeth Bennet's and Elinor Dashwood's respective temperaments broaden our understanding of the poor but middle-class woman's position? It is not enough to point to the existence of similarities or differences; you must also consider what purposes those similarities or differences might signify for the story itself.

Sample Topics:

1. **Contrasting attitudes to family:** A number of families make up the social circle in this novel: the Dashwoods, Middletons, Ferrars, Jennings, Steeles, Willoughbys, and Brandons. Compare how the story represents these families and assess the story's attitude toward the various models of family relationships in the novel.

This topic is related to the question on marriage in the section discussing themes. It would tread some of the same territory in the story, but the focus here is on contrasting the different groups to identify what might represent a good or bad model of family in *Sense and Sensibility.* Consider looking for areas of difference, as in expressions of fidelity, sympathy, or understanding. It might be worthwhile to investigate smaller groups within families, such as brothers or sisters. The sisters Steele and Dashwood, for example, provide stark contrasts in their behaviors and values.

2. **Comparing intellectual heroines in different novels:** Elinor Dashwood is one of a number of Austen's protagonists distinguished by their intelligence. Consider comparing Elinor to Elizabeth Bennet of *Pride and Prejudice* or Anne Elliot of *Persuasion.* How are they alike or different? How do they cope with the challenges of their social situation?

This topic requires you to consider how these capable women manage in a world that relegates them to the margins of domestic life. To familiarize yourself with the society in which they lived—and their social spheres are the same—do some of the research described in the section on history and context. Analyze any contrasting strategies that you see the heroines adopting. Elizabeth, for example, is far more outspoken about her frustrations than either Anne or Elinor. You might also want to consider which of your two chosen heroines seems to receive the more ringing endorsement from her narrator. Any theories about which character Austen most identified with? You will certainly need textual support for this kind of claim.

3. **Comparing Colonel Brandon and Marianne Dashwood:** Some readers have scoffed at the marriage of Colonel Brandon and Marianne as being unlikely, but one could argue that they are an ideal match. Consider their commonalities as you make a case for the suitability of this marriage.

This kind of essay makes a claim about two characters—the shared traits of Brandon and Marianne—and then asks you to analyze its verity. For areas of comparison, you might look to approaches to life, understandings of love, or personal experiences. Ultimately, this topic asks you to make a persuasive argument as you compare two different characters.

4. **Contrasting representations of the clergy in different novels:** Analyze Edward Ferrars's reasons for joining the church and compare them with the motivations of a clergyman in another Austen novel. What might Austen be saying about the profession?

Edward's desire to be a clergyman is in direct opposition to his ambitious mother's wishes, though the narrator seems to endorse his dream heartily and Elinor helps facilitate it. After analyzing Edward's reasons for wanting to join the church, compare the reasons or conduct of a church figure from another Austen novel. Mr. Collins from *Pride and Prejudice* would make an interesting contrast, since his offices have more to do with social ambition than piety. *Mansfield Park* offers points for comparison; Edmund Bertram is committed to being a clergyman, though doing so costs him the interest of Mary Crawford, the woman he loves. His desire to be a clergyman is supported by his family, and the reasons for this are worth exploring as a contrast to Edward Ferrars's situation.

Bibliography and Online Resources for *Sense and Sensibility*

Bloom, Harold, ed. *Jane Austen: Bloom's Major Novelists.* Broomall, PA: Chelsea House Publishers, 2000.

Brown, Julia Prewitt. *A Reader's Guide to the Nineteenth-Century English Novel.* New York: Macmillan Publishing Company, 1985.

Copeland, Edward. *Women Writing about Money: Women's Fiction in England, 1790–1820.* Cambridge, UK: Cambridge UP, 1995.

Fergus, Jan. "The Professional Woman Writer." *The Cambridge Companion to Jane Austen.* Eds. Edward Copeland and Juliet McMaster. Cambridge, UK: Cambridge University Press, 2006. 12–31.

Monaghan, David. "Austen's Women in a Conservative Society." *Readings on Jane Austen.* Ed. Clarice Swisher. San Diego: Greenhaven Press, Inc., 1997. 42–50.

Partikian, David. "Critical Essay on *Sense and Sensibility.*" *Novels for Students,* Vol. 18, Gale, 2003. Electronic. Literature Resource Center. Berkeley, CA: Berkeley Public Library, 30 June 2007.

Watt, Ian. "On *Sense and Sensibility.*" *Jane Austen: A Collection of Critical Essays.* Englewood Cliffs, NJ: Prentice-Hall, 1963. 41–51.

PRIDE AND PREJUDICE

*P*RIDE AND *Prejudice*, though its title resembles *Sense and Sensibility*, is not a contrast novel. Instead of the oppositions of two values (such as sense versus sensibility), Austen's second novel offers blended varieties of pride and prejudice. These two flaws are certainly marked with the two romantic protagonists (he is customarily considered to have the greater pride, she the greater prejudice), but they share these human shortcomings with each other and the other characters in the novel. The plot showcases the consequences of false impressions and misunderstandings: Pride impels prejudice; prejudice, then, impedes understanding. At the end of the novel, true knowledge overcomes with felicity the bugaboos of pride and prejudice.

In a letter to her sister, Cassandra, Jane Austen described heroine Elizabeth Bennet "as delightful a creature as ever appeared in print" (Austen 263). Austen is in accord with her readers, many of whom believe that *Pride and Prejudice* and Elizabeth Bennet are her most agreeable creations. Elizabeth is admired for her intelligence, moxie, and wit. Yet for such a perceptive heroine, it is remarkable how often her interpretations of events and people are incorrect. Her mistakes and misconceptions set in motion a great deal of conflict and dramatic energy. The novel is essentially one of discovery: As Elizabeth comes to understand the world, she also understands herself and is rewarded with a place of her own in the world.

When the novel opens, we see that Elizabeth understands her world well enough to mock it insightfully, but the wit that in Elizabeth is so charming is a flaw as well: She is teetering on the edge of cynicism. She views with an arch attitude the ridiculousness around her—her mother's cultivation of high drama and "nerves," her sister Mary's surly and pedantic sermonizing, her sister Lydia's indiscriminate giggling. Elizabeth's sense of humor is inherited from her father, who copes with his ill-suited marriage by taking a perverse pleasure in his wife's melodramatics. Mr. Bennet's character, while kind, is also defeatist: He frequently expounds on the "silliness" of his daughters, but makes no effort to correct or educate them. He speaks in witty aphorisms and quips, and there is so little that he takes seriously that he perceives the world as something of a joke: "For what do we live, but to make sport for our neighbors, and to laugh at them in our turn?" (3: 15). Elizabeth shares her father's appreciation for the absurd, but she soon becomes aware of the hazards of allowing amusement to be one's sole motivation in life. She learns the limitations of her father's sense of irony.

Before doing a general analysis of lessons, ideas, or characters, you must first contend with Austen's language. This section of the chapter demonstrates how to do a close reading of two early passages from *Pride and Prejudice,* in order to prepare for writing an essay.

One of the more important elements of this novel is the narration. To develop a good feel for the tone and meaning of this story, you must keep the narrator's sensibilities in mind. The narrator is, like Elizabeth, amused and amusing. But beneath the narrator's drollery lie serious facts. The first line of the novel, for instance, has both ironic humor and a sly truth: "It is a truth universally acknowledged, that a single man in possession of a good fortune, must be in want of a wife." The opening words of this line ape the style of a lesson, and it sounds as if we are about to learn some truth—"a truth universally acknowledged." The solemn tone of the opening clause is undercut, however, by the doubtfulness of the claim that follows it—that a wealthy man must be desirous of a wife. We wonder among whom this is a "universally acknowledged" truth. The odds are good that is it not "single men in possession of a good fortune." The more likely suspects for whom this is true are the matrons jockeying for advantageous matches for their daughters or, perhaps, those daughters themselves who have matrimony in mind. The mercenary nature of some marriages is a theme implied already. Questioning the theme of marriage results in interesting topics in social history—what is the nature and function of marriage for this society? What social pressures might explain this marriage frenzy?

The juxtaposition of the narrator's simultaneous solemnity ("it is a truth") and absurdity (that business of wealthy men wanting wives) is an example of the ironic tone that pervades *Pride and Prejudice*. Irony is loosely defined in literature as a technique whereby something contains two meanings, such as those found in innuendo, puns, Freudian slips, satire, and parody. Irony can be a slippery concept, but in this case the ironic tone is fairly straightforward: It is evident in the setting up of one expectation (it is a truth), only to deflate that expectation with a very questionable assertion (that a wealthy man must want to marry). This ironic tone runs through the novel, so you should keep your eyes open for multiple levels of meaning. The second sentence of the novel reveals the ironic tone of the first sentence building to a mock social commentary. Both sentences are quoted together here:

> It is a truth universally acknowledged, that a single man in possession of a good fortune, must be in want of a wife. However little known the feelings or views of such a man may be on his first entering a neighborhood, this truth is so well fixed in the minds of the surrounding families, that he is considered as the rightful property of some one or other of their daughters.

Social commentary is evident in the presentation of the neighbors' avid interest in the unsuspecting arrival, and a close reading of the sentences communicates the atmosphere and philosophy of this competitive society. These two sentences also yield tellingly economic and legal language. Notice the direct reference to "good fortune," but also notice that a man with such in his possession must be "in *want* of a wife" (italics added). That is to say, he must lack a wife. The economic metaphor connects to the language of legal contracts in the second sentence, in which the wealthy bachelor being discussed is considered "the *rightful property* of some one or the other" of the neighborhood daughters (italics added). Economic and legal language is the jargon of this mercantile society, which is highly conscious of economic distinctions, advantages, and motives. Money matters in *Pride and Prejudice*. After all, "It is a truth universally acknowledged, that a single man in possession of a good fortune, must be in want of a wife."

A close reading of these opening lines suggests the broadest sketch of the dramatic action to come. We anticipate that we will be reading about a small group of families and a new man in the neighborhood, a single man of "good fortune." We also get an inkling of dramatic conflicts among the families who expect that "one or other of their daughters" is to become the rightful wife of this man. In fact, such an outcome proves so "well fixed" in the mind of Mrs. Bennet that she soon proclaims to her husband that this unknown new man is a "fine thing for our girls!" Her enthusiasm flourishes though Charles Bingley—the man soon to enter the neighborhood—is unseen: Bingley's marital status and bank account are all that Mrs. Bennet's expectations require.

While the ironic tone in these first two sentences sets us up to mock the folly of zealous matrons, especially Mrs. Bennet, we eventually learn the verity of the "truth" proclaimed in the first sentence. While we, the narrator, and all right-thinking individuals know that the assertions in the first sentence are absurd, the events in the novel suggest that the men of good fortune who do materialize in the neighborhood—Darcy and Bingley—are, after all, "in want of a wife." Furthermore, while unmarried wealthy bachelors certainly do not literally belong to the community, both Darcy and Bingley are eventually married to two of the neighborhood's eligible daughters. So though the novel opens with a sense of absurdity, it closes by proving the absurdity true. Although the tone of the novel is ironic and irreverent, it is not dismissive; the narrator cannot hide the story's feelings about the very real consequences of family, love, and society.

Remarkably, in these first two lines of *Pride and Prejudice,* before a character even appears, a number of aspects of the novel are established: We are acquainted with its ironic tone; its bemused, knowing narrator; some plot hints; and a number of themes, including socioeconomic divisions, love, family, society, and social expectations. In conjunction with one another, these themes the novel's dramatic action.

Of course, you will not be aware of all these allusions in the novel's initial sentences without performing a close, careful reading of the entire work. You want to pose questions about the literature as you read any text in preparation for writing about it. In *Pride and Prejudice,* you might ask how marriage is depicted. What are its good and bad points according to the narrator? Does the novel present a suitable alternative to marriage for single women? More questions could center on the title's qualities of pride and prejudice. Which characters exemplify these qualities? What is the dynamic between pride and prejudice? How does one quality feed the other? You might also explore what kinds of lessons the characters—Elizabeth and others—learn. What encourages and what impedes understanding? These questions that the novel raises can become the core of an essay.

A slow and careful reading of *Pride and Prejudice* will better allow you to recognize the novel's patterns, issues, and ideas. Reading slowly and taking notes will make for a rich understanding of the story, while also enabling you to gather the evidence you need to write a strong essay.

TOPICS AND STRATEGIES

This section discusses various possible topics for essays on *Pride and Prejudice* and general approaches to those topics. The material below is only a place to start from, not an exhaustive master key. You should use this material to generate your own analysis. Every topic discussed here could encompass a variety of good papers.

Themes

Pride and Prejudice deals with many themes—ideas or concepts that organize and underscore the importance of the events in the novel. The section above examined some of these: marriage, social expectations, socioeconomic divisions, and others. The novel also considers ideas and practices associated with love, pride, prejudice, family, social class, and morality. Writers analyzing the novel often begin by identifying a central theme they see as important and then determine—through an essay—what the story is saying about that theme. You can identify themes by noticing the ideas, symbols, or words that are repeated in the story. In the initial chapters, for instance, there are many allusions to marriage. These allusions are not only in the first lines of the novel, they are also part of the dramatic action. With a wealthy bachelor, Mr. Bingley, newly introduced to the community comes the dream of his marrying a local young woman, a dream shared by those neighborhood matrons with eligible daughters. The mentions of Bingley and marriage are so frequently repeated that you cannot help but notice that the theme of marriage would present you with considerable material for a strong essay. This is a large theme, and you would want to focus your approach to it. You could analyze why marriage seems to be so important to this society. For information on this, you could examine the dialogues between Elizabeth and her sister Jane. You could also analyze what the novel implies are necessary traits of a good or bad marriage. Details of the Bennets' marriage would give you ample material for an essay on the consequences of an ill-suited match. Another approach to an essay on marriage would be to observe how romantic and practical understandings of marriage contrast in the novel. Each of these opposed philosophies—practical and romantic—is respectively argued for by Charlotte Lucas and Elizabeth. Does the novel wholly endorse Elizabeth's point of view, or is Charlotte's approach presented as a good solution to her difficult situation? Other themes are also worthy of analysis. Romantic notions of love, one could argue, run counter to the society in which *Pride and Prejudice* is set. How, in a society that is so mercantile and mercenary, can love and romance persevere? A cautionary word on the eponymous themes of pride and prejudice seems useful here: The concepts considered together are vast enough to undermine the focus of a good essay. Though their finer complexities do play out in tandem in the novel, in an essay of shorter length the concepts are more adeptly handled with an emphasis on one or the other concept, and so the sample topics present them here.

Sample Topics:

1. **Pride:** How does pride operate in this novel? Does it clarify or impede understanding? Is pride ever acceptable?

   This topic asks you to analyze the theme of pride as it works in the novel. The character most associated with pride is Darcy, who considers pride perfectly acceptable when there is also "understanding." One approach to an essay on this theme would be to focus on how Darcy's sense of pride changes as he develops a clearer understanding of himself. Good examples for changes in Darcy's sense of entitled pride can be found in the sections following his engagement to Elizabeth. A humorous study of pride can be found by analyzing how it operates in Mr. Collins, whom the narrator describes as a mixture of "pride and obsequiousness." There are many incidents in which Mr. Collins's pride interferes with his understanding of basic truths, such as his wife's true personality. Unaware that his wife encourages his gardening to keep him out of the house, he boasts to Elizabeth about his marriage: "My dear Charlotte and I have but one mind and one way of thinking. There is in every thing a most remarkable resemblance of character between us." Whatever approach you take to this topic, you will want to decide whether the novel presents pride as acceptable when deserved or more simply a symptom of obtuseness.

2. **Prejudice or false impressions:** How does prejudice appear in this novel? What does prejudice reveal about characters and their expectations?

When Austen first wrote *Pride and Prejudice*, she titled it *First Impressions.* That notion plays a significant role in the story's events. While false first impressions are eventually replaced with true knowledge, it is instructive to analyze the particulars of prejudice. One approach to this topic would be to focus on Elizabeth Bennet. She has good reason to think ill of Darcy after he insults her at the Assembly Room ball, but she proves herself eager to foster later misunderstandings of him. Her desire to maintain her first impression is the corollary for her mistakenly positive impression of Wickham. For evidence of this, you could analyze Elizabeth's later upbraiding of herself for misunderstanding Wickham. Ultimately, you should reach a conclusion about how first impressions or prejudice are important in this novel.

3. **Marriage:** This is a society motivated by marriage, though only a few good marriages exist in it. What do the good marriages

seem to be saying about the marriage partners? What does this novel seem to be saying about the path that leads to a happy marriage?

This topic makes an assertion about marriages in the novel. After you identify the good marriages, analyze in what ways husbands and wives contribute to their own happiness. You could, if you were talking about the Gardiners, discuss their affinity for and sensitivity to each other (sensitivity being what they *choose* to do). You would then need to discuss the second part of the topic, which asks you to consider the necessary steps for a happy marriage. What do the heroines of the novel need to endure and learn before they can be happily wed? To gain understanding of this point, consider how incomplete the knowledge of the heroines would be had they been married at the outset of the novel. If Elizabeth, for instance, accepted Darcy after his first proposal, she would have married without love. You could also approach this topic by considering how the novel presents bad marriages. What, exactly, are the ill consequences of the Bennets' marriage? Of the marriage of Wickham and Lydia? Yet another approach to this topic would be to build a topic around Charlotte Lucas's feelings on marriage. Early in the novel, Charlotte shows that she is very strategic about courtship and marriage, and she indeed makes a marriage of convenience. Does the novel disapprove of this? For evidence you would need to look for Charlotte's, Elizabeth's, and even Jane's views of marriage. Though in an unsatisfactory marriage himself, Mr. Bennet gives Elizabeth good counsel on what constitutes a happy marriage; his advice would provide excellent material for your essay.

4. **Family:** In what ways does Elizabeth's understanding of her family change during the novel? What does she come to understand about herself relative to her family?

This topic asks you to consider the significance of family for Elizabeth. To answer it, assess how she feels about and acts toward her family at the beginning, middle, and end of the novel. The middle of the novel, when she reads Darcy's clarifying letter, marks a watershed: It is here that she comes to realize the mortifying consequences of a family that does not consistently observe the rules of decorum. In this example, family represents jeopardy to Elizabeth. You would certainly want to observe how she tries to steer her father's checking of Lydia's actions. Family that represents strength is found in the Gardiners: They function as sanctuary for Jane; with Elizabeth, they enable her acquaintance with the countryside on the trip they share to Derbyshire. The Gardiners are also emissaries—and representatives of acceptable family—who facilitate her courtship with Darcy. When Elizabeth sees Pemberley for the first time and is musing on what it would have been to be mistress of it, she remembers that, in so being, her family would have been lost to her. This suggests her strong family connection, yet she seems happy to leave behind some of the Bennets upon her marriage. You will want to reach a conclusion about the ultimate significance of family to Elizabeth. What is the place of her family in her life?

Character

Because so much of the book's dramatic action is animated by the conduct of its characters, essays that examine character will be a productive means by which to analyze *Pride and Prejudice.* In the world that Jane Austen captured in her novels, character and manners were of paramount importance, especially for young women. And manners were a family affair: Families were considered connected to individuals by nearly permanent ties. If the honor of one family member was compromised, the whole family would feel the effects of it and the effects could be severe. In the case of *Pride and Prejudice,* the scandalous elopement of the youngest Bennet sister, Lydia, compromises the entire family's honor and social rank. Though Lydia is too self-absorbed to understand the consequences of her actions, Elizabeth, Darcy, Jane, Mr. Collins, and Mr. Bennet know at once that Lydia's indiscretion is likely to result in spinsterhood for her sisters. As for the future, Lydia's action could also mean the material destitution of her entire family; in the event of Mr. Bennet's death, Mr. Collins inherits the estate, and the survivors receive the smallest of annuities. Because character is so consequential in Austen's novels, there is a great deal to say about the topic in essays.

There are various approaches to essays on character. You could concentrate on character development (how Elizabeth and Jane are distinguished from each other by their respectively skeptical and accepting points of view); characterization (the reader learns about Mr. Collins from his sycophancy and ambition); or interpretations of changes in a character as the novel proceeds (the profound shift from self-assurance to humility in both Elizabeth and Darcy).

To write an essay on character, you would need to question how readers come to know various characters. How, for instance, does the narrator distinguish a character's behavior? Lydia's vapidity is clarified by her obsession with soldiers, jokes, and fun. Caroline Bingley's jealous insecurity is demonstrated by her cutting remarks about Elizabeth in Darcy's presence. To an extent, the narrator of *Pride and Prejudice* instructs us what to expect from characters. If you pay attention to the narrator's editorial comments about individuals, you will understand what the characters signify. In the first chapter, the narrator tells us that we are not to expect much in the way of genius from Mrs. Bennet: "She was a woman of mean understanding, little information, and uncertain temper. When she was discontented she fancied herself nervous. The business of her life was to get her daughters married; its solace was visiting and news." Note how in three quick sentences, the narrator dispenses with the salient points of Mrs. Bennet's character—her intelligence, her temperament, her motivations—and these qualities explain her later capricious actions and behavior. While with Mrs. Bennet's character the narrator is very straightforward, she is more circumspect about other characters. Mr. Wickham, for instance, is initially described only by his external qualities: "His appearance was greatly in his favour; he had all the best part of beauty, a fine countenance, a good figure, and very pleasing address" (1: 15). The reader is in a position similar to Elizabeth's: We may, like Elizabeth, find him appealing, but his actions will later prove him otherwise. To analyze questions of character development, look closely for distinguishing traits of language, action, or interactions with other characters. The behavior of characters with one another helps readers not only understand how characters are created, but also assess what characters signify and represent for the story overall.

Sample Topics:

1. **Elizabeth's character development:** After reading Darcy's letter to her, the letter that reveals Wickham's true nature, Elizabeth thinks: "Till this moment, I never knew myself." What does she learn about herself in this moment? How does her epiphany change her?

   To write an essay on this topic, first decide what the quote means; that is to say, in what specific ways does Elizabeth come to know herself? Does she come to understand her personality? Her motivations? Her flaws? The second part of the topic asks you to consider how her newfound knowledge changes her. How does her self-awareness reveal itself? Evidence for this can be drawn from Elizabeth's behavior and conversations with the most significant individuals in her life—her father, Jane, and Darcy. One example of a change is revealed in her conversation with her father about Lydia's trip to Brighton; though Elizabeth and her father customarily share laughs over her "silly" sisters, Elizabeth here tries and fails to make her father act with more seriousness than she probably would have before reading Darcy's letter.

2. **Mr. Collins as a character:** Most readers agree that Mr. Collins, with his bumbling ambitions, is the most ridiculous character in the novel. Though his cluelessness is operatic in its scale, he does serve a serious purpose in the story relative to his cousin Elizabeth. Analyze Mr. Collins's character as he illuminates Elizabeth's character. What could he represent to her and her family? What does he come to represent to her?

   This topic asks you to look less at Mr. Collins's character and more at what his character represents for the heroine of the story. You might consider how he contrasts with Elizabeth in dignity, values, personality, behavior, and romantic sensibilities. While he is deferential, particularly to his patroness, Lady Catherine de Bourgh, Elizabeth refuses to bow down to her social "superiors" (and Lady Catherine specifically). It is against the many contrasts between them that we come to understand Elizabeth better, though Mr. Collins himself seems remarkably unaware of their differences and is surprised that she has no interest in becoming Mrs. Collins. As the closest male relative, Mr. Collins stands to inherit the Bennet house and land. An approach to an essay could be to analyze what a marriage between Elizabeth and Mr. Collins would mean for her family on a practical level. How would it change their futures? What does it signify that even with the advantages such a union would mean for her family, Elizabeth turns Mr. Collins down flat? Furthermore, what does it mean that her father fully supports his daughter's choice? Another approach to this topic would be to consider why it is so distressing to Elizabeth when her friend Charlotte Lucas chooses to marry Mr. Collins. What does marriage to Mr. Collins mean in Elizabeth's mind? For a similar approach but using different characters, you could look at how another antagonist reveals Elizabeth's character: Caroline Bingley, Mr. Wickham, and Lady Catherine de Bourgh—antagonists all—would also be good choices for this approach.

3. **Character development in general:** How does the novel present character to the reader? What techniques does it use? Are characters transparent or somewhat concealed?

A paper on this topic would examine how Austen gives insight into character. A possible approach would be to look carefully at a pair of characters or a set of techniques and attempt to show its effects. For instance, a paper could examine how social conventions, such as dancing, reveal character. Darcy, for example, will not condescend to dance with people he does not know; Lydia will dance regardless of whether it is appropriate. Another paper could analyze how environment affects character. The narrator measures out a bit of praise for Kitty

Bennet when she is left to the company of her elder sisters. Away from Lydia, Kitty is "less irritable, less ignorant, and less insipid." Mr. Bennet's character also improves when in the good company of Bingley or Elizabeth and Darcy. A slightly different approach to this topic could look at how physical environment matters to characters: To that end, it would be worthwhile to study the characters' discussions of country life and city life.

4. **The Gardiners:** The reasonable, intelligent, easygoing Gardiners lend a sense of realism to a book filled with extreme characters. Apart from atmosphere, analyze what else the Gardiners contribute to the story and to Elizabeth's life.

This topic asks you to look at the characterization of Elizabeth's aunt and uncle Gardiner and to consider their role in her life. Your first task would include establishing how they are characterized, perhaps in contrast to Mr. Gardiner's sister, Mrs. Bennet. You might consider discussing how Elizabeth and Jane both benefit from their attentions, guidance, and generosity. The trip that Elizabeth takes with the Gardiners is especially enlightening and would provide solid evidence for your essay. Beyond bringing Elizabeth to Pemberley, how do they facilitate the courtship between Elizabeth and Darcy? In what ways is their family connection to Elizabeth a boon? It would also be worthwhile to analyze how their marriage provides the Bennet sisters with a good relationship to emulate. To that end, you would want to examine how they behave with their children, their relatives, and one another.

History and Context

Another suitable approach to the analysis of *Pride and Prejudice* is through history and context. Even a small amount of research into the historical context out of which Austen wrote this novel will greatly increase your understanding and opportunities for literary analysis. Austen's novels are informed by the events of their time—the French Revolution, the Napoleonic Wars, and the tremendous shifts in social philosophy (such as neoclassicism and romanticism) that inspired and, in some cases, culminated in these movements and military events. Studying any of these timely contexts in conjunction with *Pride and Prejudice* will help you suss out interesting connections and points of comparison. You may ask how the Napoleonic Wars, for instance, contribute to the atmosphere of the novel. The militias that are mentioned—those at Meryton and Brighton—are in place to protect England from the expected invasion from France. How might an impending attack charge the atmosphere in the novel? How does the headiness of a wartime era allow a character such as Wickham to circulate in society in spite of his profligate behavior? The battle mode of the time enabled a new degree of social mobility; we see that commanders and country gentlemen attended the same balls, hunted together, and otherwise interacted socially. Social mobility—the ability of someone such as a military officer from, generally, the middle class to ascend ranks to the upper middle class or even the aristocracy—certainly occurred during this era. *Pride and Prejudice* represents the tension that such social mobility inspired. To write an essay on social class in this novel, you could identify characters whose incomes are from trade or the law (at this time viewed as something of a trade). Bingley himself is a recent addition to the upper classes, as is evidenced by his shopping for an estate. To locate anxiety about social class, you could track the feelings of social insecurity demonstrated by Bingley's sisters. A truculent guardian of social class is Lady Catherine de Bourgh. There is a great deal to say about her feelings regarding social class and those, such as Elizabeth Bennet, who would dare to "quit [their] sphere" (3: 14). Another good topic for an essay on history would be the expectations of gender at this time. The terror that grips Elizabeth and the entire Bennet family upon hearing of Lydia's elopement tells us that Lydia's impulsive act is socially disastrous. With this last topic or any other historical topic, you would need to do some research to consider knowledgeably what *Pride and Prejudice* is asserting about the world it describes.

Sample Topics:

1. **Military context:** How does the military context affect the characters or plot of *Pride and Prejudice*? Does the novel have an opinion about the military or what it does?

This topic asks you to consider the broader context of pending war and stationed military units; your essay would require research into the military situation of the time, focusing specifically on the understandable fear of an invasion by Napoléon and on preparing for war. One tactic was to assign militias temporarily from one region of England to guard other regions (hence, the militia at Meryton is not from there, nor is it permanently stationed there). The "regulars" mentioned in the novel were part of the regular military. You might analyze how a time of near-war permitted a degree of uncustomary laxity in society. You might then examine how this atmosphere enables Wickham's disreputable behavior. To answer the final question about the novel's opinion of the military, you might look again to Wickham to assess whether he appears to be representative of the military. What are his interests? Does he take seriously his duty as a soldier? Are there more respectable examples of soldiers in the novel?

2. **Social mobility:** Where do we see anxieties about the rise of the middle class in *Pride and Prejudice*? What does the novel say about upper-class fears about class fluidity?

   There are a number of characters through which you could approach this topic. One way would be to look at how the aristocratic Darcy and Lady Catherine de Bourgh treat the new arrivals to the upper classes, such as Bingley or his sisters, Sir William Lucas, or potential members of the upper class, such as Elizabeth and Jane Bennet. Lady Catherine is outspoken in her feelings that class distinctions need to be maintained. A low point for Darcy in the novel is when, sounding very much like his aunt, he observes that his proposing to Elizabeth is a "degradation." Another angle would be to examine those of the newly minted upper class for symptoms of class insecurity. Bingley is trying to cement his social place by shopping around for an estate that would announce his family's move into the upper class. How do the Bingley sisters show a fear of being mistaken for middle class that might be customary for a newly moneyed individual? Furthermore, how may we read the Bingley sisters' opinions on walking, women, professions, education, and Elizabeth Bennet as reflecting their anxieties about their own class position? The final question asks you to make an overall assessment of the novel's presentation of social position. You might argue that the novel defends class distinctions, or you might instead argue that it lampoons class distinctions. Do you think that the novel collapses class and virtue, or does it instead present class and virtue as separate entities? Whatever approach you take, you will need to do research into social class in England during the Regency era.

3. **Elopement and sexuality:** Why is Lydia's elopement such a scandal? Analyze the social context of the era to put this scandal in perspective and explain its significance for the Bennet family.

This topic asks you to explain the context for an event in the novel. Elizabeth and the narrator provide some explanation, but you would also need to do research into social history of the Regency era in England, paying particular attention to expectations of women. Your essay should address why Lydia's actions are socially disastrous for her sisters. This will help you explain the significance of the elopement for the Bennet family. Mr. Collins writes a vicious letter about Lydia to Mr. Bennet that might very well be the voice of the status quo: In it, Mr. Collins expresses his belief that Lydia is innately bad and that, for the sake of her sisters' prospects, it would be best to disown the offending daughter. That Mr. Collins is driven by more worldly than spiritual beliefs is also made manifest in his comments: "The death of your daughter would have been a blessing in comparison to this." If you read closely other conversations and letters that are exchanged around this topic, you will see that there is a great deal of fear about Lydia's sexual conduct, and these conversations tell us that this society vigilantly, even obsessively, protected its honor and bloodlines. The narrator alludes to this when she discusses the melodrama that the Longbourn neighbors hoped for with Lydia. You might choose to discuss the novel's opinion of Lydia's conduct. What are we to make of the book's last words on Lydia's life with Wickham? Is she punished for her scandalous conduct?

Form and Genre

Form and genre provide useful ways of thinking about literature. Form is the shape and structure of a literary work; genre is the kind, or classification, of a literary work. Though technically independent of the content of literature (meaning that freedom or natural beauty, for instance, are ideas that can be communicated in various forms), form and genre are used deliberately by authors to further the ideas in and strengthen the dramatic impact of their stories. *Pride and Prejudice* is fiction and, more specifically, it is a novel. This may seem too straightforward an observation, but it is a fruitful start for an essay on form. Essays could look at how Austen's novel is shaped. Scholars consider her a master of realism and *Pride and Prejudice* an especially accomplished example of the realism genre, yet in its broadest outlines, this novel resembles a fairy tale. Both *Pride and Prejudice* and "Cinderella," for example, feature a worthy heroine, an antagonistic mother figure, an ineffectual father figure, difficult sisters, and a future husband with a castle as the rewards of tribulations bravely borne. An essay could explore how Austen manages to make a Cinderella story seem realistic. Do some characters counterbalance the caricatures? What events seem in keeping with the life of a young woman of the period (social calls and dancing) instead of that of a fairy tale heroine (incantations and helpful birds)? Another topic on form could explore more general questions, such as how Austen achieves comic effects in her writing.

Sample Topics:

1. **Realism of *Pride and Prejudice***: In terms of some of its extreme character types and its overall plot, *Pride and Prejudice* could have tipped into the realm of fairy tales; yet the novel is considered an accomplished example of realism. How does it achieve its verisimilitude?

Verisimilitude is defined as the appearance of truth or authenticity in art. This topic guides you to consider how Austen crafts verisimilitude in her story. One way into an essay on this topic would be to analyze what makes Elizabeth's Cinderella story believable. To do this, you would first need to examine in what specific ways *Pride and Prejudice* resembles a fairy tale, then analyze how its preternatural elements are replaced with realistic ones. Scholars of fairy tales track the trials that fairy tale heroes undergo before they are rewarded; generally, these tests are of devotion, courage, intelligence, and the like. In what ways is Elizabeth tested? In what ways is she rewarded? What kind of poetic justice is awarded to the characters overall? Another approach would be to consider how realism is used in characterization. You might analyze the cast of characters and find realistic counterparts to the more extreme characters. You might, for instance, consider how Elizabeth Bennet, Charlotte Lucas, the Gardiners, or Georgiana Darcy serve as counterparts to the extremes of Mrs. Bennet, Mr. Collins, Caroline Bingley, or Lady Catherine de Bourgh. Another approach would be to examine the narration for signs of realism. How, for instance, does the narrator's wry, sometimes sarcastic voice keep the dramatic events and the characters grounded in a recognizable reality?

2. **Comic effects in *Pride and Prejudice***: Why is *Pride and Prejudice* so amusing? Analyze some of the techniques Austen used to achieve the novel's sense of humor.

This broad question asks you to survey and analyze the means by which Austen achieves the comedy in *Pride and Prejudice*. You could choose a single technique—such as satire, parody, understatement, hyperbole, caricature, burlesque, or irony—and track its use in the novel. Depending on the length of your essay, you could select two or more techniques and discuss them together. You will, of course, need to do some background reading on the techniques you select and identify places in the novel where you see the techniques in action. It might also be worthwhile to consider the humor in the novel. Are there, for instance, places where the humor is suspended? Are there sections where the irony gives way to earnestness? The conclusions you reach about humor in this novel will reveal what it values. What does it not laugh at?

3. **Use of letters:** How is the use of letters significant to the novel?

This topic involves considering how letters affect the novel or provide some of its effects. Consider, for instance, the letters written by Mr. Collins, Lydia, or Darcy. Your central analysis should argue what purpose these letters perform. Why did Austen use these letters? Do they aid in plot and characterization? Letters certainly allow characters to communicate what they would not be able to do in polite company. How might the letters allow Austen to include information in her story that propriety prevents her narrator from revealing outright, such as Wickham's scandalous conduct? Your conclusion should make a general assessment explaining how letters are significant in *Pride and Prejudice.*

Language, Symbols, and Imagery

Language, symbols, and imagery are some of the creative means by which authors convey feelings or ideas that would, if simply announced, be undermined in terms of their imaginative and evocative power. All writers, and those of imaginative fiction especially, use language deliberately. They choose words based on their connotative meanings. In Jane Austen's work, language is especially meaningful. She uses the words and even the patterns of language—such as sentence structure—to convey information about characters and situations. Character development, as was discussed in the section on character, is partly constructed by what a character says. Communication style—either by conversation or by letter—conveys character. Elizabeth and her father are both astute readers, and their awareness of Mr. Collins's intellectual limitations is triggered when they read over not only the content, but also the unnecessarily deferential, overly complicated, and obtuse language in his introductory letter:

> If you should have no objection to receive me into your house, I propose myself the satisfaction of waiting on you and your family, Monday, November 18th, by four o'clock, and shall probably trespass on your hospitality til the Saturday . . . following, which I can do without any inconvenience, as Lady Catherine is far from objecting to my occasional absence on a Sunday, provided that some other clergyman is engaged to do the duty of the day. (1: 13)

Elizabeth interprets his style of address correctly: "He must be an oddity, I think . . . There is something very pompous in his stile" [*sic*]. Mr. Bennet also observes in Mr. Collins's style of writing "a mixture of servility and self-importance." An essay could insightfully explore the intersections of language and character in *Pride and Prejudice*. How does language reveal character? What style of language does the narrator endorse or criticize? Another approach to an essay on language in this novel could focus on conversational style as a symbol of affinity. There are characters that understand one another intuitively. An essay could explore how the novel crafts communication style to reflect affinity.

Symbols, usually used in conjunction with imagery, are objects, either animate or inanimate, that writers also use to convey ideas. Austen does not use a great deal of overt imagery in her writing; similes, metaphors, and outright symbols are rare. There are, however, objects in the story that the characters understand symbolically. Consider, for instance, houses in *Pride and Prejudice*. Elizabeth's acquaintance with Darcy's estate, Pemberley, initiates her full understanding of the true Darcy. An interesting essay could explore how Pemberley is analogous to Darcy's character. Even just focusing on the views out of Pemberley's windows could provide more than enough information for a worthwhile essay on what this estate communicates to Elizabeth about Darcy. The best essays on symbolism look at imagery and analyze it in relation to a novel's larger ideas. When you are asked to discuss symbolism, you are being asked to discuss what something signifies in light of the entire work.

Sample Topics:

1. **Communication style:** Each character's speaking and writing style in *Pride and Prejudice* is distinctive. Choose two or more characters and assess what their language and communication styles reveal about them. What style of communication does the narrator appear to endorse?

This topic asks you to analyze styles of expression. The narrator herself could be considered a character for this topic; she surely speaks in a distinctive style that is deft, incisive, wry, and clever and uses irony, inference, understatement, and other forms of quiet conviction. The narrator also proves an amusingly biting and acute reader of events and individuals, as when she observes of the general reception of the news of Lydia's marriage to Wickham that it would been "more for the advantage of conversation" had Lydia become a prostitute or had a child out of wedlock (3: 8). Another character well worth analysis is Mr. Collins, an inveterate name-dropper who speaks in epithet and whose syntactical subordinations are feats of obfuscation. Elizabeth, Darcy, Mrs. Bennet, Mr. Bennet, and Lady Catherine de Bourgh all have speaking and communication styles that reflect their personas; reading closely any of their styles reveals a great deal about their characters. Another approach to this topic would be to study the imagery in the language of different characters. Lydia's motivations are revealed through her reliance on words having to do with pleasure. Mr. Collins is obsessed with appearance and social hierarchy, as is revealed through his repetition of words related to flattery, condescension, and deference. Lady Catherine de Bourgh's fearsome opinions on class distinctions are shown in her uses of the language of pollution and corruption. Studying the language of other characters is equally worthwhile. What language style and character do you think the novel endorses? Base your conclusion on your insights into the narrator.

2. **Affinity in conversation:** How does conversational style reveal affinity between and among characters?

Though Elizabeth remains unaware of it for much of the book, the conversations, repartee, and debates that she and Darcy engage in show how well they are suited to each other. Their communication style is a kind of courtship ritual from which other characters are excluded, as we see, for instance, when Miss Bingley, "tired of a conversation in which she had no share," suggests music as an alternative to Elizabeth's and Darcy's debate. What Elizabeth does not at first understand is how her discussions with Darcy are about values they both share. Other characters with shared values have an instinctive and immediate understanding of one another. An essay could explore the affinity of values demonstrated by Mrs. Bennet and Mr. Collins, Elizabeth and Colonel Fitzwilliam, or Jane and Bingley.

3. **Houses:** In what ways do the featured estates—Pemberley, Rosings, Netherfield—symbolize their occupants?

The three estates mentioned in this topic in many ways stand in for their occupants. Rosings is as fussy and oppressive as Lady Catherine de Bourgh; Netherfield is as newly occupied as Bingley's family is among the ranks of the upper classes. About Pemberley there is the most to say because it is the estate that Elizabeth views with the keenest interest; when she first sees it she is conscious that "of this place" she "might have been mistress." What she observes of the Pemberley grounds is that "She had never seen a place for which nature had done more, or where natural beauty had been so little counteracted by an awkward taste." An essay could fruitfully explore how Pemberley works as a means by which Elizabeth finally understands Darcy's qualities as a gentleman of stability, responsibility (to land and family), intelligence, and aesthetic appreciation. Another approach to this topic would be to focus on one element of the house, such as the gardens, the rooms, or the views. How might one of these aspects of the house signify the overall qualities of Darcy to which Elizabeth is attracted?

Comparison and Contrast

Comparing components of a story to explain and analyze the similarities or differences among them is a useful approach to writing an essay. Remember to avoid simply creating a list of similarities or differences in a work; instead, take the necessary step of commenting on your observations. To begin a comparison/contrast essay, you might compare characters with each other: How does Mrs. Bennet compare with Caroline Bingley? With Mr. Bennet? How does Elizabeth Bennet compare with Charlotte Lucas? You could also compare characters (or other elements of the story such as themes or events) across different Austen novels. For example, how do the villainous suitors compare with one another in *Sense and Sensibility* and *Pride and Prejudice*? How is conceit depicted differently in *Pride and Prejudice* and *Persuasion*? The challenge of this kind of essay is to decide what the similarities or differences you identify might mean. These are the questions that make essays compelling and the ones that will have different answers for each writer. To answer these questions, you might find it helpful to think about what kinds of effects Austen achieves by producing either similarities or differences among the elements of her stories. How, for example, do Elizabeth Bennet's and Marianne Dashwood's respective temperaments broaden our understanding of Austen's versions of love?

Sample Topics:

1. **Comparing Wickham and Willoughby:** Both *Pride and Prejudice* and *Sense and Sensibility* feature roguish suitors who are proven threats to young women. Consider their respective characters and assess which is the more unsavory. What subjects do characters such as these enable Austen to explore in her novels?

This topic asks you to observe two young men whose good looks and "pleasing address" prove specious. In fact, in their respective novels, each cad poses a serious threat to the well-being of the main family. Compare the threats that they represent and argue for which man—Willoughby or Wickham—is the more despicable. Does it make a difference that Willougby is shown to have sincerely loved Marianne, while Wickham's feelings for Lydia seem more casually carnal? In your essay, it would be worthwhile to analyze what these characters allow Austen to explore in her novels. What does it mean, for instance, that these intelligent, physically appealing, and charming young men are such adept dancers and conversationalists, but so irresponsible with money and honor? What do the heroines learn from their experiences with such men?

2. **Comparing proposals:** In this novel there are a number of marriage proposals, some of which we see firsthand and some of which are reported to us. What does this novel suggest are the qualities of an ideal proposal?

This topic asks you to read closely the proposals that take place throughout the novel. You should consider Mr. Collins's two proposals, Bingley's proposal to Jane, and Darcy's two proposals to Elizabeth. Does the novel imply a causal link between the kind of proposal and the kind of marriage that those individuals are likely to enjoy? According to your findings, what proposal is presented as the ideal one? In your analysis, consider notions of true love, respect, practical arrangement, affinity, values, and modes of expression as practiced by the participants.

3. **Comparing Elizabeth's and Jane's styles of expression:** Elizabeth and Jane contrast each other in their philosophies and conduct. How are their styles of expression analogous to their characterization? Do their styles of expression adjust as their characters change?

To address this topic you would need to identify passages that illustrate Elizabeth's and Jane's different speaking styles. Elizabeth's sometimes cynical, often wry temperament is reflected in her expression of witty judgments and strong language, while Jane's optimistic sentiments are reflected in her somewhat innocent assessments of the world. Your essay should locate sections where the sisters' reactions to events are contrasted. You might look, for instance, to the section following Darcy's revelations about the duplicitous Wickham. Other illuminating sections relate to the sisters' feelings of love and conduct. Your analysis should show whether their styles of expression adjust as their characters change.

4. **Comparing lessons learned by Elizabeth and Darcy:** Compare the lessons Elizabeth and Darcy learn about themselves. Are their flaws eventually corrected?

To answer this topic it would be best to work from the conclusion of the story and then look back at sections related to Elizabeth and Darcy's expressions of self-awareness. Identifying what mortifies Elizabeth and Darcy about their earlier pronouncements and actions will help you understand the lessons that each felt it necessary to learn. This might be a place where the eponymous themes—pride and prejudice—are discussed. Is Darcy's lesson related to his pride? Is Elizabeth's lesson related to her prejudice? Finally, you will want to assess whether their flaws—as they see them—are corrected by the end of the novel. How do their learned lessons enable their union and felicity?

Bibliography and Online Resources for *Pride and Prejudice*:

Austen, Jane. *Pride and Prejudice.* New York, W.W. Norton and Company, 2001.

Folsom, Marcia McClintock, ed. *Approaches to Teaching Austen's* Pride and Prejudice. New York: Modern Language Association of America, 1993.

Gill, Richard, and Susan Gregory. *"Pride and Prejudice." Mastering the Novels of Jane Austen.* New York: Palgrave-Macmillan, 2003. 123–73.

Gray, Donald. Preface. *Pride and Prejudice.* By Jane Austen. 3rd ed. New York: Norton, 2001. vii–viii.

Kelly, Gary. "Jane Austen Biography." Retrieved 24 July 2007. <http://people.brandeis.edu/~teuber/austenbio.html>.

Pinion, F. B. *"Pride and Prejudice." A Jane Austen Companion: A Critical Survey and Reference Book.* London: Macmillan, 1973. 92–100.

Teachman, Debra, ed. Pride and Prejudice: *A Student Casebook to Issues, Sources, and Historical Documents.* Westport, CT.: Greenwood Press, 1997.

Van Ghent, Dorothy. "On *Pride and Prejudice*." *The English Novel: Form and Function.* New York: Harper and Row, 1953. 99–111.

MANSFIELD PARK

*M*ANSFIELD PARK (1814) is probably Jane Austen's most challenging work for a contemporary reader, in part because the novel only parses out the pleasures we expect from an Austen novel. It is overtly moral and only infrequently witty. Its villainous characters are more vivacious—and in many ways more likable—than its heroes. Even the protagonist confounds convention with her passive nature: Events happen less because of Fanny Price and more to her. This lack of agency is in direct opposition to the heroine of Austen's previous book, *Pride and Prejudice*, in which Elizabeth Bennet's intelligence, humor, vitality, and initiative help her overcome the challenges she encounters. Though displaying none of Elizabeth's energy, Fanny Price tenaciously weathers far more challenges and injustices than Elizabeth ever did. Fanny is practically orphaned when, at age nine, she is removed from her home and adopted by wealthy relatives who, though they "never meant to be unkind . . . [neither did they] put themselves out of their way to secure her comfort" (1: 2). Fanny suffers the petty cruelties of her Aunt Norris, is often treated as a servant, and is frequently overlooked (sometimes literally) by the members of her adopted family.

Fanny accepts all of these difficulties stoically and feels neither outrage nor indignation at her lot. Her nature is not conventionally heroic: She is insecure, quiet, complacent, physically weak, and cripplingly shy. It is worth questioning why Austen would write a novel around such a character. You may find that Fanny's inaction creates space for other characters and ideas to play out. You may also find that Fanny's quiet introspection models the thoughtful morality that the novel advocates. Your questions and conclusions about the novel's challenges may well generate ideas for an essay on *Mansfield Park*. No matter what analytical approach you take to the novel, you must contend with Austen's language. This section demonstrates how to do a close reading of a part of *Mansfield Park* to prepare for writing a strong essay.

When doing analysis of any Austen novel, it is helpful to remember that language is character and character is everything. Therefore, you should pay attention to the nuances of dialogue and narration. One of the most interesting aspects of Fanny's dialogue is her lack of nuance: She is utterly straightforward. This style proves to be a sign of her moral strength, a strength that is highlighted when she refuses to participate in the play that the young people promote at Mansfield Park. A number of elements of the play scheme are morally dubious. One problem with the plan is that the family would be acting frivolously while the patriarch, Sir Thomas, is making the dangerous trip home from the West Indies. A second issue is that the play itself is of questionable propriety (it involves children born out of wedlock and seduction). Finally, there is the problem of decorum disregarded by individuals who would be voicing and acting the roles of indecent characters. Fanny is not wholly aware of all these problems, but when she is asked to participate, she declares "I cannot act" (1:15). While the reader may very well (and very insightfully) interpret the multiple significances of this statement—that Fanny is too earnest, for example, to pretend to be anything but what she is—Fanny herself is making a simple and literal declaration. There is no artifice, nuance, or ulterior motive in Fanny's character or dialogue.

In contrast to Fanny Price's simple style of rhetoric is that of the Crawford siblings, who both use an agile, ironic, and witty speaking style that is featured prominently during preparations for the play. Mary and Henry Crawford are sophisticated urbanites whose whirlwind arrival at Mansfield Park initiates the Bertrams' discord, jealousy, upheaval, and eventual estrangement. Mary and Henry's presence generates dramatic action and undermines the tranquility of Mansfield Park; to understand their place in the book it is important to delineate the traits associated with them. One of their most distinguishing characteristics is their speaking style: Both Crawfords excel in rhetorical gymnastics—sometimes for its own pleasures and sometimes to manipulate or obfuscate—and their speeches are characterized by suggestion, pun, innuendo, and double meaning. Mary Crawford, Fanny's foil and romantic rival, is a master of language. When Mary is given the part of Agatha, the young woman who seduces her tutor, she asks which of the men will be playing the part of the tutor by asking, "What gentleman among you am I to have the pleasure of making love?" (1: 15). The carnal suggestiveness of this question is not lost on Edmund, the individual she is interested in, and the double meaning of her query renders him shocked yet intrigued. The other significant element of her line is its casual nature, its glib treatment of love and sex. Her language reveals that she is comfortable crossing the lines of playing (in drama) and being (in life); this is a talent that the novel presents as a sign of a morally suspect nature. Mary's language—its irreverence, wit, and charm—later costs her Edmund's love when she describes her brother's scandalous affair as "folly" (3: 17). It is here, finally, that Edmund understands the amoral heart of the woman with the great turn of phrase.

Within the challenges of *Mansfield Park* rest opportunities for excellent analysis. An essay might grow from questions you pose about Fanny's unconventional heroism or about the benefits of prominently featuring such a character in this novel. What do Fanny's silences allow us to notice about other characters? Does the narrator's approval of Fanny ever turn into impatience? You might also analyze how, though quiet, Fanny is strong enough to resist the fearsome family pressure exerted on her to accept Henry Crawford's marriage proposal. Another character worthy of analysis is Henry. Does he genuinely change into someone who would truly appreciate Fanny, or is his interest transient? Opportunities for broader analyses are in the study of the novel's themes and contexts. How, for example, does the narrator present the ideas of acting, art, truth, nature, and colonialism? A slow and careful reading of *Mansfield Park* will better allow you to recognize the patterns, issues, and ideas in the novel. Reading slowly and taking notes will make for a rich understanding of the story, while also enabling you to gather the evidence to write a strong essay.

TOPICS AND STRATEGIES

This section of the chapter discusses various possible topics for essays on *Mansfield Park* and general approaches to those topics. Remember that the material below is only a place to start from, not an exhaustive master key. Use this material to generate your own analysis. Every topic discussed here could encompass a variety of good papers.

Themes

Mansfield Park deals with many themes—ideas or concepts that organize and illuminate the importance of the events in the novel. The section above briefly examined some of these: morality, acting, heroism, and others. The novel contains many more ideas, including those related to setting, behavior, love, education, social class, vocation, stewardship, and home. Writers analyzing the novel often begin by identifying a central theme they see as important and then determine—through an essay—what the story has to say about that theme. You can identify themes by noticing the ideas, symbols, words, or activities that are repeated in the story. In the initial volume, for instance, the dramatic action is centered around the play *Lovers' Vows* that the less serious young people are committed to staging. Amid the dialogue about play choice, casting, and staging, there is a great deal of discussion about acting. Numerous aspects of acting are discussed, such as whose social role should prevent their acting, whose acting is atrocious, and who is too capable an actor. These many discussions show clearly that acting is a theme of this novel. You may follow the characters' leads as you choose an approach to the theme of acting. Noticing how the risks of acting seem different for men and for women, for instance, forms one approach to this topic. Another approach could examine what it means in the novel to be too good an actor, as Fanny observes of Henry Crawford and Maria Bertram. Other themes could be approached in similar ways. You could approach the theme of home by observing how Fanny comes to understand home and then analyze her opinion relative to those of other characters and the narrator. Thematic approaches also blend with the philosophical approaches described below.

Sample Topics:

1. **Acting:** When the young people decide to stage a play at Mansfield Park, they dedicate their time and energy to discussions about acting. What is the significance of acting in this novel? How does the idea of acting run counter to the novel's values of truth and moral probity?

Whichever approach to this topic you choose, be aware of the contents of the play because the play's roles and action parallel and inform the events in the novel. The novel contains allusions to the play's contents, but it would be worthwhile to locate a synopsis of *Lovers' Vows,* a play that was popular during Austen's lifetime (see, for instance, Gill and Gregory or Pinion). One approach to this topic would be to look at how the play permits an atmosphere of abandon, such as is registered in Maria Bertram's behavior. Though engaged to another man, Maria is deeply attracted to Henry Crawford, and the two contrive to be cast in roles that allow their flirtation to express itself by physical touch and declarations of love that would be scandalous offstage. Fanny believes that Maria Bertram acts the scenes of intimacy "too well." How else does acting in the play permit immodest and immoral behavior? Acting in this novel blurs the lines between honest and dishonest conduct. Where in the novel do we see truth sacrificed to acting? Though she "cannot act," Fanny is aware of the risks that the play poses and the larger implications of acting. Fanny watches with great interest Henry Crawford's acting in the play and thinks that, though she dislikes him as a man, she admires him as an actor. Is she, then, right to suspect later that his declarations of love are mere acting? You will want to reach an overall conclusion about how acting relates to the novel's values of truth and morality.

2. **Home:** Home is of particular importance to Fanny, who is transplanted from her modest birth home to grand Mansfield Park at age nine. How does her understanding of home change over the course of the novel?

   This topic involves looking specifically at the importance of one theme for the novel's protagonist. You would want to first identify Fanny's understandings of home at the beginning of the novel to more substantively assess how her feelings change about what constitutes a home. When she later returns to her hometown of Portsmouth, she is surprised by how quickly she realizes that she feels no innate connection with it: "Portsmouth was Portsmouth; Mansfield was home." What, in Fanny's later view, constitutes home? Another approach to the theme of home would be to analyze how it relates to the notion of a "proper place." To that end, what is the significance of Fanny's eventually taking her place as a true member of Mansfield Park? Yet another approach would be to contrast Fanny's views of home with other characters' views. In contrasting Fanny's views with those of the peripatetic Henry Crawford, for instance, we recognize Fanny's valuing of stability. Does the book also champion stability and home or dynamism and adventure? Is it significant that unfortunate events await those who leave Mansfield Park?

3. **Education:** *Mansfield Park* is a novel of education for not only its protagonist but also the entire Bertram family: They eventually learn to recognize the value of Fanny. How does her outlook and understanding educate her adopted family? More generally, how does the novel characterize a good education?

An essay on this topic might begin by analyzing Fanny Price's education and understanding of the world. You might look to her perceptiveness of the feelings of those around her and her sometimes lyrical observations of the natural and social worlds. You might also examine her deferential attitude to Edmund, who acts as her teacher. Her commitments to reading and observing also reveal a mind that is cultivating itself. Contrasting Fanny's use of her education to that of her cousins, Maria and Julia Bertram, or of Mary Crawford is instructive; the trip to Sotherton Court contains ample opportunities to observe Fanny's deep appreciation of the world around her, while Maria, Julia, and Mary are instead focused on their individual ambitions. To analyze how Fanny educates her family, it would be useful to consider how Fanny affects Sir Thomas and Edmund, both of whom learn by her example. Another approach to this topic could focus solely on Fanny and her evolving understanding of the value of education. In what specific ways does Fanny's teaching of her sister Susan help Fanny come to realize the importance of an education? Your conclusion should demonstrate an overall understanding of the role of education in this novel.

4. **Charm:** Why is charm presented here as a dangerous trait? In what ways does charm threaten characters?

It is telling that so many of the most charming characters in this novel are also the most duplicitous and, perhaps, nefarious. The novel, in fact, presents charm and moral integrity as opposed and mutually exclusive traits. To address this topic you need to identify sections in which a charming character threatens to undermine the principles of a moral character. You might, for instance, analyze how Edmund is particularly vulnerable to Mary's charm. Another approach might analyze how Henry's charm functions. The principled Fanny Price is always aware of the morally slipshod natures of the Crawford siblings, but even she seems to weaken in her resistance to Henry's charming behavior. Your essay should analyze charm's machinations in this novel, while also showing how charm effectively obscures moral danger.

Character

Because so much of the novel is focused on the conduct and manners of its characters, examining character is a productive means by which to analyze *Mansfield Park*. Essays can focus on questions of character development (such as how Austen distinguishes Edmund from his brother Tom by their respective treatments of Fanny), means of characterization (such as the way the reader understands Aunt Norris by her cruel castigations of Fanny and her general pettiness), or interpretations of changes in a character as the novel proceeds (such as the profound shift from gruffness to tenderness in Sir Thomas).

To write an essay on character, you should assess the novel by questioning how readers come to know various characters. How, for instance, does Austen distinguish a character's behavior? Fanny Price's fragility is seen in her physical weakness and emotional timidity. Mr. Rushworth's limited intelligence is made manifest by the narrator's pointing out Rushworth's inability to follow simple topics of conversation. Lady

Bertram's mental and physical inertia is demonstrated by her constant napping and her persistent need to ask her husband what she thinks. Edmund's generous heart shows itself in his thoughtfulness toward both Fanny and Mary Crawford. Aunt Norris's selfishness is ironically hinted at when she repeatedly alludes to it: "My own trouble, you know, I never regard" (1: 1).

To an extent, the narrator instructs you what to expect from characters, and if you pay attention to the editorial comments about individuals, you will understand what the characters signify. When introducing Aunt Norris, for instance, the narrator asserts the character's motivating principles: "As far as walking, talking, and contriving reached, she was thoroughly benevolent, and nobody knew better how to dictate liberality to others: but her love of money was equal to her love of directing, and she knew quite as well how to save her own as to spend that of her friends" (1: 1). In this description, we see that Aunt Norris's great loves are meddling and hoarding money, and so they prove in her conduct. Her desire to dictate generosity and expense to others helps explain what would otherwise appear a philanthropic gesture, the act of proposing that Fanny Price be adopted into the Bertram household. Aunt Norris's cruel castigations of Fanny are some of the most dramatic lines in the novel. Meditating on how they reveal truths about Aunt Norris, or what larger purpose she serves in the novel, can lead to a good thesis. To analyze questions of character development, look closely for distinguishing traits of language, action, or interactions with other characters. Tracking the ways characters behave with one another helps readers not only understand how characters are created, but also assess what characters signify and represent for the story overall.

Sample Topics:

1. **Henry Crawford's character development:** Does Henry change over the course of the novel, and if so, how?

   Henry Crawford is an interesting character. He is not handsome, but he exudes charisma and is, Mary tells us, the world's "most horrible flirt." He charms the Bertram sisters for sport and then later decides that he will entertain himself by making Fanny fall in love with him. When he finds himself in love with Fanny's goodness and sweet temperament, he surprises his sister, himself, and the reader. What are we to make of his change of heart? Does the narrator characterize his changes as in earnest or are they superficial? You will certainly want to address the significance of his affair with Maria, the affair that eliminates the possibility of his having a relationship with Fanny. How does this ill-advised relationship fit into the larger scheme of Henry's character?

2. **Aunt Norris as a character:** Aunt Norris is probably the most villainous of all Austen's characters. To what does the narrator ascribe her villainy, and what is the role of her character in the story of Fanny Price? In what ways does Aunt Norris's eventual self-exile from Mansfield Park seem appropriate for her character?

This is an evaluative topic requiring you to analyze Aunt Norris in two ways: in terms of explaining her character and in terms of her role in the novel. Pay attention to how the narrator explains Aunt Norris's actions. An example of the narrator's accounting for her is given above in the introduction to this section. Another example comes much later, when the narrator remarks that Aunt Norris "disliked Fanny, because [Aunt Norris] had neglected her." Does this explanation help you understand Aunt Norris's cruelties to Fanny? Aunt Norris's role, you could argue, is either divisive or galvanizing for the Bertram family and for Fanny Price especially. That Aunt Norris eventually chooses to leave Mansfield Park could be seen as a triumph for Fanny and the values she represents. Your conclusion could discuss whether Aunt Norris's choice of self-exile is appropriate to her character.

3. **Sir Thomas's character development:** How does Sir Thomas change over the course of the novel? What is the significance of these changes?

To write an essay on this topic, you need to decide not only what types of changes Sir Thomas undergoes but also to discuss his initial behavior. Before his significant changes, he demonstrates a tendency to be dictatorial in conduct and intimidating in manner. The narrator observes that Sir Thomas terrifies Fanny when she arrives at Mansfield Park because, though he wants to be welcoming, "he had to work against a most untoward gravity of deportment." His return from Aruba signals a marked shift in his behavior, though he changes even more in his outlook before the end of the novel. What is the nature of his realizations in the aftermath of Maria's affair with Henry and Julia's elopement? What regrets does Sir Thomas have about his parenting? How does his understanding of Fanny change? A strong essay will assess how Sir Thomas's growth relates to the novel's larger themes of authority, discipline, and duty.

4. **Character development in general:** How does the novel present character to the reader? What techniques does it use? Are characters transparent or somewhat opaque?

A paper on this topic would examine how Austen gives insight into character. A possible approach would be to look carefully at a pair of characters or a set of techniques and show what effects each has. For instance, an essay could study how behavior, such as the treatment of Fanny, reveals character. The Bertram sisters, for example, are all but incapable of noticing Fanny, while Edmund is attentive to her. Another paper could analyze how letters—their content, style, and exchange—reveal a great deal about characters. You might focus on Lady Bertram's or Mary Crawford's letters: Both characters' true natures show themselves in their letters.

History and Context

Another suitable approach to the analysis of *Mansfield Park* is through history and context. Even a modest amount of historical research into the world of this novel will provide great returns in understanding and analytical opportunities. *Mansfield Park* is Austen's most historically rich novel. It refers to international affairs such as those related to the United States, the British Empire, slavery, the East and West Indies, and the Mediterranean. The novel does not focus at great length on these places and subjects, but clearly shows how colonialism was part of the English citizen's mindset. More lengthy attention is given to local affairs. The context of the English estate system, for instance, is an interesting subject. *Mansfield Park* is, after all, named for a country estate, and much of the novel's tension turns on the questions of proper management of an estate and family. Another way to analyze the context of the novel would be to study the play *Lovers' Vows* (1798), by Mrs. Inchbald, which the young people are eager to stage. After researching the contents of the play, you would be able to discuss knowledgeably how that particular play provided Austen with her material for the dramatic action in her story.

Sample Topics:

1. **Slavery:** What are we to make of the mentions of slavery in *Mansfield Park*? Where are anxieties about slavery expressed and to what end?

   This topic asks you to reach conclusions about the significance of the references to slavery in the novel. You would need to research the slave trade and the abolitionist movement in England: The Slave Trade Act outlawed slave trafficking in 1807, but slavery itself was not fully abolished in England until 1833. *Mansfield Park* is set in the midst of the abolitionist movement, but the exact dates of the novel are uncertain. This makes conclusive assertions about the novel's views on slavery somewhat enigmatic. Nevertheless, a strong paper can analyze how anxieties about slavery are expressed in the story. You should analyze the dinner conversation when Fanny asks her uncle about slavery in Antigua—where he owns a sugarcane plantation—and her question is met with "dead silence." Sir Thomas's reasons for traveling to Antigua are connected to labor problems there that might very well be related to the aftermath of slavery. He brings his elder son, Thomas, to Antigua, but circumstances that are dangerous or "unfavourable" compel Sir Thomas to send his son back to England. The mentions of Antigua suggest threat, and it is in these mentions that anxiety about slavery resides. Some scholars see in Fanny an analogue for slavery. If you were interested in that line of inquiry, you would need to identify places where Fanny's situation loosely parallels those of slaves.

2. **Colonialism:** The British Empire was at the height of its power when *Mansfield Park* was written, and symptoms of colonialism pervade the novel. How is colonialism an important aspect of the cultural context of the story?

An essay on colonialism in *Mansfield Park* would require research into the British Empire during the Regency era. A good encyclopedia will help you gain a sense of the scale and administration of colonial Britain. The Caribbean, also called the West Indies, is of particular importance because the Bertram family owns a plantation in Antigua. This plantation is valuable enough to the family to risk the travels that managing it requires. To address how colonialism materialized in England, you should identify how products from these distant locales circulate through households; one example of this is the shawls that Lady Bertram wants William Price to procure for her in the East Indies. Even the ubiquitous tea and less common coffee are goods acquired through colonialism (some would say these goods drove colonialism). William and the Royal Navy, of which he is a member, represent an important arm of the colonial administration of Britain. How is the navy shown to be an integral aspect of English society? You might research how the navy represented an avenue for professional advancement for the middle classes. How does this fact show colonialism's integral presence in England?

3. **The context of *Lovers' Vows*:** This novel includes long sections on acting, the theater, and one play in particular. How does *Lovers' Vows* inform the context of *Mansfield Park*?

This topic asks you to study the play that the young people of Mansfield Park prepare to stage. Your first step would be to research the substance of the play (a synopsis of which can be found in Gill and Gregory or Pinion). Next, you should analyze the aspects of the play that relate to the larger themes in *Mansfield Park*. Why do you think Austen chose this particular play? What elements of the play allow Austen to explore the ideas that she includes in her novel?

4. **The estate:** *Mansfield Park* is named for an estate, and much of its dramatic action relates to the proper management of that estate. What kind of commentary does the novel make about the traditional estate?

For this broad topic, the writer might focus on a few elements and evaluate the novel's position on them. One approach might be to include close readings of the estates described in the novel: Mansfield Park, Sotherton, and Everingham. Which estate is the most capably managed and how does the narrator suggest this? Lady Rushworth's ignorance of the identities of the family members in portraits, for example, seems indicative of an estate whose occupants have lost touch with their traditions. Sotherton Court, indeed, has many symptoms of an ill-managed estate. Sir Thomas is a capable steward of his estate, but he sees it compromised in his prolonged absence. How does his absence contribute to the degradation of his house and family? These examples might form the core of an essay that argued for the novel's presentation of estates as tenuously held entities. Another approach might be to do close readings of the estate holders, instead of the estates themselves. What does it mean for the estate's future, for instance, that Tom Bertram, the eldest Bertram son, incurs such large gambling debts? A conclusion for any approach to this topic should include a discussion of why the novel is so focused on the estate tradition: How might Austen's discussions of estates relate to the novel's values of family, home, or morality?

Philosophy and Ideas

Another approach to forming an argument about *Mansfield Park* would be to explore its many philosophical ideas. This approach is related to the thematic approach described above in that it tracks an idea in the story, but the result of this kind of essay would demonstrate how you see the story commenting on the idea in its more general form. Austen was of an age that debated the morality—the rightness and wrongness—of actions and beliefs, and many of the ideas in this novel have moral connotations: character, responsibility, ethics, conduct, and the stewardship of the land. *Mansfield Park* is considered the most morally insistent of Austen's novels, in part because protagonist Fanny Price is so focused on moral probity. Fanny is—because of her nature and situation—often on the fringes of the action and so is often in a position to be Mansfield Park's moral arbiter; an example of this is seen when she is recruited to assist with preparations for the play in which she refuses to act. Her close observations of the actors and their roles allow her to assess the group's actions in the form of constructive criticism:

> She was invested, indeed, with the office of judge and critic, and earnestly desired to exercise it and tell them all their faults; but from doing so every feeling within her shrank, she could not, would not, dared not attempt it; had she been otherwise qualified for criticism, her conscience must have restrained her from venturing at disapprobation. (1: 18)

Fanny here is shown to think like a judge, but her retiring nature and sense of decorum prevent her from offering opinions. While Fanny sees faults, she does not mention them because "her conscience must have restrained her from venturing at disapprobation." She thinks in terms of morality, and this determines her actions and behavior. Planning an essay around a moral issue in *Mansfield Park* must certainly include analysis of Fanny's point of view, but the entirety of Fanny's moral vision is too broad a scope for a short essay. More feasible would be an essay that focused on one of Fanny's values by analyzing how that value functions in the novel. Constancy, for example, is a quality that she values and finds lacking in Henry Crawford.

Other promising philosophical ideas reveal the moral issues that are couched within general philosophies about everyday life. For example, an essay could examine the philosophies of landscape design discussed by the characters in the novel. At this time in England, groups disagreed on the function of the grounds surrounding estates. Was the correct design a traditional one that promoted the vistas to and from the mansion itself, or should grounds instead look natural and help the mansion blend in with the picturesque landscape? These questions were paralleled in philosophical debates about England itself: Was it a country in need of radical change or one that needed to preserve its traditions? The revolutions in France and the United States gave rise to some of these questions. In *Mansfield Park,* an interesting thesis could be generated by observing which characters speak to the need for either stability or change in landscape aesthetics.

Sample Topics:

1. **Fanny's moral outlook:** Consider one of Fanny's prized values—constancy, selflessness, duty, and obedience are some of these—and analyze how that value is presented. Does the narrator sometimes disagree with Fanny's values?

   There are many aspects of Fanny's moral identity on which an essay could concentrate. If you wrote about selflessness, you would have an opportunity to discuss how Fanny observes characters acting out of self-interest and how the book presents those characters as perhaps suffering because of their actions. If you wrote about duty to family, you might analyze how Fanny herself suffers when the family's goals run counter to what she considers to be morally correct. In rejecting Henry Crawford, she incurs the stunned disapproval of both Sir Thomas and Lady Bertram, her surrogate parents. She is also prevented from fully explaining her dislike of Henry because to do so would reveal the improper behavior of her cousins Maria and Julia. In the intersection of Fanny's and the narrator's views you will find the evidence you need to support this essay. Another approach to an essay on Fanny's moral outlook might simply observe which of Fanny's values are validated by the events in the novel.

2. **Landscape aesthetics in *Mansfield Park*:** Why does *Mansfield Park* pay so much attention to landscape design? How does the philosophy of landscape design resonate with ideas or characters in the novel?

The leading landscape designers of this time are mentioned by name in the sections pertaining to the Sotherton Court visit. You would need to do background reading about individuals such as Capability Brown, an influential designer who believed in "improving" grounds to such an extent that he would remove cottages and even hillsides if their form or situation did not agree with his aesthetic goals (Gill and Gregory 198). You can construct a strong thesis by considering how the characters discuss "improvements" and how the narrator represents these ideas. An example of this is when Mr. Rushworth expresses his desire to make large-scale changes to his estate, Sotherton. Rushworth's vapidity and insecurity motivate him to follow trends eagerly. His outlook is opposed to Fanny's—she sees some of his remodeling proposals as bordering on criminal. When he casually ponders removing the avenue, a stately row of mature trees bordering a path—a landscape feature that was symbolic of the order and stability of an estate—Fanny passionately descries the notion. Where do we see that the narrator prefers that estates be maintained for their traditional advantages? More generally, how does this outlook on landscape design reveal characters' values?

3. **Fanny as the conscience of *Mansfield Park*:** In what ways is Fanny vindicated as the conscience of Mansfield Park?

This topic requires a close reading of the end of the novel, with special attention paid to the way that Fanny's examples and beliefs help to resolve the divisive issues that beset the Bertram family. How does the family patriarch, Sir Thomas, come to embrace Fanny's values? How are Fanny's impressions of the Crawfords proved to be correct in the novel's resolution? You might explore how her associations with order, tranquility, and stability remedy the family's problems. You should pay special attention to those places where the narrator implies that Fanny is shown to be a true daughter of Mansfield Park.

Language, Symbols, and Imagery

Language, symbols, and imagery are some of the creative means by which an author conveys certain feelings or ideas that would, if simply declared, be less effective in their imaginative and evocative power. All writers, and those of fiction especially, use language deliberately and choose words based on their connotative meanings. As you read fiction in preparation for writing about it, be alert to the connotative meanings of words, even as you register the surface meaning of language in order to follow the plot itself. *Mansfield Park* is distinguished from Austen's other novels by its more prominent incorporation of symbolism to further its ideas. While it does not include figurative language such as similes and metaphors, Austen's novel does promote its ideas through entities that come to represent more than just the entities themselves. This is accomplished via houses, outdoor spaces, indoor rooms, and objects.

The outdoor spaces at Sotherton Court are especially rich in symbolic import. The young people—the Crawfords, the Bertrams, Rushworth, and Fanny—move through the spaces of the woods, walks, and gardens, and as they do so their character traits materialize. All of these physical spaces take on figurative meanings. In the Sotherton outdoors even the characters appear aware of the multiple significances of their actions and words. Henry Crawford, for instance, who has been aggressively flirting with Maria, points out that she should overlook her fiancé's personal shortcomings by instead focusing on the beauty of the grounds and home that are to be hers upon her marriage to Rushworth: "Your prospects . . . are too fair to justify want of spirits. You have a very smiling scene before you." Henry, here, is using language with double meanings: "Prospects" means both the views they are looking at and her future prosperity; the "smiling scene" too suggests a propitious future "before" her. Maria is alert to his multiple meanings: "Do you mean literally or figuratively? Literally, I conclude. Yes, certainly, the sun shines and the park looks cheerful. But unluckily that iron gate . . . give[s] me a feeling of restraint and hardship" (1: 10). After Maria shifts away from her literal interpretation of Henry's words, she moves to her figuratively rendered emotional state of mind: Though her financial prospects look bright, her emotional prospects look dark. The gate of her present situation, the fettered behavior that her engagement requires, gives her "a feeling of restraint and hardship." Their path is literally blocked by a large, locked gate at this moment, and though Rushworth has hastened back to the house to get the key, Maria chooses simply to climb over the gate that symbolically restrains her so that she and Henry can continue on their way. Fanny recognizes the hazards of this symbolic act, but is unable to prevent her cousin's crossing over: "You will hurt yourself. . . . You had better not go." The symbolic significance of Maria's act is profound: She is bypassing the rules of decorum to find a private space in which she can be alone with Henry. Later in the novel, she will bypass her marriage restrictions to pursue an affair with Henry. Maria does hurt herself, as Fanny predicts. An essay built around the symbolism of the physical spaces and barriers at Sotherton Court could look to both the actions there and later events to find how the two resonate with each other. A strong analysis of an indoor space could focus on Fanny's room at Mansfield Park: How does it reflect Fanny's character? Looking for connections between characters and indoor spaces could also examine how houses mirror their occupants. Another symbolic space in the novel is London. There is a great deal to say about how it is characterized. Yet another essay on symbolism might analyze the necklace dilemma that Fanny has to negotiate.

Sample Topics:

1. **Outdoor spaces:** The outdoor spaces of *Mansfield Park* see some of the most symbolic action in the novel. Examine a garden, wood, or path and analyze how the space is characterized and how it connects to the larger ideas in the novel.

    This topic allows you to explore the symbolically fertile grounds of Sotherton Court as discussed in the introduction to this section. You could concentrate on how the characters' natures are illustrated by their symbolic actions while in the woods, on the paths, or sitting on a bench as an uncomfortable witness to the behavior of others (as Fanny does). Why do you think Austen places these activities outside? What is the significance of the character's later leaving Sotherton Court in such ill humor? What realizations have they had about themselves that are left unresolved? The outdoor spaces at Mansfield Park, the Grant's parsonage, or Portsmouth also provide interesting ideas for an essay.

2. **Indoor spaces:** How do indoor spaces in *Mansfield Park* symbolically describe their occupants? What is the significance of your chosen indoor space in terms of the larger ideas or events in the book?

For this topic you could examine the significant interiors at Sotherton Court, the Price's house at Portsmouth, the Grant's parsonage, or Edmund's parsonage at Thornton Lacey. All of these houses magnify the personalities and values of their occupants. Looking at rooms within houses is a worthwhile method for approaching this topic. You might study, for instance, Sir Thomas's billiard room, the one that is made into a theater in his absence. Another interesting indoor space is Fanny's bedroom and the east room, the one-time schoolroom that is later considered hers. The east room has especially powerful symbolic overtones, both in how her decorations reflect her personality and because of what takes place in that room. Sir Thomas's epiphany about Aunt Norris's cruelty begins in the east room when he sees that she has instructed that there never be a fire there, though Fanny uses the room often. What is the significance—both for Fanny and for Aunt Norris—of his ordering a fire always be lit thereafter? Other significant events center around the increased traffic that the room sees as the book progresses. How do the nature of those visits from Edmund, Mary Crawford, and Sir Thomas speak to Fanny's growing value at Mansfield Park? Your essay should also discuss the significance of the indoor space in light of the novel's larger ideas or values.

3. **The necklaces:** The necklaces that Fanny receives from the Crawfords and Edmund are heavily symbolic. How do the gifts reveal the aims and natures of the gift givers? What does Fanny's use of the necklaces symbolize about the gifts?

One approach to this topic would be to analyze how these gifts were bestowed on Fanny. The giving of the Crawford's necklace is complex, while Edmund's gift is both straightforward and, perhaps, portentous in the accompanying note that Edmund gives to Fanny. How do these gift-giving ventures reveal the characters involved? Another analysis could focus on why, exactly, Fanny considers the Crawford necklace inappropriate. Does the narrator share Fanny's discomfort about the necklace? Yet another approach to this topic could focus on the solution to the necklace dilemma that seems providential. (Providence is the idea that a caring God guides the actions and fortunes of humans; in other words, that fate—such as inappropriate necklaces not fitting—is God's doing.) You might tie this possible example of providence to other examples that save Fanny from difficult circumstances, such as Sir Thomas's returning just as Fanny is tempted to participate in the play, or Henry Crawford and Maria's embarking on their affair just when Fanny is tempted to fall for Henry. This last approach utilizes a symbolic situation, the dilemma of the necklaces, as a bridge to a larger idea in the story, that of providence in Fanny's life.

4. **London:** How is London characterized in *Mansfield Park*? What does it symbolize for the events and characters of the novel? Consider how events that take place in the city affect country life.

To write an essay such as this, begin by identifying where the novel either represents or discusses London, then observe what kinds of judgments that characters and the narrator offer about the city. You might consider analyzing events that originate in London or values associated with the city. Mary Crawford, a denizen of the city who comes to Mansfield Park, is closely associated with London's culture and style. How do her values threaten the culture of the countryside? Nearly all of the events that debilitate the Bertram family—Maria and Henry's affair, Tom's illness, Julia's elopement—take place in London. It would be worthwhile to consider why the novel was shaped in this way. Another approach would be to focus solely on how the novel characterizes the landscapes of the country and the city (including Portsmouth). Just observing how the physical properties of setting are characterized by the narrator will reveal how the novel's values align with those it associates with the countryside.

Comparison and Contrast

Comparing components of a story to explain and analyze the similarities or differences among them is a useful approach to writing an essay. Avoid simply creating a list of similarities or differences in a work; instead, be sure to comment on your observations. To begin a comparison/contrast essay, you might compare characters with each other: How does Lady Bertram compare with Aunt Norris? With Mrs. Price? How does Henry Crawford compare with Edmund Bertram? With Mr. Rushworth? You could also compare characters (or other elements of the story, such as themes or events) across different Austen novels. For example, how do the love interests of the heroines compare with one another in *Mansfield Park* and *Pride and Prejudice*? How do the depictions of love resemble each other in *Mansfield Park* and *Persuasion*? The challenge of this kind of essay is to decide what the similarities or differences you identify might mean. These questions make essays compelling, and they will have different answers for each writer. You might find it helpful to think about what kinds of effects Austen achieves by producing either similarities or differences among the elements of her stories. How, for example, do Elizabeth Bennet's and Fanny Price's respective temperaments broaden our understanding of what it means to be a heroine? It is not enough to point to the existence of similarities or differences; you must also consider what purposes those similarities or differences might signify for the novel itself.

Sample Topics:

1. **Comparing love in different novels:** Love is the primary motivation in all of Austen's novels, but the kind of love in each novel varies. Choose another one of the novels and compare *Mansfield Park*'s representations of love with it. How are they alike or different? What kind of commentary on love can be drawn from this kind of comparison?

Such an essay requires you to analyze novels for their overall representations of romantic, family, or sibling love. You might make an argument for the variety of love that is represented as the strongest or most important in two or three novels. Another approach would be to compare romantic love in two or three books. Consider, for instance, the paucity of romance in *Mansfield Park,* compared with that in *Pride and Prejudice.* Why would romantic love make such a minor appearance in *Mansfield Park*? A related question: How is it significant that in a novel with so little romance there is a suggestion of Fanny's being pregnant on the last page? Is there a difference in Austen's novels between romance and marriage?

2. **Comparing unheroic heroines:** Austen used unheroic heroines in *Northanger Abbey, Mansfield Park,* and *Persuasion.* What is the effect of these unheroic heroines on their stories? How do they enable Austen to explore ideas related to realism?

This topic requires an assessment of the effects and significance of the protagonists in *Northanger Abbey, Mansfield Park,* and *Persuasion.* Why would Austen write novels about such guileless and sometimes passive protagonists? In what ways do these protagonists propel the themes of their novels? For example, Fanny's quiet earnestness looks positively pleasant compared to the frenetic wit of the Crawford siblings. In *Northanger Abbey,* Catherine's guilelessness contrasts with Isabella's calculation. In *Persuasion,* Anne Elliot's humility is a welcome contrast to her family's arrogance (known by others as the "Elliot pride"). Some scholars have noted that these heroines contribute to Austen's innovations in realism. You might explore how Fanny, Anne, and Catherine lend realism to their novels. You should pay attention to the role of these protagonists in their own novels, as well as compare the protagonists to one another.

Bibliography and Online Resources for *Mansfield Park*

Byrne, Sandie, ed. *Mansfield Park: A Reader's Guide to Essential Criticism.* New York: Palgrave-Macmillan, 2005.

Donoghue, Denis. "A View of *Mansfield Park.*" *Critical Essays on Jane Austen.* Ed. B. C. Southam. London: Routledge, 1970. 39–59.

Gill, Richard, and Susan Gregory. *"Mansfield Park." Mastering the Novels of Jane Austen.* New York: Palgrave-Macmillan, 2003. 179–240.

Pinion, F. B. *"Mansfield Park." A Jane Austen Companion: A Critical Survey and Reference Book.* London: Macmillan, 1973. 101–13.

Southam, Brian. "The Silence of the Bertrams." Excerpt. Ed. Harold Bloom. Jane Austen: Bloom's Major Novelists. Broomall, PA: Chelsea House Publishers, 2000. 59–60.

Wilshire, John. *"Mansfield Park, Emma, Persuasion." The Cambridge Companion to Jane Austen.* Eds. Edward Copeland and Juliet McMaster. Cambridge: Cambridge UP, 2006. 58–83.

EMMA

IT IS in *Emma* (1816) that we see Jane Austen in top form and on the verge of a renown about which she felt ambivalent. Austen was proud of her work and gratified to hear positive responses to it, and while she was enthusiastic about the more financially certain future that a greater readership promised, not all aspects of fame appealed to her. One of the unwelcome marks of her considerable popularity is seen in the dedication of *Emma* to the Prince Regent, one of the more dissipated and least beloved members of the royal family at that time (he continued to be disliked later as King George IV). Although Austen had thought a simple dedication sufficient to her royal obligation, her publisher overruled with a lavish inscription that contains three references to "his royal highness" (Tomalin 248–50). Austen's notice by those around the royal family shows that while her fame as a novelist was growing, her private life as a writer was slipping away. Soon after *Emma* was in print, J. S. Clarke, the Prince Regent's chaplain and librarian, wrote Austen letters offering both praise and plotlines for future novels, books that would have sounded very much like the life and times of J. S. Clarke himself. Austen fended off Clarke's suggestion—that she write a "Historical Romance, illustrative of the History of the august house of Cobourg"—by protesting her inability to write something beyond her knowledge or inclination: "I must keep to my own style & go in my own Way [*sic*]; and though I may never succeed again in that, I am convinced I should totally fail in any other" (Parrish 350–51).

Austen was not entirely convinced that she would succeed with *Emma*. In a letter to her sister, Austen wrote that Emma was a character that no one but she would like, and the author did indeed set up a challenge for herself by designing a protagonist who is so flush with good fortune (Parrish viii). In literature, conflict is customarily the shaper of identity and the creator of action, but in this novel we have a protagonist who enjoys a quiet life of placid happiness: "Emma Woodhouse, handsome, clever, and rich, with a comfortable home and happy disposition, seemed to unite some of the best blessings of existence; and had lived nearly twenty-one years in the world with very little to distress or vex her" (3). While the words *distress* and *vex* hint at the possibility of both, neither prospect proves radically destabilizing to Emma or her world. This is a book of comfortable people in a lovely place, and where discomfort occurs, a salve soon follows. Emma's mistakes furnish the dramatic action of the story, and while she does misstep, misunderstand, and misspeak, all that she does wrong is soon made right.

In *Emma*, Austen disposes of the moralizing tone that she used in *Mansfield Park*, her preceding novel. All of Austen's literary fortes are on superlative display in *Emma*: comic situations, ironic narrative, deft sketches of country life, insightful representations of family dynamics, realistic situations, characters, and dialogue, and the slow burn of worthy and healthful love. Before doing a general analysis of lessons, ideas, or characters, you must first contend with Austen's language. This section demonstrates how to do a close reading of a few early passages from *Emma* in order to prepare for writing an essay.

Emma begins with the protagonist feeling the effects of a vacuum in her life. It is the evening after her governess and friend, Anna Taylor, marries. Though Emma Woodhouse is happy for her friend, she is also aware of the loss that this poses for her personally: "she was now in great danger of suffering from intellectual solitude. She dearly loved her father, but he was no companion for her. He could not meet her in conversation, rational or playful" (5). A close reading of this passage reveals that Emma is an individual whose time and intelligence are idle: She is lonely and bored. Into this personal void soon walks the humble Harriet Smith, a young and pretty boarder at the local girl's school. While Harriet is delighted simply to be invited to visit Hartfield, the Woodhouse home, Emma decides that she will dramatically transform Harriet Smith. The narrator adopts Emma's point of view to describe these plans:

> *She* would notice [Harriet]; she would improve her; she would detach her from her bad acquaintance, and introduce her into good society; she

would form her opinions and her manners. It would be an interesting, and certainly a very kind undertaking; highly becoming her own situation in life, her leisure, and powers. (20)

This passage illustrates how closely the narrator adopts the point of view of Emma herself. Notice that in this passage where Emma decides that Harriet Smith will be the project to occupy her now empty hours, there is no intervening voice opining whether this project is, in fact, "a very kind undertaking": This is Emma's opinion. The bulk of the novel is told in this style, which blurs the lines between a separate entity—what we generally think of as a third-person narrator—and the protagonist herself. This form of narration, generally termed free indirect speech, is one that Austen mastered in her novels.

The effect of free indirect speech in this novel is that we have first-hand insight into Emma's feelings and opinions, though we are also in the position of realizing how often she is mistaken or misguided. In examples of textbook dramatic irony, Emma's mistakes are often clear to the reader, though not to Emma herself. An example of this irony is in the quoted passage above. In it, we learn that Emma feels that her desire to transform Harriet Smith is "highly becoming her own situation in life, her leisure, and powers," though we know that the sensible Mr. Knightley has already declared disruptive and interfering Emma's meddling in people's lives.

Considering the themes present in passages and discussed by characters is an important task of close reading. In the above passage, Emma's marked class consciousness is shown when she thinks of "her situation . . . [and] powers." Emma here articulates her society's belief that the rich should think of the poor as a responsibility; in its basest form, this belief reads the poor as children who needed to be taken care of. This paternalism is an ideology that contemporary readers are likely to take exception to, but the notion of paternalism and the belief that social class was a relatively fixed category—that the poor, the middle class, and the wealthy naturally occupy different levels of society—are ones that Austen weaves throughout the story. As a student of literature, your job is to track the patterns of ideas and assess how the novel presents them. You might, for instance, notice whether Emma's feelings of paternalism are questioned or validated by the events and narration in the novel.

Emma's feelings are accessible to us, and so are those of other characters. The narrative's third-person point of view absorbs the points of view of the characters she is describing—this is the technique of free indirect speech—and so we are presented with the hysterical philosophies of Mr. Woodhouse. Mr. Woodhouse is one of Austen's great comic figures, a character who fears all food that is not gruel, or at least boiled, and who shudders at the dangers he perceives in drafts, weather, marriages, and late nights. The narrator provides a view into Mr. Woodhouse's mind by describing his feelings about suppers, a meal shared in the evening:

> Upon such occasions poor Mr. Woodhouse's feelings were in sad warfare. He loved to have the [table]cloth laid, because it had been the fashion of his youth; but his conviction of suppers being very unwholesome made him rather sorry to see any thing [*sic*] put on it; and while his hospitality would have welcomed his visitors to every thing [*sic*], his care for their health made him grieve that they would eat. (21)

Here the reader is able to see key points in his characterization: both the health fears that preoccupy Mr. Woodhouse and the absurdity of his preoccupation. The narrator uses the hyperbolic style of Mr. Woodhouse's own thinking; his "feelings" are, after all, in "sad warfare" about his divided commitment to both gracious hospitality and the physical well-being of his guests. He likes to see the table prepared for guests, to have "the cloth laid," but it "grieve[s]" him that his guests "would eat" the food that lies upon it. Between these two, for him, untenable positions, he is stuck, and this is just one example of the inertia that, ironically, motivates him. The novel will show that Mr. Woodhouse is driven by the desire to avoid change at all costs. Free indirect speech in the novel guarantees that we understand Mr. Woodhouse and even sympathize with him, even if we cannot imagine inviting him to a dinner party.

There are many opportunities for analysis within Emma's quiet world. An essay might analyze the book's form and organization and identify how the novel's events provide resolutions to conflicts. Are all its resolutions realistic? You might also look to characters for good topics to analyze. Which characters embody the novel's values? How do some characters, such as Frank Churchill, show themselves to be antagonistic to the novel's values? Opportunities for broader analyses are to be found in the study of the novel's themes and contexts. How, for example, does the narrator present the ideas of truth, understanding, love, community, and class? There is a great deal to say about socioeconomic class in this highly class-conscious novel. What are we to make of those moments in the novel that testify to the existence of poverty and despair? Is the narrator critical of a society that tolerates the existence of have-nots, or does the narrator accept poverty as natural? The physical landscape is also worth investigation. How does small and idyllic Highbury affect its denizens?

A close and careful reading of *Emma* will better allow you to recognize the patterns, issues, and ideas in the novel. Reading slowly and taking notes will make for a rich understanding of the story, while also enabling you to gather the evidence you need to write a strong essay.

TOPICS AND STRATEGIES

This section discusses various possible topics for essays on *Emma* and general approaches to those topics. The material below is only a starting point, not an exhaustive master key. You will want to use this material to generate your own analysis. Every topic discussed here could encompass a variety of good papers.

Themes

Emma deals with many themes—ideas or concepts that organize and underscore the importance of the events in the novel. The preceding section touched on some of these: socioeconomic class, comfort, fears, meddling, and family. The novel also considers the ideas of love, poverty, marriage, and community. Writers analyzing a novel often begin by identifying a central theme and then determine—through an essay—what the story is saying about that theme. You can identify themes by noticing the ideas, symbols, or words that are repeated in the story.

While reading *Emma* you will notice that the characters and narrator frequently use language that describes rank in their society. The words *sphere* and *level*, euphemisms for position in the social hierarchy, for instance, are often repeated. When Knightley and Emma are disagreeing about the marriageability of Harriet Smith and Mr. Martin, they are largely disagreeing over whether the social rank of these two individuals is compatible. While Knightley feels "the advantage of the match . . . to be all on [Harriet's] side," Emma is convinced that Harriet is Mr. Martin's superior: "Mr. Martin may be the richest of the two, but he is undoubtedly her inferior as to rank in society.—The sphere in which she moves is much above his.—[The marriage] would be a degradation" (55). This exchange reveals a great deal about how class-conscious this society is. All of the characters are as knowledgeable as Mr. Knightley and Emma in the ways and means of social rank. We see in this exchange that marriage suitability is primarily determined not by mutual love, but by rank in society and that the best marriages will be ones that provide a social or material "advantage." We also see that socioeconomic class is not determined solely by wealth, but also by social contacts. Emma believes that though Robert Martin has more material wealth than Harriet, she has the advantage in social wealth. When Emma says that the "sphere" in which Harriet moves is "much above [Robert Martin's]," she is talking about the people with whom Harriet associates. And when she is talking about Harriet's higher "sphere" of acquaintance, Emma is referring to herself.

Socioeconomic class is a large topic in *Emma,* and you should focus your approach to it judiciously. An interesting essay might explore not only the centrality of socioeconomic class in this novel and for this protagonist, but wherever class is trumped by merit or where the novel's events show how social levels overlap. Another approach to an essay on this topic would be to focus solely on social climbing. Who are the social upstarts and why are they considered such? More general themes at work in this novel include comprehension/understanding, community, and marriage.

Sample Topics:

1. **Socioeconomic class:** What is the role of socioeconomic class in *Emma*? How does class affect the behavior of characters? Does the novel criticize or endorse the social hierarchy?

    There are a number of ways you can narrow this very broad topic. One approach would be to focus on Emma and her sense of social roles. She is certainly the most class-conscious of Austen's protagonists, so focusing on her opinions and actions would provide ample opportunities for an essay. At this time in England, many believed that the gentry (of which the Woodhouses are members) had the benefits of wealth, but also the responsibility to care for those in the lower classes. This is a form of paternalism, a belief that privileged members of society should take care of the less fortunate of that society. How do we see paternalism in Emma's actions? One example is when Mr. Knightley chastizes Emma for her lapse in responsibility as a wealthy woman when she is unkind to Miss Bates, a poor woman probably soon to be even worse off. Mr. Knightley reminds Emma that the poor deserve perhaps even more respect than an individual of equal rank. Does the novel present Emma's other examples of paternalistic altruism as redemptive? Another approach to this topic might use *Emma* as a sociological document by focusing on characters who have ascended or descended the social ladder: Are characters' moves through ranks reckoned as merited or unjust? How does the novel chart the methods by which characters gain social power? Based on the information in *Emma*, how long does it take to ascend the ranks? You might consider discussing the socially ambitious Eltons, the Sucklings, the Bateses, the Westons, or Mrs. Churchill. For a case study, you could look to the example of Mr. Weston, whose biography illustrates the steps he took for social success. Whatever your approach, you should identify and read closely the fascinating ways that characters discuss society and rank. Your essay should certainly assess what the novel ultimately says about society. To that end, it is worth noting whether characters marry within or outside of their rank. Does the novel disagree with this hierarchical arrangement of society?

2. **Poverty:** Poverty is a much stronger presence in *Emma* than in Austen's other novels. Are these examples of poverty at odds with the idyllic comfort of the Woodhouses? What are we to make of the symptoms of social desperation in this otherwise Edenic corner of England?

   This topic asks you to concentrate on the depiction of poverty in the novel and to assess what this might signify for the novel more generally. One example is when Emma and Harriet Smith visit the "poor sick family, who lived a little way out of Highbury." Other scenes of poverty's effects are registered when Harriet is accosted by "gipsies" [*sic*] and when John Abdy is no longer able to care for his elderly father. Closer to home for Emma are the examples of poverty's impact on the Bates women. One approach to this topic would be to focus on women and poverty. Emma ruminates on the differences among women's paths. For herself, she sees that her wealth ensures her social status irrespective of marital status: "It is poverty only which makes celibacy contemptible." Jane Fairfax, who has no fortune, is on the brink of hiring herself out as a governess, a job that is presented here as a wretched one. No matter what approach you take, your essay should assess how poverty helps us better understand the world depicted in the novel. Does poverty serve as a foil to the Woodhouses' wealth, or does it instead constitute a threat to the comfort of Highbury?

3. **Community:** How is the idea of community shown to be valuable in *Emma*? What threatens community?

This topic asks you to analyze how community functions in the novel. Specifically, you are asked to track how community is presented as an important value for the society of Highbury. You should search for examples that show how a unified community enables felicity, or, conversely, how a disconnected community invites unhappiness. The outing to Box Hill, for example, illustrates the perils of social disarray. What decisions do we see characters making out of a desire to preserve community? It would also be useful to identify any threats to community. Frank Churchill, for instance, is a threat to community because so many of his actions exclude or upset other characters. A good conclusion would show how community is preserved and strengthened at the end of *Emma*.

4. **Marriage:** The disagreements between Emma and Mr. Knightley—principally on Emma's matchmaking—ensure that we are privy to many debates about what constitutes an appropriate

match. From these debates and the events in the novel, what do we decide *Emma* is saying about a good marital match?

This topic poses a general question about a main feature of the dramatic action in *Emma*—the choosing and acquiring of an appropriate marriage partner. An essay on this topic might focus on one or two partnerships and analyze how they are presented as appropriate or not. The Eltons' marriage, for instance, is presented as distasteful because their courtship seems so calculated and clichéd. By contrast, how does the novel show that the marriage of Robert Martin and Harriet Smith is appropriate? The marriage of Mr. and Mrs. Weston? A particularly fascinating marriage is the climactic one: that of Knightley and Emma. A good essay would include a discussion of their marriage and how it speaks to the novel's larger themes of community, truth, and parity.

Character

Because so much of the novel focuses on the conduct and manners of its characters, examining character is a worthwhile means by which to analyze *Emma*. Essays can focus on questions of character development (how Austen distinguishes Mr. Knightley from Mr. Elton by their respective treatments of Harriet Smith); characterization (the way the reader understands Miss Bates's love of anything by her rambling soliloquies on everything); or interpretations of changes in a character as the novel proceeds (the marked shifts from artlessness to artfulness and back again that we see in Harriet Smith).

To write an essay on character, you need to assess the novel by way of questions about how readers come to know various characters. How, for instance, does Austen distinguish a character's behavior? That Isabella is her father's daughter is seen by their shared hypochondria and anxiety. Mrs. Elton, with her penchant for dropping the names of her wealthy friends, the names of their great estates, and the kinds of posh carriages they own, is distinguished as having a particularly unappealing kind of social ambition. We understand Mr. Knightley's character by his showing Emma the respect of an intelligent, well-intentioned individual, even as he corrects and upbraids her. Though we never hear him speak directly, Mr. Martin's solid values and manners are demonstrated by reports of his words and deeds, and the description of his well-run, modest, and pretty Abbey-Mill Farm. Mr. Martin is, in fact, one of many peripheral characters distinguished solely by what other characters say about them. Some of these ancillary characters are stock ones, such as Serle, the cook, in whom the overly cautious Mr. Woodhouse puts such faith that he has no qualms about offering a small soft-boiled egg to a guest, since "Serle understands boiling an egg better than any body" (1: 3). In this case, we see that though a stock character, Serle is useful for understanding other characters like Mr. Woodhouse; in speaking of Serle, Mr. Woodhouse is revealing his fear of strangers, as well as his own fear of food. *Emma* presents a large number of characters that talk about a great number of characters.

To an extent, we are instructed what to expect from characters. If you notice the narrator's descriptions of individuals, you will understand what the characters signify in the novel. When introducing Mr. Woodhouse, for instance, the narrator asserts his character is one that requires "support. He was a nervous man, easily depressed; fond of every body that he was used to, and hating to part with them; hating change of every kind" (1: 1). Mr. Woodhouse is rather childish: He needs taking care of in the same way that a toddler needs to be protected from the elements, from upsetting stimuli, and from certain people. In spite of his immaturity, Mr. Woodhouse is not represented as flawed, but instead as vulnerable. His character, then, is most significant to the novel by our registering how others treat him. We are led to disapprove of Frank Churchill's having fun with Mr. Woodhouse's phobia of unhealthy atmospheres by the young man's hinting that at dances one runs the risk of people opening windows and letting drafts in on a warm room. Instead, we approve of Mr. Knightley's patient treatment of Mr. Woodhouse, his calming the older man's fears, his providing appropriate means of quiet entertainment during the visit to Donwell Abbey. As you prepare to write an essay on character development in *Emma*, consider the larger purposes a character serves. Look closely for distinguishing traits of language, action, or interactions with other characters. Tracking the ways characters behave with one another helps the reader not only understand how characters are created, but also assess what characters signify for the story overall.

Sample Topics:

1. **Emma's character development:** In what ways does Emma change over the course of the novel? In what ways does she remain the same?

   To write an essay on a topic such as this, first identify which of Emma's qualities or beliefs change during the novel. For example, you might look to dialogue where she expresses her feelings about love and matrimony, for instance, or to her internal dialogue where she reflects on herself and her own motives. *Emma* is in some ways a coming-of-age novel, and it might be useful to consider how Emma grows up. What half-baked beliefs or tendencies does she eventually dispense with? What laudable qualities from her youth—such as her kind attention to her father—does she maintain? An essay on this topic would have to examine how Emma speaks as much as how she behaves over the course of the novel.

2. **Character development in general:** How does the novel present character to the reader? What techniques does it use? Are characters transparent or veiled?

   A paper on this topic would look at how Austen gives insight into character. A possible approach would be to look carefully at a pair of characters or a set of techniques and attempt to show its effects. For instance, a paper could examine how social conventions, such as conversation, reveal character. Emma, for example, likes to gossip with Frank Churchill, but she is frustrated that Jane Fairfax, with her "odious composure," will not condescend to this kind of unburdening conversation. Another essay on conversation might examine how topics of discussion show a character's mental or psychic preoccupations: The topics of Mr. Woodhouse, for instance, are illuminating, if limited, as are those of Miss Bates. What might favorite topics of conversation show us about character?

3. **Harriet Smith as a character:** What kind of figure is Harriet Smith? How does she change over the course of the novel? What is the significance of these changes?

Harriet Smith is admired by other characters for her innocence and artlessness, but she is inadvertently transformed into a more ambitious individual by Emma's machinations. To discuss this topic you would need to start with its first question, which asks you to consider what kind of figure Harriet is. You might consider, for instance, what she represents to Emma. How is Harriet a kind of blank slate for Emma? If she is simply a project to Emma, what kind of project is she? The remainder of the topic asks you to analyze the behavioral changes that Harriet cycles through and the significance of those changes. What does it mean that Harriet later adopts Emma's philosophies when the younger woman elects to set her sights on Mr. Knightley? You might also consider what it means for the novel's larger themes that Harriet eventually marries the farmer, Mr. Martin, and is folded into a humble class that Emma does not socialize with.

4. **Frank Churchill as a character:** Frank Churchill's deceptions disrupt the community of Highbury in many ways. How is he represented as antithetical to the village's values? Is he ultimately assimilated into the community?

This topic asks you to explore the different ways that Frank Churchill disrupts the Highbury world, a place that relies on truth and transparency. It would be useful to consider disruptions both literal (such as moving around furniture) and symbolic (such as pretending he disapproves of Jane Fairfax, the woman to whom he is secretly engaged). Churchill's many ruses and secrets are good sources of evidence for his deceit, and you might look to his flattery, flirtation, teasing, and love of games. Your essay should identify ways that his deceptions potentially undermine Highbury society. How does his presence negatively affect Emma, her father, or the Westons? Frank Churchill does confess his sins in a letter that appears contrite, but Mr. Knightley, an embodiment of Highbury values, is not impressed by the contents or execution of the letter. Would you say that Frank Churchill is ultimately assimilated into the happy, honest world of Highbury? Can he be forgiven?

5. **Offstage characters:** Emma features a tremendous number of characters that we hear about, but never hear from. Choose a small number of these characters and analyze their significance for the overall novel.

This topic allows you to explore the many minor characters who figure in the novel but are never brought onto the main stage. Mr. Knightley's reported conversations with William Larkin and Robert Martin, for instance, demonstrate Knightley's appreciation of good men, no matter their social class. Mrs. Elton's ramblings on her relatives, the Sucklings, enable us to see how ambitious and materialistic she is. The world of the Sucklings, too, allows us to imagine how unpleasant Jane Fairfax's tenure would be if she were employed as governess to one of their set. Mr. Weston's unburdening of himself about Mrs. Churchill shows that she is an individual whose obsession with socioeconomic class diminishes her humanity. Your essay would need to show what significance your chosen characters contribute to the novel's ideas.

History and Context

Another productive approach to the analysis of *Emma* is through history and context. Even a small amount of historical research into the novel's world will yield great returns in terms of both understanding and opportunities for analysis. Though provincial in its locale, the forces of the larger world noticeably impinge on the community of Highbury. For one example, the sense of national character, of Englishness, in *Emma* is pronounced. Consider the narrator's devotional description of Donwell Abbey's situation: "It was a sweet view—sweet to the eye and the mind. English verdure, English culture, English comfort, seen under a sun bright, without being oppressive" (3: 4). Both the repetition of "English" and the content of the observation—the pleasantness of the scene—tell us that this England is a terrestrial heaven. Mr. Knightley, the owner of Donwell Abbey, also makes many references to Englishness as it relates to behavior, and he takes a swipe at Frank Churchill when he suggests that the younger man's behavior is more French, perhaps, than English. Research into national identity at this time, and possibly English francophobia, would enable you to discuss knowledgeably how this book presents the idea of Englishness. Other approaches to history and context in *Emma* could examine the social issues and pastimes in the novel. You could do research, for instance, on governesses to help put into context why that occupation is so dreaded by Jane Fairfax and those who care for her. Research into the many games played in *Emma* would help you understand and analyze how they further the themes and dramatic situations in the novel.

Sample Topics:

1. **Englishness:** How does this novel characterize what it means to be English?

   Mr. Knightley, Emma, and the narrator all refer to Englishness. *Emma* is highly conscious of its Englishness, but what does that mean? To answer this topic, you would need to both track the novel's discussions of Englishness and research the social climate at the time. A good encyclopedia of English history will discuss English reactions to the Napoleonic Wars, and a history of England will yield notions of English autonomy. *Emma* takes place after the fall of Napoléon (1815), but Francophobia and the belief in English difference remained and, some would argue, continues today. Ultimately, your essay should connect how the sense of being English (or being in England) relates to the novel's larger themes.

2. **The governess trade:** When Emma is appalled that Mrs. Elton would dare to mention Mrs. Weston's having been a governess, we deduce that the position of governess was not a lofty one. Why does being a governess conjure up such dread for the women in this novel?

Governess was one of the few jobs available to educated, middle-class women who were poor. There are a number of indications in the book that being a governess was thought a terrible fate: Jane Fairfax's comparing it to slavery is just one example. Emma proclaims that governesses should earn five times whatever they make. To analyze this topic, you need to research women's history in England to understand the reputation and circumstances of being a governess. Julia Prewitt Brown, for instance, discusses the desperation of many governesses (63). Another approach to considering the governess's lot would be to compare the discussion of it in *Emma* with representations of it in other novels of this approximate period. Written 30 years after *Emma*, Charlotte Brontë's *Jane Eyre* (1847), for instance, represents the challenge of being a governess and also records the dubious reputation of governesses. Your essay should explore not only what being a governess entailed in England at this time, but also how such a job is significant to this novel. How, for instance, does being employed to help another's family break up the community that Mr. Woodhouse so prizes?

3. **Games in the novel:** *Emma* is riddled with word games, board games, and puzzles. How does Austen use these games? What thematic or dramatic purposes are served by these recreations?

An essay on *Emma* and its games would need to research the many games that are mentioned, such as charades, enigmas, riddles, backgammon, and acrostics. A good edition of *Emma* (such as a Norton Critical edition) includes footnotes on these games that will help direct your research. Once you have gained an understanding of the games, you can analyze how the novel uses them. Do some games hurt or exclude people, while other games bring characters together? You might also consider how fond of games certain characters are. Emma asserts that she prefers open, honest communication, yet she is a master of most enigmatic, interpretive games. What does it mean that Frank Churchill is so preoccupied by gaming, punning, and puzzling? You might also think about how the novel is itself a riddle: Doesn't the narrator deliberately withhold information about plot that misleads the reader about what is happening? A more focused approach would be to concentrate on one or two games and track how they connect to the novel's larger themes.

Philosophy and Ideas

Another approach to forming an argument about *Emma* would be to explore the philosophical ideas in the novel. This approach is related to the thematic approach described above in that it tracks an idea in the story. But the result of this kind of essay would demonstrate how you see the story commenting on an idea in its more general form. Emma, an inconsistent philosopher, forms an interesting and complete contrast to Fanny Price, the protagonist of Austen's previous novel, *Mansfield Park*. Where Fanny is nearly paralyzed into inaction by her beliefs, Emma's beliefs yield to her dynamism, impulsiveness, and energy. In fact, Emma sometimes even speaks against her own beliefs, as when in a debate with Mr. Knightley, and "to her great amusement," she realizes that she is arguing a tack that is opposite to "her real opinion" (1: 18). Though Emma seems, according to Mr. Knightley, a creature of "whim and fancy," she is also principled and consequently mortified when she missteps. Identifying and tracking a character's understanding of duty and morality can form the basis of a very worthwhile essay on philosophy and ideas. One of the principles that Emma never shirks from is her duty to her father. She believes, and the novel supports this, that he would not be able to manage without her. So she pledges never to leave him, a pledge that contributes to her conviction that she will never marry. Though Mr. Knightley dismisses Emma's antimarriage philosophy as meaning "nothing," Emma makes very good arguments for why she will avoid marriage. The antimarriage sentiments in this novel are remarkably well argued for a work that is so focused on marriage, and these are well worth building an essay around. An essay on philosophy and ideas could also analyze the application of an idea in the story. The psychological notion of projection is displayed many times in *Emma*. In a novel that contains so much misinformation, characters often resort to projecting their own beliefs onto the events and people around them.

Sample Topics:

1. **Duty:** Mr. Knightley's many corrections of Emma are generally done out of his sense of duty, a belief in the rightness of his conduct. Select one of the characters in the novel and analyze how duty motivates that character's actions.

   Promising characters to discuss in connection with this topic include Jane Fairfax and Emma. Once you select a character, track how duty dictates his or her actions. Emma, for example, shows a remarkable sense of duty to her father, though she criticizes herself when her actions interfere with her sense of duty to other women and with her duty as a woman of means. An essay might analyze how her beliefs and behavior become more aligned over the course of the novel. Another character to discuss in light of this topic is the highly principled Mr. Knightley. Does his behavior or sense of duty change? Jane Fairfax is the most enigmatic character because we do not have much access to her inner thoughts, but her later actions, her remorse, and her words show that she has a very pronounced sense of morality.

2. **Psychological projection:** *Emma* contains many examples of what psychologists call projection, the attribution of one's feelings to other people or things. Mr. Knightley quotes from a poem that speaks to the idea of projection when he wonders, am I "myself creating what I saw" (3: 5)? Where do you see projection in action, and how does this phenomenon function in the novel?

   The psychological concept of projection occurs when we project our feelings onto other objects or other people. A person who perceives a rainy day as matching his sad or happy feelings is projecting. In *Emma* a great deal of projection takes place and the details of these projections are significant both in terms of characterization and action. An essay could focus on how projection is used to comic effect, such as when Mr. Woodhouse refers to the elated newlywed Mrs. Weston as "poor Miss Taylor." Because he laments her loss and cannot imagine anyone choosing to leave Hartfield, Mr. Woodhouse projects his sadness onto her. Projection is also used humorously in Mrs. Elton's soliloquy about strawberry picking at Donwell Abbey. Another focus for an essay on projection could discuss how, in the absence of information, characters formulate theories about events that match their own state of mind. Both Mr. Knightley and Emma do this kind of projection, particularly when attempting to discern what, exactly, is happening with Jane Fairfax or Frank Churchill.

3. **Antimarriage philosophy:** Though Emma does eventually marry, she argues throughout the novel that marriage is not for her. Are her antimarriage sentiments sensible? What do Emma's antimarriage theories reveal about socioeconomic class?

Mr. Knightley is dismissive of Emma's proclaimed refusal ever to marry, but it is difficult to dismiss the good reasons why she sees no personal benefit in marriage. An essay that discusses the antimarriage philosophies in the novel would need to focus on Emma's conversations with Harriet Smith, Mrs. Weston, and Mr. Knightley. Your essay should include a discussion of socioeconomic class relative to this subject. We have examples of what it means to be single and poor, after all, in Miss Bates, as well as the specter of impoverished singleness looming for Jane Fairfax. Your essay would certainly need to examine the reasons why Emma forsakes her long-held philosophy of celibacy. What changes her mind?

Form and Genre

Form and genre provide productive ways of thinking about literature. Form is the shape and structure of a literary work; genre is the kind, or classification, of a literary work. Though technically independent of the content of literature (meaning that romantic love or natural beauty, for instance, are ideas that can be communicated in various forms), form and genre are used deliberately by authors to help further the ideas in and strengthen the dramatic impact of their stories. In the case of *Emma*, the genre is fiction, specifically, a novel; yet even more specifically, it is a comic bildungsroman. These observations may seem too straightforward, but they are good starts for an essay on genre. Essays could examine how Austen's novel is formed and how its effects are created. It is easy to see that *Emma* is an accomplished novel, but trying to understand just what makes it so engrossing is a question that scholars have pondered and one that you yourself could explore in an essay. You might locate a quality of the novel that you find particularly interesting or enjoyable and analyze how that quality works in the novel. In her introduction to *Emma*, Terry Castle discusses the sources of some of the novel's pleasurable effects, such as its organization. Castle points out that one of the most pleasant elements of the story is its structural and dramatic equilibrium (xxi); as is true in most comedies, including Shakespeare's, in the end, all's well. This pleasant equilibrium is evident in *Emma*'s many resolutions. The community is unified and strengthened by the story's events: The many marriages at the end of the novel, in fact, leave none of the principal young characters unmarried; Emma's father, a character dependent on stasis, is incorporated into his daughter's marriage with minimal disruption to his life; the characters from the area remain there; characters who had been crossing class lines are restored to their original sphere.

Another interesting topic on form concerns Austen's narrative style in *Emma*. As was discussed in this chapter's introduction, the narration often adopts the point of view of a character through free indirect speech. We see many examples of this style throughout the novel, including the following, which shows Mr. Woodhouse's dislike of marriage asserted by the narrator: "Matrimony, as the origin of change, was always disagreeable" (1: 1). The narrator here makes what appears to be a general statement about matrimony, the "disagreeable" "origin of change," when in fact it is the philosophy of Mr. Woodhouse himself. An essay on free indirect speech might explore how this particular style of narration allows the reader complete access to some characters, but not others.

Sample Topics:

1. **Resolutions:** The final chapters of *Emma* are distinguished by many resolutions. Discuss the kinds of conflicts that the action of the novel had stirred up and analyze how equilibrium is ultimately reestablished in Highbury.

This topic asks you to analyze the extended falling action that leads to the novel's end. Your essay would need to work somewhat deductively by locating how the ending's events resolve conflicts previously established within the main action of the novel. In other words, your essay would look to the resolutions at the end of the novel in order to identify the earlier conflicts in the novel. One example of this is Harriet Smith's marriage to Robert Martin. Their union resolves the conflicts that had centered on Emma's influence on Harriet, particularly in Emma's gambit to usher Harriet across class lines. While there is a reestablishment of class divisions in the Harriet and Emma plotline, there is—when Mrs. Churchill dies—a relaxing of inappropriate divisions in the Churchill and Weston plotlines. Other examples of resolution are those surrounding Frank Churchill and Jane Fairfax. How does their engagement resolve the conflicts around Jane's future? How does Frank's confession to Mrs. Weston resolve his conflicts among him and the Westons and the larger Highbury community? Your essay should include discussion of the resolution that Emma's marriage to Mr. Knightley represents.

2. **Narrative style:** How does the narrative style, frequently termed free indirect speech, function in this novel?

Preparatory to your analysis, consider how your understanding of Mr. Woodhouse, for example, would be changed had the novel been a more straightforward third-person narration, or had it been a first-person narration from, say, Mr. Knightley's or Emma's point of view. This kind of thinking will prepare you to understand how the narrative style of *Emma* is important to the novel. An essay on this topic needs to show how free indirect speech, as defined in the chapter's introduction, functions in this novel. Your essay should give examples of this style of narration and, in your close readings of those examples, show how the style contributes a particular atmosphere or familiarity with characters. How, for instance, does free indirect speech enable us to see both Emma's flawed thinking and her good impulses? How does this kind of narration help us understand and not judge negatively Mr. Woodhouse's many fears and neuroses? You will want your essay to reach a conclusion about how the narrative style is significant to the novel overall.

Language, Symbols, and Images

Language, symbols, and imagery are some of the creative means by which an author conveys certain feelings or ideas that would, if simply announced, be undermined in terms of their imaginative and evocative power. All writers, and those of imaginative fiction especially, use language deliberately, they choose words based on their connotative meanings. In Jane Austen's work, language is especially meaningful. She uses the words and even the patterns of language—such as speaking styles—to convey information about situations and characters. Character development, as previously discussed in the section on character, is partly constructed by what a character says. This is especially true for Austen's characters. Communication style—either in conversation or letter—reveals character. Frank Churchill's letters are closely read and remarked on by seemingly all the principal characters of the novel, and their reactions to his style show that language is considered an embodiment of the person himself. Mr. Knightley, never a fan of Frank Churchill, comments on a letter as he reads it: "Humph!—a fine complimentary opening:—But it is his way" (3: 15). Emma is as grudging in her praise of Mr. Martin's letter to Harriet, though she concedes that it shows the feelings of a sensible man. There are abundant examples of the communication style of Miss Bates because she is, as she says of herself, a "talker" (3: 5). Her optimism and humility are evident in her speeches, which have no overarching organization. The punctuation of her speeches is principally dashes, which indicate associative, not hierarchical, thought processes. An essay could insightfully explore the connections of language and character in *Emma*. How does language reveal character? What style of language does the narrator endorse or criticize? How, for instance, do we understand the narrator's disapproval of Mrs. Elton's style of communication?

Jane Austen does not generally use a great deal of overt imagery in her writing: Similes, metaphors, and outright symbols are few. However, in *Emma* many of the characters themselves use figurative language, and observing the particular language they use yields significant insights. You will notice, for instance, that characters speak of others as belonging in spheres, ranks, and levels or remark that some individuals are unequal or incongruous. This motif, or repeated imagery, relates to hierarchy. An essay could also analyze how characters use this kind of imagery to describe class. Symbols, usually used in conjunction with imagery, are objects, either animate or inanimate, that writers also use to convey ideas. In *Emma*, you might focus an essay on the way that children or food perform symbolic meaning for characters. The best essays on symbolism examine imagery and analyze it in relation to a novel's larger ideas. When you are asked to discuss symbolism, you are being asked to discuss what something signifies in light of the entire work.

Sample Topics:

1. **Style of expression:** The speaking and writing styles in *Emma* are distinctive to each character. Choose two or more characters and assess what their language and communication styles reveal about them. What style of communication does the narrator appear to endorse?

   This topic, related to characterization, asks you to analyze styles of expression. An essay on this topic would focus on two or more characters and analyze how their communication style is distinctive from others. You might track the logic of Mr. Woodhouse, the vivaciousness of Harriet Smith, or the ramblings of Miss Bates. How is each of these characters' speaking style distinctive? Mr. Knightley's honesty and good sense, for instance, are echoed in his incisive and straightforward speaking style. Another character well worth analysis is Mrs. Elton, who speaks in clichés, is an inveterate name-dropper, and tends to refer to people by their informal names, which shows her presumptuousness. Basing your conclusion on your insights into the narrator's opinions, what language style and character do you think the novel endorses?

2. **Hierarchical imagery:** The characters in this novel use hierarchical, even mathematical, imagery in their dialogue. Where do you see this imagery and what does it signify?

This topic prompts you to look for a specific variety of imagery and to analyze its use in the novel. Your essay should include instances of this imagery; your close readings of these examples will provide you with the substance of your analysis. One example of mathematical imagery is seen when the ambitious Mr. Elton asserts why Harriet Smith's social class makes her an inappropriate mate for him: "Every body [*sic*] has their *level*: but as for myself, I am not, I think, quite so much at a *loss*. I need not so totally despair of an *equal* alliance, as to be addressing myself to Miss Smith!" (1: 15; italics added). You might find that the characters who most rely on mathematical imagery, such as Mr. Elton, are the most conscious of class differences. Why do you think these characters use euphemisms of hierarchy?

3. **Children:** How do children function as symbols in this novel? What do children symbolize?

To answer this topic properly, you will need to reach conclusions about the novel's main themes and values. Then you will be able to analyze how children function as symbols here. Some main themes in the novel include community, love, family, and fidelity. How might children be symbolically meaningful in light of one or more of these themes? What might be significant about Mrs. Weston's having a child? Another approach to this topic would be to consider the symbolism of how characters treat children. To that end, what is significant about Mr. Knightley's ease with his nieces and nephews?

4. **Food:** Mr. Woodhouse is fixated on food: its preparation, its quantity, its taste, its being offered to guests as a gesture of hospitality. What does food symbolize for Mr. Woodhouse?

This topic directs you to focus on one symbol as it functions for one character. It would allow you to explore the often comical philosophies that Mr. Woodhouse espouses about gruel, boiling meat, and sweets, such as cake, that he considers pure poison. Considering his thoughts and speeches on food, what do you think food represents to him? Why does he often attempt to prevent others from eating? Why does he refuse to believe that the children of his cherished apothecary, Mr. Perry, were seen eating cake? Your analysis should include discussions of Mr. Woodhouse's character to explore insightfully what food means to him.

Comparison and Contrast

Comparing components of a novel to explain and analyze the similarities or differences among them is a useful approach to writing an essay. Remember to avoid simply creating a list of similarities or differences; instead, you must comment on your observations. To begin a comparison/contrast essay, you might compare characters with each other: How does Mrs. Elton compare with Emma Woodhouse? With Mrs. Cole? How does Emma compare with Jane Fairfax? You could also compare characters (or other elements of the story such as themes or events) across different Austen novels. For example, how do socially ambitious characters compare with one another in *Sense and Sensibility* and *Emma*? How is merit depicted differently in *Emma* and *Mansfield Park*? The challenge of this kind of essay is to decide what the similarities or differences you identify might mean. These questions make essays compelling. They will have different answers for each writer.

Sample Topics:

1. **Comparing father-daughter relationships:** Both *Pride and Prejudice* and *Emma* feature close relationships between the heroine and her father. Compare these relationships and reach a conclusion about the significance of these relationships.

This topic asks you to assess the father-daughter relationships in two novels and to reach a conclusion about their significance. One approach could observe how the fathers influence their daughters. Another approach might show how the daughters act as parents to their fathers. You might also attempt to reach a conclusion about why Austen arranged these relationships as she did. Why, do you think, did she design these particular characters to have such strong father-daughter relationships instead of mother-daughter relationships?

2. **Comparing Emma and Mrs. Elton:** Though Emma thoroughly dislikes Mrs. Elton, we cannot help noticing that they share a number of similarities. In what ways are they alike? What is the significance of their similarities? Does Emma notice any reflection of herself in Mrs. Elton, a recognition that causes a change in her behavior?

This topic asks you to compare two characters and to identify the ways in which a sympathetic and an unsympathetic character overlap in terms of their behavior and beliefs. The principal similarity between the two characters is in their deciding to "better" a younger woman of lesser fortune: in Emma's case, this is Harriet Smith; in Mrs. Elton's case, Jane Fairfax. You might approach this topic by focusing solely on these projects. What do they tell us about Emma's and Mrs. Elton's ambitions and egos? Another approach might be to look only at the shared beliefs of Emma and Mrs. Elton. Does one's snobbery seem worse than the other's, or just less concealed? Finally, consider the significance of their similarities for Emma's character development. Does she recognize how closely she resembles her detested doppelgänger, and does this change her behavior?

Bibliography and Online Resources for *Emma*

Castle, Terry. Introduction. *Emma*. By Jane Austen. New York: Oxford UP, 1995. vii–xxviii.

Duckworth, Alistair M. "Games as a Device in Austen's Novels." *Readings on Jane Austen.* Ed. Clarice Swisher. San Diego: Greenhaven Press, 1997. 93–102.

Gill, Richard, and Susan Gregory. *"Emma." Mastering the Novels of Jane Austen.* New York: Palgrave Macmillan, 2003. 243–305.

Holm, Catherine Dybiec. "Critical Essay on *Emma." Novels for Students* 21. Thomson Gale, 2005. Electronic. Literature Resource Center. Berkeley, CA: Berkeley Public Library, 24 Aug. 2007.

Lane, Maggie. *Jane Austen's World.* London: Carlton Books, 1996.

Marsh, Nicholas. *Jane Austen: The Novels.* New York: St. Martin's Press, 1998.

McMaster, Juliet. "Class." *The Cambridge Companion to Jane Austen.* Eds. Edward Copeland and Juliet McMaster. Cambridge: Cambrige UP, 2006. 115–30.

Polhemus, Robert M. *Comic Faith: The Great Tradition from Austen to Joyce.* Chicago: University of Chicago Press, 1980.

Trilling, Lionel. Introduction. *Emma.* By Jane Austen. Cambridge, MA: Riverside Press, 1957. v–xxiv.

PERSUASION

*P*ERSUASION (1817) begins not with attention to the protagonist, Anne Elliot, but to her flawed family. Anne's father, Sir Walter Elliot, spends his idle hours perusing the only book he reads, the Baronetage, which records the histories of England's aristocratic families. The section that describes his own family gives him the most satisfaction, and his "interest" in it "never failed" (1: 1). Sir Walter's gazing into the Baronetage at his own name parallels his frequent staring into mirrors, both acts being exercises in self-regard. Sir Walter is, as the narrator informs us, "the constant object of his warmest respect and devotion." Anne's older sister Elizabeth, nervously watching the rapid approach of her 30th birthday and fretting about its expected effect on her marriage prospects, shares her father's concern for self and disregard for her sister. Anne is of negligible presence and importance; according to her solipsistic father and older sister—sounding just like the villains of "Cinderella"—Anne is "only Anne."

Persuasion resembles "Cinderella" in the characterization of its vain, thoughtless family villains and also in some of its themes. Like Cinderella, Anne Elliot was once loved and valued by a mother, now dead, who was kind and had "softened, or concealed" her husband's failings. Unlike Cinderella, Anne Elliot suffers a second serious loss. Eight years before the novel begins, when Anne was "a very pretty girl," she fell in love with a worthy naval officer of modest means, Captain Frederick Wentworth. Reluctantly persuaded by her mother's best friend, Lady Russell (an unhelpful fairy godmother figure) that the marriage would be inappropriate, Anne gives up the engagement; Captain Wentworth, infuriated by the rejection, goes off to the high seas to fight France, make his fortune, and forget Anne Elliot. Now, all these years after that second loss, the novel begins. Anne still loves Captain Wentworth, and her family offers only noxious, if familiar, distractions. Austen experiments with the form of the Cinderella story by describing what happens when "happily ever after" does not follow the hero and heroine's recognition of true love, but instead is suspended until their wisdom, experience, and good fortune bring them together again.

Perusasion is considered by many critics to mark a turning point in Austen's writing. The much delayed love story is just one shift in Austen's work, which previously featured stories of young love. An essay on this novel might focus on how its form shows changes relative to Austen's earlier works. To that end, you might examine how the events in the novel are organized: Analyzing the effect of the novel's opening focus on unsympathetic characters might be one way to do this. Before reviewing the themes, form, and other larger literary elements of *Persuasion*, it is necessary to consider the particulars of Austen's language. This section gives an example of close reading, a skill that, once acquired, will help you generate analysis and find the evidence you need for essay writing.

A close reading of any work of literature requires concentration on the significances of passages. You locate significances by paying particular attention to word choice, ideas mentioned by characters, and narrative opinion. Close readings of passages yield material on multiple subjects. The following passage, where Anne ruminates on the advantages of young love and marriage, speaks to characterization, narrative style, philosophy, and theme:

> How eloquent could Anne Elliot have been,—how eloquent, at least, were her wishes on the side of early warm attachment, and a cheerful confidence in futurity, against that over-anxious caution which seems to insult exertion and distrust Providence!—She had been forced into prudence in her youth, she learned romance as she grew older—the natural sequel of an unnatural beginning. (1: 4)

The most traditional, reliable, and often fruitful method of close reading is found in tracking the diction in this or any other passage. A close reading of the diction here immediately relays an understanding of this passage. Anne's enthusiasm for young love is shown in the words used to describe it positively: *warm, cheerful, confidence*. The words associated with forestalling love in favor of ruthless "caution" are, by comparison, negative: *over-anxious, insult, exertion, distrust, forced, unnatural*.

This passage suggests how Anne's sacrificing of her first love changed her. The narrator is simultaneously presenting Anne's point of view and commenting on her experience. We are alerted to the passion of Anne's personal opinions in the passage's use of exclamation marks and dashes, but we also hear the narrator's independent assertion about the effects of prudence in youth causing romance in maturity ("the natural sequel to an unnatural beginning"). The narrator's comment here gives us information on how Anne's background has affected her outlook: That because of her experience of giving up Captain Wentworth, she is now a believer in "early warm attachment" and "romance."

This passage also describes Anne's philosophical understanding of life when it describes her feelings about Providence; more commonly called Divine Providence, it is a belief that God determines fate. The "over-anxious caution" impeding young love here alludes to Lady Russell's caution on Anne's behalf. Such caution is characterized as blasphemous and unnatural, since it "distrust[s] Providence." This implicitly refers to the keenly felt loss of Captain Wentworth, but, moreover, points us to the larger themes of fate and chance, two ideas prominently displayed in a novel so conscious of life's vicissitudes. It is best, in Anne's mind, to have a "cheerful confidence in futurity"; in other words, since fate is not ours to determine, the best philosophy is to embrace what already exists and have "confidence in" the future.

While reading closely, you want to think about what interests you. Those topics that most engage you will be those on which you will write a strong analysis. In this quoted passage, you might find that you are most drawn to the philosophical ideas. In this case, an analysis of fortune, chance, and providence would make for an excellent essay on *Persuasion*. Another worthwhile topic could be love and romance. How might punctuation, sentence structure, or syntax convey the rushes of passion that course through this novel? No matter what analytical approach you eventually take to the novel, a slow and careful reading of *Persuasion*'s language will enable you to recognize its patterns, issues, and ideas. Reading slowly and taking notes will make for a rich understanding of the novel, while also enabling you to gather the evidence you need to write a strong essay.

TOPICS AND STRATEGIES

This section discusses possible topics for essays on *Persuasion* and general approaches to those topics. The material below will guide your own approach to an essay on *Persuasion,* but it is not an exhaustive master key. Use this material to generate your own analysis. Every topic discussed here could encompass a variety of good papers.

Persuasion deals with many themes—ideas or concepts that organize and underscore the importance of the events in the novel. The section above briefly examined some of these: loss, vanity, fate, and love. The novel contains many more ideas, including those related to romance, literature, the gentry, home, isolation, constancy, time, and, of course, the eponymous theme of persuasion. Writers analyzing the novel often begin by identifying a central theme and then determine—through an essay—what the story is saying about that theme. You identify themes by noticing the ideas, symbols, or even words that repeat in the story.

Literature is a prominent theme in *Persuasion,* a fact attested to by its many references to prose, poetry, and history. Anne Elliot is certainly Austen's most literary heroine. Tracking her ideas about literature could form the basis of an interesting essay on the role that literature plays in the novel. For Anne's character, literature is both a means of understanding and a source of psychic comfort. Anne distracts herself with lines of poetry during the walk where she sees her beloved Captain Wentworth paying attention to Louisa Musgrove. The poetry Anne thinks of matches her feelings of missed opportunity and loss: "The sweet scenes of autumn were for a while put by—unless some tender sonnet, fraught with the apt analogy of the declining year, with declining happiness, and the images of youth and hope, and spring, all gone together, blessed her memory" (1: 10). This passage encapsulates the autumnal feeling of much of the novel where Anne's mental focus is on the past, on how her life might have been different had she not refused Captain Wentworth eight years ago. Here, autumn is literally part of the setting, but it is also the melancholy season that speaks to her retrospective mind: "the declining year, with declining happiness," the time after "youth and hope, and spring" is gone, the tawny declension of her life. Observing the vital Captain Wentworth with the vivacious Louisa Musgrove, Anne, diminished and isolated, retreats to the comfort offered by "tender sonnets."

In this kind of literary relief, however, Anne recognizes a risk. It is on this very topic, after all, that she counsels the mourning Captain James Benwick that, because of his passionate nature, he should take care to prevent wholesale emotional abandon by rationing his poetry consumption: "the strong feelings which alone could estimate it truly, were the very feelings which ought to taste it but sparingly" (1: 12). Though she recognizes her own weakness for poignant poetry, to Captain Benwick she "ventured to recommend a larger allowance of prose in his daily study; and on being requested to particularize, mentioned such works of our best moralists, such collections of the finest letters, such memoirs of characters of worth and suffering . . . as calculated to rouse and fortify the mind by the highest precepts, and the strongest examples of moral and religious endurance" (1: 11). This or any of the many discussions of literature in *Persuasion* could form the basis for an essay. You might consider how the characters look to literature to understand their world, or alternately, how literature bolsters or debilitates certain individuals. Other themes could be approached in similar ways: You could approach the theme of persuasion by assessing whether the events in the novel suggest that the act of being persuaded is always a sign of personal weakness, as Captain Wentworth believes. Another approach to an essay on theme could analyze what the novel seems to be saying are the qualities needed to weather loss and life's other vicissitudes properly. Thematic approaches also blend with the philosophical approaches described below.

Sample Topics:

1. **Literature:** *Persuasion* features Austen's most literary heroine, and the novel contains discussions of both poetry and prose. What, according to this novel, is the function of literature for individuals and society?

   To address this topic, begin by identifying where the novel shows characters either reading or debating about literary topics. Because there are so many scenes in which literature or reading is central, you should first assess how these scenes are significant and then decide in what direction you want to take your analysis. One approach might be to discuss how literature serves as a kind of companion for certain characters (as discussed in the introduction to this section). Another approach might be to discuss how literature is represented as playing a social role: It is shown, for example, to be a clearinghouse of social history from which individuals extract precedent and fact. There is an example of this at the end of the novel, when Anne and Captain Harville debate historical representations of women's constancy. Specifically, Anne takes exception to literary depictions of women, since "Men have had every advantage of us in telling their own story. . . . the pen has been in their hands." How is Anne's rebuttal to Captain Harville a commentary on the larger role of literature in society? Whichever approach you take, you should reach a conclusion about how literature is significant to the ideas in this novel, or to the characters more generally.

2. **Loss:** Anne Elliot, Captain Wentworth, Captain Benwick, and Mrs. Smith all experience the loss of a loved one at the hands of death or other forces. What, according to this novel, is the best way to weather such tragedies? Is loss a different proposition for men than for women?

To address this topic, examine closely both how characters cope with loss and how they discuss it. Anne Elliot's injunctions on fortitude to the suffering Captain Benwick is one area that yields useful material on how the novel presents ways of coping with tragedy. Mrs. Smith, Anne, and Captain Wentworth all seem to rise naturally to the challenges of loss. From your assessments of their particular approaches to dealing with loss, develop a thesis about how to weather loss and, perhaps, more general challenges in life. An ambitious essay might also consider how social expectations affect the different coping strategies available to women and to men. Consider, for instance, the contrasting cases of Anne and Captain Wentworth: While he distracts himself from his heartbreak by swashbuckling for the Royal Navy, her role in society requires that she retreat to a quiet, domestic life.

3. **Persuasion:** Yielding to persuasion is a proposition on which Anne and Captain Wentworth disagree. What do the events in the novel tell us about the force of persuasion?

An essay on this topic might start by viewing closely those scenes in which persuasion is discussed. For example, there are two extended sections in which Anne thinks about the advantages and disadvantages of persuasion. In one section, she reflects on Lady Russell's convincing her not to marry Captain Wentworth; in another section, she evaluates the causes of Louisa Musgrove's fall from the Cobb at Lyme. In the second instance, Louisa, a character who has prided herself on her unyielding determination, suffers a grievous injury because of her refusal to be persuaded. When Captain Wentworth tells Louisa that the jump she is attempting is too dangerous, she peremptorily refuses to be convinced, and in so doing invokes two traits that point to her stubborness: "I am *determined*. I *will*" (1: 12; italics added). To discuss this topic, your essay would need to reach a conclusion about how persuasion is ultimately presented in this book. Does the novel suggest that there are certain times when one should yield to persuasion, and times when one should ignore advice? Explain your response.

4. **Social climbing:** Social ranks in this novel are in flux, and the novel seems to approve of some examples of social ascendancy. Analyze the novel's views on warranted and unwarranted social climbing.

An essay on this topic would focus on examples of social climbing, a phrase that often has negative connotations, but in *Persuasion* is not always such a bad thing. One approach could draw comparisons among the examples provided by Mrs. Clay, Colonel Wallis, and Mr. Elliot and those of the Crofts, Charles Hayter, and Captains Wentworth and Benwick. Pay attention to the narrator's opinions about who merits social ascendancy and why. An ambitious essay might also consider Anne Elliot, a daughter of the gentry, and how her social rank changes in the novel. That she all but effectively relinquishes ties to the gentry suggests that worthy characters, such as Anne, might well choose to dispense altogether with the old social hierarchy.

Character

Because so much of the novel's events are based on the conduct of characters, examining character is a worthwhile means by which to analyze *Persuasion*. Essays can focus on questions of character development (such as how Austen distinguishes Captain Wentworth from Charles Hayter by their respective conduct during Anne's childcare challenges); means of characterization (such as the way the reader understands Lady Russell's preoccupation with appearances by her gravitating to the attractive but duplicitous Mr. Elliot); or interpretations of changes in a character as the novel proceeds (such as in the case of Anne Elliot, whose initially retiring manner becomes significantly more active and outspoken).

To write an essay on character, assess the novel by questioning how readers come to know various characters. How, for instance, does Austen distinguish a character's behavior? The Musgroves' informality and warmth is demonstrated by their inviting others to their boisterous family get-togethers and their disinterest in ambitious marriages for their daughters. That Captain Wentworth's spirited nature is sometimes also rash is indicated by his often rushing to and from places: to sea, to a grieving friend, away from Lyme, to Bath. Mary Elliot Musgrove's immature solipsism is shown by her belief in her persecution, as well as her general peevishness. Captain Harville's dedication to his family and his industriousness are demonstrated by the many improvements he makes to his small home in Lyme. Mrs. Clay's fawning attentions to Elizabeth and Sir Walter suggest that she has ambitions and is seeking social advancement through marriage to Sir Walter. Mr. Elliot's own ambition, to block Mrs. Clay's efforts to marry Sir Walter and secure Kellynch Hall with an heir, is revealed not by his conduct (though we have our suspicions), but by the revelations made about him by Mrs. Smith.

To an extent, we are instructed what to expect from characters, and if you note the narrator's editorial comments about individuals, you will understand what the characters signify in the novel. When introducing Sir Walter, for instance, the narrator decisively asserts that "[v]anity was the beginning and the end of [his] character; vanity of person and of situation" (1: 1). Sir Walter's vanity, then, explains both his conduct and his character. His fixation on appearance and beauty suggests that he has lost all but the most surface understanding of an exalted position in society. If a portrait of the gentry, Sir Walter certainly makes it look ridiculous, but if the portrait of nobility is embodied in Lady Dalrymple and her daughter, the depiction is even more harsh: "[T]hey were nothing" (2: 4). With *Persuasion* Austen launches criticism aimed at the English status quo; single representatives of the classes, therefore, have broader significance. Whether considering characters individually or as symptoms of their sphere, be sure to look closely for distinguishing traits of language, action, or interactions with other characters. Tracking how characters behave with one another helps the reader not only understand how characters are created, but also assess what characters signify and represent for the story overall.

Sample Topics:

1. **Anne's transformation:** Does Anne Elliot change as a character during the novel, or does she just become more noticed by the world around her?

   Though the narrator's attention is squarely on Anne Elliot throughout the novel, it is remarkable how much more central to the action Anne is in the book's second half. While in the novel's beginning we are frequently reminded that Anne is considered inconsequential by many, the second half of the novel shows that she is considered essential to both action and individuals. To tackle this topic you should establish first how Anne's marginalization is evident: Where is she ignored, unheard, disregarded? Then you will want to analyze those sections that show how powerful she has become. The scene at the Cobb, for instance, demonstrates how all individuals look to the steady and capable Anne for guidance. Many other scenes show Anne's gaining power that you will want to read closely for evidence. Ultimately, you want to theorize a response to the question posed about Anne's transformation. Does Anne change, or those around her?

2. **Captain Wentworth as a character:** That Captain Wentworth is an admirable character is made clear by his many good deeds to his friends and—we are led to believe—the nation in its defense against France. What does he have to learn about himself before he is ready to acknowledge his love for Anne and—most important—deserve her love?

To write such an essay, you first need to find evidence to support the topic's assertion that Captain Wentworth is a worthy character, examples of which will be found in reports of his kindness from his friends. The next step would be to analyze in what ways he lacks insight into himself. In what understanding is he deficient? It is telling that, when discussing his ideal mate, he describes Anne's qualities without seeming to realize he is doing so. One approach to this topic would be to work backward from the realizations he has at the end of the novel. Another approach might be to discuss how Captain Wentworth's character—so well suited to wartime—has to adjust to peacetime.

3. **Character development in general:** How does the novel present character to the reader? What techniques does it use? Are characters transparent or somewhat veiled?

A paper on this topic would look at how Austen gives insight into character. A possible approach would be to study a pair of characters or set of techniques and show what effects they have. For instance, a paper could examine how activities, such as walking, reveal character. Sir Walter's obsession with male and female beauty is such that he strolls the streets of Bath counting handsome faces. Though he is generally disappointed by what he sees, he reveals his own desire to be counted a handsome face by commenting on how often he believes he is looked at. Walking in Bath for Anne and Lady Russell is also instructive for discussions on characterization: Lady Russell is invigorated by the bustle and mercantile splendor of Bath, while Anne is invigorated only when she sees a loved one on the street. Another essay might explore how character development is established in group situations. To that end, you might explore how characterization crystallizes in the scene on the Cobb at Lyme, or on the walk near Uppercross.

4. **Mrs. Smith as a character:** What role does Mrs. Smith play in *Persuasion*? How does she help us understand Anne? How does Mrs. Smith's life experience illuminate the themes of the novel?

Mrs. Smith, Anne's former school friend, allows us access to Bath's wider social world, one that includes the lower classes. An essay on Mrs. Smith could explore not only her character, but also the characters that we become acquainted with because of her, such as her landlady and her nurse. If Sir Walter embodies the gentry's anemic soul, what are we to deduce about the lower classes by looking at the figures connected to Anne's former school friend? The question about Mrs. Smith's role in Anne's life could be explored by considering either what Anne learns from Mrs. Smith's example or how the information from Mrs. Smith's world helps Anne better understand her own. The last question could encompass an entire essay. An essay could explore how Mrs. Smith's life experience helps illuminate themes, such as loss, fortune, and luck. How is it significant that Mrs. Smith's fortune is recouped by Captain Wentworth?

History and Context

Another worthwhile approach to the analysis of *Persuasion* is through history and context. Even a small amount of research into the historical context out of which Austen wrote this novel will offer significant returns in both understanding and opportunities for literary analysis. Austen's novels are informed by the events of their era—the French Revolution, the Napoleonic Wars, and the tremendous shifts in social philosophy (from neoclassicism to romanticism) that resonated with, inspired, and sometimes culminated in these popular and military events. Studying any of these contexts in conjunction with *Persuasion* will help you locate connections and points of comparison that can form the basis of a strong essay.

One approach to an essay on history and context could be to focus on how the end of the Napoleonic Wars contributes to both the atmosphere and the dramatic action of this novel. The postwar atmosphere in *Persuasion* shows an England infused with new energy. One example of this is found in Captain Wentworth, who insists to his sister that he has returned to England ready to marry the first woman that catches his eye. The economic benefits of the end of the war are mentioned by Sir Walter's business adviser, Mr. Shepherd: "This peace will be turning all our rich Navy Officers ashore. . . . Many a noble fortune has been made during the war" (1: 3). In this case, Mr. Shepherd is describing how Sir Walter might be in a good position to secure a wealthy tenant for Kellynch Hall. By arranging for a military man's tenancy of an estate, Mr. Shepherd is, probably unknowingly, facilitating a secondary change: that of the entrance of wealthy military men into the upper ranks of society. One of Sir Walter's objections to the navy is that it creates upheaval in the social hierarchy, that it is a means of "bringing persons of obscure birth into undue distinction" (1: 3). An essay might examine accounts of English naval officers to study how the wars did exactly what Sir Walter feared.

More interesting areas for research on history and context could be those of fashion and resorts, two subjects related to the infamously profligate Prince Regent. Bath, a spa town during Roman times, was fashionable again at the end of the 18th century, but was losing its elegant edge during Austen's lifetime, in part because the Prince Regent moved his court to Brighton. An essay on resort towns in England might focus on how Bath is characterized in this novel, or how the denizens of such fashionable places are represented. With this last topic or any other historical topic, you would need to do research to consider knowledgeably what *Persuasion* is demonstrating about the world it describes.

Sample Topics:

1. **The Royal Navy:** The dramatic action of *Persuasion* is largely oriented around the navy and the presence of naval officers back

from their triumphs against the French. What kind of commentary does the novel make about the Royal Navy?

The naval contexts of this novel are extensive, and there are numerous opportunities for analysis. A general topic might explore the practices of the navy at this time. An encyclopedia entry about the Royal Navy will give information to help you write an essay about how fortunes, such as those of the Crofts or Captain Wentworth, were made. Another topic might explore how not just material, but also social fortunes were made. Such an approach would enable you to discuss how the upper echelons of the British class system were breached by individuals such as the legendary Lord Horatio Nelson, whose spectacular wartime accomplishments at sea brought him fortune, fame, and aristocratic titles, in spite of his humble birth. Studying the experiences of more ordinary sailors would also be interesting in light of *Persuasion.* For what kinds of individuals was the navy a suitable employment? What might the career of an ordinary man look like? How did naval families manage in wartime? Whatever approach you take to this topic, you should reach a conclusion about what Austen's novel is ultimately saying about the navy and its role in society. Why is one of the novel's final comments, then, a reference to the navy?

2. **Veterans:** How are those sailors whose fortunes were not made by the war characterized in this novel? What are we to make of Captain Harville and his impoverished living conditions? What is *Persuasion* suggesting about such men and their situations?

To answer this topic, your essay should analyze the depictions of impoverished veterans, such as Captain Harville. He is a sympathetic character because he is amiable, domestic, and deserving. How have his experiences changed his life and that of his family? Captain Wentworth talks about Harville and other naval officers he has known as men who deserve more from their country than they received. Does *Persuasion* suggest that England has not treated these men fairly? Is Austen challenging her country to do better by them? Further evidence for their merit can be found by examining Anne's patriotic meditations on the navy's contributions to England.

3. **Fashion:** Once in Bath, Sir Walter's already considerable obsession with beauty and fashion reaches epic proportions. Why does a resort town like Bath bring out Sir Walter's worst variety of shallow conceit? How do historical dandies help us better understand the social commentary that Austen's novel makes?

Sir Walter's vanity, particularly in the sections of *Persuasion* set in Bath, remind many historians of the Regency era's vogue for excessive fashion, resorts, and the decadence associated with the Prince Regent (later, King George IV). An important figure in the Prince Regent's life, Beau Brummell, was famous for his influence on fashion and his fixation on appearance. In these aspects he resembles Sir Walter. An essay on this topic could look to either the Regency era's interest in fashionable resort towns (such as Bath or Brighton) or dandyism. Should you choose the latter topic, there are a number of readily available books on Beau Brummell and the Prince Regent. Materials on the Prince Regent will also give you information on Brighton, the seaside town that he helped popularize. Research on the habits of these prominent figures will help you reach conclusions about what kind of social or political commentary Austen was registering by making Sir Walter such a dandy. It might be useful to consider how the fashionable types in this novel are set up as contrasts to the less fashionable navy men.

Philosophy and Ideas

Another approach to forming an argument about *Persuasion* is to explore the philosophical ideas in the novel. This approach is related to the thematic approach described above in that it follows an idea in the story, but the result of this kind of essay would demonstrate how you see the novel commenting on an idea in its more general form. Because of her experience and nature, Anne is a philosophical character. She reflects a great deal on what she sees, knows, and deduces from circumstances. Many of

her meditations are internal—since she has no one in whom to confide
or discuss her ideas—but she proves a good listener to herself. The mental process by which she understands Captain Wentworth's continued
affection for her is illustrative of her logical turn of mind. After a conversation with him at the concert, she reasons:

> His choice of subjects, his expressions, and still more his manner and look,
> had been such as she could see in only one light . . .—sentences begun
> which he could not finish—his half averted eyes, and more than half
> expressive glance,—all, all declared that he had a heart returning to her at
> least; that anger, resentment, avoidance, were no more; and that they were
> succeeded, not merely by friendship and regard, but by the tenderness of
> the past; yes, some share of the tenderness of the past. She could not con-
> template the change as implying less.—He must love her. (2: 8)

Here Anne retrospectively gathers evidence—topical, physical, emotional—and reaches a conclusion that is sensible and exhilarating: "He
must love her." That he loves her is a fact Anne arrives at only after reflection and consideration. Her need for introspection is repeated many
times, such as when, after hearing the story of Mr. Elliot's reprehensible
treatment of Mrs. Smith, Anne "went home to think over all that she had
heard" (2: 10). Anne is so thoughtful and introspective a character that a
study of any of her philosophical observations—on constancy, pride, her
father's character, the moral mandate of counsel—will furnish the mate
rial for a good essay on ideas in the novel.

The application of Anne's philosophy does change; it becomes less
introspective and more articulated as the novel reaches its conclusion.
The philosophical debate that she and Captain Harville enter into is one
place where Anne's ideas about love, history, and gender are clearly and
insightfully expressed. Her ideas about love and gender are noteworthy,
for they simultaneously testify to difference and parity: "I believe you
[men] capable of every thing great and good in your married lives. . . .
All the privilege I claim for my own sex (it is not a very enviable one, you
need not covet it) is that of loving longest, when existence or when hope
is gone" (2: 11). Captain Harville argues that the love of a man is a more
fixed emotion, but Anne makes a very good case for women who "lov[e]
longest . . . when hope is gone." The representations of gender in the more

general sense are worth exploring in this novel. Other ideas also worth investigating are related to the novel's wartime background. There is an implicit understanding that fortune and luck are variables that sailors and their dependents must contend with. Another idea worth exploring is the psychological notion of narcissism. In Sir Walter, we have a classic case study.

Sample Topics:

1. **Gender:** Anne is highly aware of the way that gender affects individual lives. What is her philosophy on gender? How might her philosophy affect her conduct after she marries Captain Wentworth?

As the introduction to this section discusses, Anne is philosophically minded, and some aspects of life that she observes are how men and women behave and how they are allowed to behave. Her discussions with Captain Harville show that while Anne is aware of how the experiences of men and women are different, she also recognizes the heroism of both. To write an essay on this topic, you will want to read closely the debate between Anne and Captain Harville, as well as track her reflections on how gender matters elsewhere. Her reflections on Captain Benwick's situation as a young man who has suffered a loss are illuminating. Also informative are Anne's observations of Admiral and Mrs. Croft, a couple who enjoy complementary gender parity. Do the Crofts represent an ideal couple that Anne would like to emulate? Does their childlessness seem attractive to Anne or not? Once you decide what Anne's overall philosophy is about gender roles, you can theorize about how she might practice her beliefs in her married life.

2. **Providence, justice, or luck?:** Characters in *Persuasion* have dramatic experiences: fatal storms at sea are narrowly averted; illness snatches away a loved one; two dissimilar individuals are thrown together into a circumstance from which a lifetime union follows. To what are we to ascribe these events: to divine providence, to cosmic justice, or to just dumb luck?

This topic asks you to reach a conclusion about what motivating forces are at work in the novel. To decide this, you would need to locate the stories of dramatic good fortune or reversals of fortune, and read closely how the relevant character interprets its cause. One example is after the engagement of Anne to Captain Wentworth, when he declares: "'I have been used to the gratification of believing myself to earn every blessing that I enjoyed. I have valued myself on honourable toils and just rewards. Like other great men under reverses,' he added with a smile, 'I must endeavor to subdue my mind to my fortune. I must learn to brook being happier than I deserve'" (2: 11). In this case, Captain Wentworth muses that luck is the determining factor, far outstripping the effects of his merit, or "just rewards." Anne herself ruminates on luck and circumstances; after being flattered by Mr. Elliot, for example, she wonders what her feelings for Mr. Elliot might have been "had there been no Captain Wentworth" (2: 9).

3. **Carpe diem:** How does this novel showcase the "seize the day" philosophy of carpe diem?

With a protracted war in the recent past, the focus on war in *Persuasion* is palpable. There are constant reminders that life can change in an instant. The transience of happiness is understood implicitly by Anne, whose own happiness eight years earlier evaporated, seemingly forever, because of the bad advice of a trusted friend. Where do we see her carpe diem philosophy at work? Admiral Croft expresses his own belief in seizing the day when he tells Anne what naval marriages customarily look like: "We sailors, Miss Elliot, cannot afford to make long courtships in time of war" (1: 10). What other examples are there of the sense of urgency implicit in a carpe diem philosophy? Is it this sense of urgency that makes love and kindness that much sweeter in the novel?

4. **Narcissism:** How is Sir Walter's narcissism demonstrated to be a debilitating character flaw? Consider the ways in which his

pathological self-regard shows itself and in what ways it diminishes his humanity.

Sir Walter's self-regard is the motivating force in his character. As the narrator tells us, "[V]anity was the beginning and the end of [his] character; vanity of person and of situation" (1: 1). He is a static character and consequently shows no development in the novel, but his characterization is interesting in part because it demonstrates the narcissistic personality. Narcissism is an extreme form of self-regard. One of the ways that it manifests itself is in the belief that one's values and interests (particularly about oneself) are shared by the rest of the world. One of the interpersonal limitations this creates is a lack of empathy. To answer this topic, you could do a little research into narcissism as a psychological disorder, then observe how Sir Walter's opinions and actions are impeded by his narcissism. How does *Persuasion* present Sir Walter's extreme variety of self-love as preventing his being fully human?

Form and Genre

Form and genre provide instructive ways of thinking about literature. Form is the shape and structure of a literary work; genre is the kind, or classification, of a literary work. Though technically independent of the content of literature (meaning that love, for instance, is an idea that can be communicated in various forms), form and genre are chosen deliberately by authors as they make decisions about how to arrange their stories. *Persuasion* is a novel. This facile observation might still provide the basis for an essay on form; for instance, an essay could examine how Austen's novel is structured. *Persuasion*'s overall structure—how its beginning, middle, and end are composed—is worthy of analysis. The opening, for instance, presents Anne's flawed family, though most of the novel is almost solely focused on Anne. An essay might review what benefit this structural choice presented to Austen. How might this approach suggest Anne's virtual isolation?

Another way to look at *Persuasion* would be to consider how the novel evokes certain generic conventions, such as those in a fairy tale or, in its mood, those of an elegy. An essay might also explore how the author uses certain techniques, such as eavesdropping or gossip. In spite of her high principles, Anne manages to hear a great deal of secondhand information. How does Austen manage to maintain both Anne's moral probity and her access to prohibited information? An example of eavesdropping is found when Anne overhears Captain Wentworth's conversation with Louisa Musgrove. Another example of eavesdropping is when Captain Wentworth overhears Anne's debate with Captain Harville about women's constancy in love. This scene is pivotal because without his listening in, Captain Wentworth would not have heard Anne's testaments to undying love. In an essay about gossip, it might be useful to consider Mrs. Smith's opinion: "Call it gossip if you will; but when nurse Rooke has half an hour's leisure to bestow on me, she is sure to have something to relate that is entertaining and profitable; something that makes one know one's species better" (2: 5). Are there indications that Austen herself subscribes to Mrs. Smith's philosophy—that gossip is both diverting and edifying?

Sample Topics:

1. **The novel's opening:** Why does the novel begin with a discussion not of the heroine, but of her flawed family? What effect does this have on the beginning of the novel? What does it mean that the family virtually falls out of the narrative for large sections and is essentially absent from the novel's ending?

   This topic requires that you draw conclusions about the organization of *Persuasion*. To write an essay on this topic, you should read closely the opening chapters and consider how the novel might have been changed in terms of its focus and meaning had the opening been arranged differently. It would also be worthwhile to study the presence of Elizabeth and Sir Walter Elliot as the novel unfolds. Why might they be so dramatically marginalized in different sections of the novel? What effects on the action or themes are created by their absence or presence?

2. **Elegiac mode:** An elegy is a lament for a person or a time that is lost; a mode is a particular style of a work of art. Where do

we see the elegiac mode in *Persuasion*? What is the effect of the elegiac tone of this novel?

To write an essay on this topic, you should research what constitutes an elegy. A handbook of literary terms will give you sufficient information about this genre and this form. For the purposes of an essay, you would need to understand that an elegy is a celebration of something or someone lost; by its nature, it looks retrospectively at its subject. How is Anne's main focus retrospective? Examples for this are found where she reflects on how things in her life might have been different. She often laments the loss of places and people, such as when she says good-bye to the happiness she felt at Uppercross: "An hour's complete leisure for such reflections as these, on a dark November day" (2: 1). Here the season helps signal the elegiac mood. In part because of its often dreary weather, autumn is frequently featured in English poems about loss. Ultimately, you would need to decide how the elegiac mode contributes meaning to *Persuasion*. Does it make the felicitous ending more meaningful or does it seem unrealistic?

3. **Eavesdropping/gossip:** Eavesdropping and gossip play pivotal roles in the novel because only the information secured through these questionable means permits the judicious conclusion of the novel. How does the novel maintain the heroine's moral authority, despite of her trafficking in illicit information?

   This topic makes an assertion about eavesdropping and gossip. The first thing an essay should do is establish how these sources of information affect the novel. You could discuss such scenes as Anne overhearing Captain Wentworth and Louisa talking, and then analyze how this information propels either the plot, certain themes, or Anne's character development. Other relevant scenes include those with the gossip-loving Mrs. Smith or Captain Wentworth's eavesdropping when Anne is talking to Captain Harville. How are these scenes significant to the story? This topic also asks you to consider how Anne's moral authority is never compromised even though she is hearing things she ought not. How does the novel manage this? An ambitious essay might speculate about Austen's views on gossip. Are there signs here that she endorsed the telling of untoward stories?

4. **Language of passion:** Read closely passages that describe significant feeling and analyze how Austen conveys passion.

The mental confusion that desire can cause is demonstrated in dialogue between Captain Wentworth and Anne Elliot. How does the novel's arrangement of syntax, punctuation, and ellipses render the feelings of romantic love? In addition to exploring the passionate feelings that Austen shows, discuss what feelings or experiences Austen seems reluctant to show.

Language, Symbols, and Imagery

Language, symbols, and imagery are some of the creative means by which an author conveys certain feelings or ideas that would, if simply declared, be weakened in terms of their imaginative and evocative power. All writers, and those of fiction especially, use language deliberately. They choose words based on their connotative meanings. As you read fiction in preparation for writing about it, be alert to the connotative meanings of diction even as you register the surface meaning of language to follow the plot itself. *Persuasion* is distinguished from Austen's other novels by its more prominent incorporation of symbolism. While she does not rely on figurative language such as similes and metaphors, Austen does use images, incidents, and diction to reinforce her ideas.

Persuasion centers on past events, regrets, and ruminations on lost opportunities. Austen uses reminders of these themes in imagery related to the passing of time. An example of this kind of imagery is seen on the trip to Lyme when the narrator observes a beach that is the "happiest spot for watching the flow of the tide, for sitting in unwearied contemplation" (1: 11). Tides, regular events of every day, themselves suggest the passing of time. Focusing on seasonal cycles is another example of temporal imagery.

Sir Walter's fixation on appearance and age is another obvious example of the passing of time. He thinks "himself and Elizabeth as blooming as ever, amidst the wreck of the good looks of every body else; for he could plainly see how old all the rest of his family and acquaintance were growing. Anne haggard, Mary coarse . . . and the rapid increase of the crow's foot about Lady Russell's temples had long been a distress to him" (1: 1). Sir Walter, of course, is interested only in the most superficial changes, while the book and its heroine are, by contrast, concerned with the deeper significance of change and transience.

The term *bloom*, which Sir Walter believes he is still enjoying, is an example of word choice that does double-duty: It is both a colloquial expression that describes a phase of life when one is young and at the peak of one's form, while it also alludes to flowering plants and, more symbolically, growth. An essay might focus on this particular variety of nature imagery, perhaps as it relates to Anne. Her bloom, the narrator initially observes, is behind her, yet there are many places toward the end of the novel where she seems to have regained her bloom. When Lady Russell compliments her, Anne hopes "she was to be blessed with a second spring of youth and beauty" (2: 1). She herself thinks in terms of natural imagery when she considers the future of Captain Benwick: "I cannot believe his prospects so blighted for ever. . . . He will rally again, and be happy with another" (1: 11). In light of his gender and youth, Anne considers Captain Benwick's prospects healthy, not "blighted" like a diseased plant. Whatever approach you take to an essay on language, symbol, or image, you should reach a conclusion about the significance of your symbolism. When you are asked to discuss symbolism, you are being asked to analyze what something signifies in light of the entire work.

Sample Topics:

1. **Time imagery:** How does the imagery related to time and its passing resonate for this novel's themes? Does the time imagery change as the novel approaches its felicitous conclusion?

   To write an essay on this topic, you should first locate events or images that speak to the passing of time. You might find that those events that most remind Anne of her regrets—such as witnessing Captain Wentworth's attentions to Louisa Musgrove—are the sections that most focus on how time is passing. Your essay should also discuss whether the time imagery shifts as events become more propitious at the end. As Anne's regrets soften, does the novel's consciousness of time become less pronounced?

2. **Places in the novel:** *Persuasion* is a novel with multiple settings and no fixed home. Consider how one or two of those settings are characterized and reach a conclusion about what those settings represent for the heroine or the novel.

To address this topic, you should first consider the variety of places that Anne travels to and from in this novel. The principal locales include Kellynch Hall, Uppercross, Lyme Regis, and Bath. Each of these places makes a strong impression on Anne, and the narrator's descriptions will help you analyze what these locales represent to her and the novel. An essay that focuses on Anne's least favorite city, Bath, might consider how it is characterized as a place that prizes social rank and fashion, values that are antithetical to Anne's. An essay that focused on Lyme Regis might describe what Anne learns to regret after witnessing the bonhomie among the naval officers.

Comparison and Contrast

Comparing components of a story to analyze the similarities or differences among them is a useful approach to writing an essay. Avoid simply creating a list of similarities or differences; instead, take the crucial step of commenting on your observations. To begin a comparison/contrast essay, you might compare characters with each other: How does Lady Russell compare with Mrs. Musgrove? With Mrs. Harville? How does Captain Wentworth compare with Mr. Elliot? You could also compare characters (or other elements of the story, such as themes or events) across different Austen novels. For example, how do depictions of nature compare with one another in *Mansfield Park* and *Persuasion*? How do the obstacles to love resemble one another in *Persuasion* and *Sense and Sensibility*? The challenge of this kind of essay is to decide what the similarities or differences you identify might mean. These questions make essays compelling and will have different answers for each writer. To get to these answers, you might find it helpful to think about what kinds of effects Austen achieves by producing either similarities or differences among the elements of her stories. How, for example, is moral strength depicted differently in Anne Elliot and Fanny Price? It is not enough to point to the existence of similarities or differences; you must also consider what purposes those similarities or differences signify for the novel overall.

Sample Topics:

1. **Contrasting romanticism in *Sense and Sensibility* and *Persuasion*:** Analyze the different presentations of romantic sensibilities in these two novels. After assessing the ways in which they are different, consider how their distinctive representations function in each novel.

   To answer this topic properly, you should first consult a handbook of literary terms to find a definition of what is commonly called romanticism. With a working definition in mind, consider the romantic elements of each of these novels. In *Sense and Sensibility*, the high feeling, quoting of heartfelt poetry, and love of nature are often mocked, when not represented as profoundly irresponsible. Consider why you think, by contrast, Anne Elliot's pronounced romantic sensibilities are represented as poignant. To that end, think about how Anne's and Marianne Dashwood's respective modes of conduct are different.

2. **Contrasting the navy and the gentry:** Analyze Austen's contrasting representations of the navy and the gentry in this novel. To what values of the navy is she sympathetic? Ultimately, what social commentary does she make by opposing these groups?

   This is a potentially broad topic, because the navy and the gentry are drawn as absolute opposites. The challenge of this topic is to focus on how these two groups are opposed. You might, for instance, concentrate on how their leisure time is spent differently; for example, Sir Walter's mirror gazing and immersion in the *Baronetage* contrast unfavorably with Captain Harville's construction of improvements to his house.

You might also consider the occupancy of Kellynch Hall: How does the residence of the Crofts compare with that of the Elliots? Who is the more responsible resident? Ultimately, you want to reach a conclusion about the social commentary Austen might be making here. If the navy is indeed the more responsible group, is she suggesting something so radical as the elimination of the gentry? Could she be saying that the gentry's weakness will be its doom and that it will be phased out and replaced by a meritocracy? Any comprehensive social criticism you think Austen is making will need the support of the narrator's commentary.

Bibliography and Online Resources for *Persuasion*

Austen, Jane. *Persuasion.* Norton Critical Edition. Ed. Patricia Meyer Spacks. New York: Norton, 1995.

Grey, J. David. "Military (Army and Navy)." *The Jane Austen Companion with A Dictionary of Jane Austen's Life and Works.* Ed. J. David Grey. New York: Macmillan, 1986: 307–13.

Hopkins, Robert. "Moral Luck and Judgment in Jane Austen's *Persuasion.*" *Nineteenth-Century Literature* 42 (1987): 143–58. Rpt in *Persuasion.* Ed. Patricia Meyer Spacks. New York: Norton, 1995. 265–74.

Parker, Keiko. "'What part of Bath do you think they will settle in?': Jane Austen's Use of Bath in *Persuasion.*" *The Jane Austen Journal,* Annual 2001 23. Thomson Gale, 2005. Electronic. Literature Resource Center. Berkeley, CA: Berkeley Public Library. 15 Sept. 2007.

Sales, Roger. "Persuasion: The War and the Peace." *Jane Austen and Representations of Regency England.* New York: Routledge, 1996.

Wiltshire, John. *Jane Austen and the Body.* Cambridge: Cambridge UP, 1992.

INDEX